'Convoi Exceptionnel'
A Mongol Rally Adventure
The Mongol Rally – 2018

&

'A beginners guide to the Mongol Rally'
Thinking of taking on the challenge?

Alastair Cameron.

Convoy: A group of vehicles, typically motor vehicles or ships, traveling together for mutual support and protection

Printed in the United Kingdom
First Printed 04/2019
ISBN13: 978-1-5272-3954-8
Self-Published, Amazon UK & Amazon Kindle.
First Edition
abrucecameron@gmail.com
https://www.facebook.com/TeamAwayFK/

Dedication

This book is dedicated to my beautiful wife and children.
Caroline, I wish you were with me on this most amazing
adventure. You were supportive, brave and inspirational.
Thank you for letting me chase my dream.
Kids, I hope you one day find yourself on the Mongol Rally, I
can't wait to bore you to death with the same stories over
and over again until the end of my days!

&

Everyone from Convoi Exceptionnel. Thanks for making this
adventure a truly once in a lifetime experience. I hope we
convoy again soon.

Preface.

"Look around you, our entire planet is known and monitored, mapped by hand, by plane and satellite. Our world seems controlled and predictable, but humans need the thrill of discovery, children love to play hide and seek but we fear to venture without technologies tether. We have forgotten we need adventure, we need to get lost, we need to get stranded, we need to live by our wits or we will lose them. Evolution has made us this way, we are wired to survive, designed to explore otherwise we die. The Mongol Rally is not another health and safety course, this is an adventure." – The Adventurists.

Like all good stories, this one starts with a kick ass friendship; I met Lee at University, he was extremely easy to get along with, a real top bloke with the sort of 'do a favor for anyone' attitude whilst expecting nothing in return. We were both studying Performing Arts and Technical Theatre at the University of Cumbria, drinking heavily four times a week, playing stupid pranks on each other and throwing endless downtime hours into Xbox and computer games. (Euro-Truck Simulator 2 being our favorite)
When we weren't studying or virtually crossing Europe in a MAN Truck from the comfort of our bedrooms we would be out in the beauty of northern England or Scotland. We would either jump into the back of Lee's car or he would take lead and I'd follow him on my Suzuki GS500 Motorcycle.
I often favored motorcycles over cars, I didn't go for my car license until the age of 23, but I passed my motorcycle test as soon as I could at 17. I felt that the freedom of a motorcycle was nothing in comparison to the comfort of the car. Little

did I know that I would be proved wrong in such a short time.

This book is the story of 'Convoi Exceptionnel' Two best friends Alastair and Lee from Team: Away from Keyboard tackling the 2018 Mongol Rally in a 1995 Ford Fiesta MK3 driving from Blackpool (UK) to Ulan Ude (Russia) via Mongolia. Creating the most amazing friendships, traveling over 1/3 of the globe and supporting two amazing charities.

Everyone who attempts the Mongol Rally is downright stupid! Nothing can prepare you for what is to come, the highs are high and the lows are low, it's physically and mentally challenging every day. I mean, who would pay thousands of hard-earned cash to drive across the largest land mass in the world with 4 changes of clothes and a travel toilet whilst only eating boiled noodles? I hope by the end of this book the answer is you!

It's truly incredible, on the rally you really start to realize that nothing is impossible. That the world is a beautiful & wonderful place filled with amazing, helpful and inspirational people, but at the same time it's completely terrifying and that looking down the barrel of a loaded gun from a smirking border guard doesn't get easier the 2nd time. It's these stories that make the rally yours, they make them unique and individual, not one person on the trip had the same experience as me, that's how fantastic it is. I could set off again tomorrow on exactly the same route but I'd find different problems, meet different strangers and come home with a thousand more memories.

Whilst undertaking this adventure myself and Lee promised each other we would blog as much as we could, keeping the

memories fresh and as thrilling as the moment we lived them. It's regretful to say that every night we sat down and did nothing of the sort, there was just too much to do.
So, the blogging was sparse, sorry.
The rally really takes it out of you, however we did find the time to write as much as we could, thanks to the 36-hour Turkmenistan Ferry and between every pothole bounce whilst driving on the long-broken roads of Kazakhstan.

I wrote these notes as a memory for myself, so I could look back through them and remember a snippet of the trip that wouldn't come to mind without that little bit of extra information. I never intended to create a book but with the stories I told and the information about the trip Lee so incredibly gathered, I couldn't think of a better way to share them with the world. I will be 100% honest and tell you every story how it was; I won't glorify anything or add things in to make it more interesting, because I don't have too. The Mongol Rally is the most random, interesting and stupid thing I have ever attempted, it's no gap year in search of enlightenment funded by mummy and daddy, this my friends, is an adventure! Here's how it all went down...

An introduction to the Mongol Rally

The Mongol Rally is a truly epic trans-continental adventure set up by *The Adventurists,* it's where you take the smallest, crappiest car you can find and drive it all the way to Mongolia. You can go whatever way you wish, north, south, east or west and take as long as you desire! It doesn't matter if you are by yourself or in a team of 5 there are only 3 rules.
1) The car must have an engine size of 1.2 or less.
2) You are completely on your own with no backup.
3) You must raise a minimum of £1000 for charity.
That's it.
Three rules to follow for a huge adventure like that, no health and safety, no risk assessments and no hand holding. The Adventurists know how to put on an adventure!
It cost us £575 to sign up as a team of two, this gave us access to the huge Facebook page with thousands of members, those who are taking part that year and those who have done it in the past. Along with that you get an amazing launch party, a beach party, two t-shirts and three stickers for your car. I know it doesn't sound like much, but the support and information from rally veterans really was priceless. That and you get to see the progress of other people who are doing the rally with you that year. It's amazing how many times myself and Lee looked at the page for advice or information to see someone saying *"Just got three jerry cans and a sump guard fitted"* that usually made Kevin (The Mongol Rally organizer) appear with a comment such as *"Pontins is down the road if you want an easy holiday."*

Although you are traveling around the world in a terrible car, you really want to plan and prep as much of the gear you possibly can, however when you start to do this, you start to do the opposite of what the rally is about.

The Mongol rally is about breaking down in the middle of nowhere, jumping on the back of nomad horse to the nearest hut and trading your shoes for a new alternator that isn't even for your car. Then getting lost on the way back to your car due to lack of water and somehow managing to kick your car back into action.

The less you take, the more you need, the more you need the more you stop, the more you stop the more interactions you have with people, cultures and countries. The Mongol Rally is not a race, it's far from it, it's an adventure.

Every year since 2004 the Mongol Rally has ran, starting with an entry of six teams, all the way to 2018 when 300 teams had signed up. It's becoming ever so more popular each year, the thirst for adventure has caught on and people can't get enough of it.

Chapter 1 – How not to buy a car

After many years of saying *"one day this will be us"* I finally persuaded Lee commit to the rally. I commented on a Facebook post by The Adventurists saying *"Sign up now with me, don't even think about it just say yes!"* After forgetting all about it and waiting three days I opened Facebook again to see *"YES"* on the post. What a fool, he had no idea what he had just signed up for, of course he knew it was an epic road trip around the world but did he really know that he would be squatting in the woods up to six times a day and spending more time under the car fixing it than driving it? Of course not.

It took him so long to reply because he was currently working as a lighting designer on Explorer of The Seas, Royal Caribbean Cruise Ships. That's where he met his beautiful partner Mica, she loved the idea of an adventure but didn't seem too keen on the idea of Lee getting lost or hurt, you could easily see that they cared a lot for each other.

I can't comment on how they both felt about the dangers of the rally, but I sure can about my partner, Caroline.

She hated the idea of me going and leaving her and the children behind, but couldn't have been more supportive, she was so inspiring and willing to help make it happen whenever or however she could, she was truly incredible by instantly offering to sort out or logos, car graphics and full team branding.

It was on a dull September evening in 2017 Lee drove to Blackpool to come visit me and the family, it was the first time he was able to meet them all because of his life on ship.

After stepping through the door within seconds the baby was crying because she didn't like his beard and the ales were open. We had ordered pizza and had a quick a catch up when in all the excitement the convocation turned instantly to about the rally,

"But what car would we take?
It's a long way you know mate!
But what are the rules again?
It's a really long way you know mate?"

I think Caroline and Mica thought this was just an idea at first, I'm pretty sure they thought we would have gotten over the idea soon, realized how silly it was and just continued on with our lives. To be honest I'm sure there were times myself and Lee even considered it.

Lee had one contract left to complete on the ships which he would start at the end of January and finish around March, then he was free. I on the other had had a lot of work to come, but due to my overtime and the buildup of hours working overtime I had, I realized that I was owed around 9 weeks off work, just enough to do the rally. I just had to get my boss on my side.

We spoke all evening about the rally, looking at Google maps and flicking through Caravanistan.

For those of you who don't know what Caravanistan is, it's the holy grail of adventure information, from travelers all across the world. They tell you all the information you are unsure about such as what borders are open to only locals, the roads that actually exist and time frames through certain areas. You may think that using this is against rally spirit, but you have to know all of this information beforehand to get your visa dates correct for each country, if you mess this up then you pretty much can't get to the finish line, you have to know your entry and exit dates and have them in a 'doable' time limit or your rally could be over before it began.

By the time the weekend was over, we had agreed our roles in preparation of the rally. I would do everything at home such as find the car, take it all apart, learn everything I could and put it back together. I would also look into sponsorship, equipment and graphics. Lee's job was to do everything he could from afar, (as being on a ship at sea, what more could he do?) he would research each country, decide the visa dates, research entry documents and all information needed for ferry crossings, plot it all out on Excel sheet ready for when he returned so we could get the visas sorted as soon as possible.

The rally started to feel real as we started to let everyone know about our adventure, our friends and families would shrug it off at first with comments such as *"that's an interesting idea"* not knowing we were already in stage one of planning. But the more they shrugged, the more they sniggered, the more I wanted to show them how real and how sure I was about it all.

Without thinking another second, we signed up before anyone could talk us out of it. Firing our deposit over to The Adventurists, our Mongol Rally adventure had begun.

Lee headed off home with adventure in mind, meaning that rally preparations began almost instantly. Before he would head back on ship just after Christmas, we both agreed that It would be a good idea if we both kept an eye on eBay and auto trader for something interesting. Covering the north and south of England meant we would hopefully find something soon. Silly and wacky ideas such as a Russian tank and at one point we even considered and were planning on viewing an Airport Staircase vehicle. However, after finding out that their top speed was a measly 28 mph and would beach on 'any' incline, we looked elsewhere. Lee was particularly interested in finding the car, the enthusiasm he showed towards the trip was incredible, he even went out of his way learn the difference and benefits between a carburetor and a fuel injection engine because his mechanical knowledge was close to none-existent.

He would phone me with lists of cars that I should look out for and how 4-wheel drive would be such a huge advantage. *"STOP."*

I had to remind him that this was The Mongol Rally. We didn't want 4-wheel drive, because that would make the trip that bit more comfortable, *"we need to break our comfort zones and take the 'worst' car we can find."*

Lee seemed to understand what I was saying and respected my opinion. That was one of many great attributes about Lee, he would always listen to what you had to say, before telling his opinion and then coming up with a fair, reasonable compromise. He wasn't one to put his foot down; he would always be understandable and react accordingly.

The search went quiet for a while until one day I got an eBay listing through from him, *"It's perfect"* it read.

VW Polo Breadvan 1.2, it certainly looked the part but I'd never heard of one before. With my love for motorbikes, a few years before the rally I had built one from the parts I had lying around. I built a hardtail chopper and since that day my interest in mechanics ran wild. So much so I started to service my old Fiat Punto, learn how to do a complete oil change, change a few ignition coils, anything I could do to it without having to get specialized tools. So, with all of these cars I was being sent, Lee was also being subliminally asking me *"Can you learn to fix this?"*

I did all the research I could within a few evenings as the auction had almost ended, parts were cheap, parts were parts were available and the Haynes manual was ordered. I gave Lee the go ahead and £750 later we were the owners. At least, I thought we were.

Lee woke up to a message from the eBay seller the next morning that read,

"Oh, I didn't realize you were an actually bidder, because you hadn't bid before the winning bid, I thought you were having me on, so I retract your bid and I've sold it to the last bidder for £730, sorry."

We were devastated.

It was in such a good condition and we were looking forward to seeing what the old VW had to offer. We just had to let it go, we were refunded and the quest to find the car began again, we were so lucky to see that another VW polo Breadvan had just been listed. It was a newer model, better condition, less miles, roof rack already installed, steel rims not alloy it was a blessing in disguise that we lost the first one, buy it now £750. SOLD.

We pressed buy it now without even a viewing, Lee messaged the seller to let him know he was 100% non-fiction. Before we knew it, the seller responded saying *"brilliant to hear from you so soon, no need to send the deposit, just bring it all with you in cash when you come to pick it up"*. We really couldn't believe our luck; the curse for the VW Bread-van had been lifted.

A few days had passed after Lee had text the owner asking what day he could pick it up however we receded no reply.

He tried again a few days later and was greeted with a brief reply that read something along the lines of *"will sort this at the weekend, just a bit busy at the moment".*

Lee was not for giving up, he added the car to the insurance and goggled where the owner lived, or at least the town, then text him saying *"brilliant will see you at the weekend."* He drove about 100 miles from his house in Kent with his dad to they could view the car before buying but no luck. He wouldn't pick up his phone or reply to his texts. In Lee's anger he sent me a text reading, *"I think this guy isn't genuine and is having me on, I've driven to his town and he won't reply to my texts or calls, don't think I'll find him unless I start knocking on doors, I think it's a dead end"*

However, in his anger, Lee made one fatal mistake and accidently sent it to the owner of the car. Within seconds he replied with *'I am genuine, how dare you come to my town looking for me when we haven't agreed a date, blah blah blah',* until he finally refused to then sell it to us.

Annoyed and defeated Lee drove home empty handed; We believed at this point maybe the VW bread-van wasn't the car we should take on the rally. With our hearts in our hands we agreed that we would widen our search from now on but if we happen to see a Bread-van, take a peek.

About a week of searching countless websites turned up nothing of interest, just some old rust bucket barn finds and a tiny little Subaru.

'PING'

"What about this mate, it looks like a right good choice"

I opened the webpage to see the tiny little Scooby I was looking at already, the Subaru Vivo, it got its name VIVO

because in roman numerals, that's how many CC's it had. 658cc, that's no misprint. I really mean it 658cc. (43bhp) It was a tiny little car that neither of us had ever heard of.
"NO."

Was my instant reply, *"I've never worked on a Subaru, It's the worst looking car I have ever seen, its fuel injection and its 0-60 of close to impossible would extend our rally by at least another week or two!"*

Lee quickly replied backing himself up, *"Just have a look over it, sleep on it mate and let me know in the morning",* I agreed and went to bed a little grumpy, I couldn't believe what Lee was suggesting, but at the same time I thought back to what I had said in the first place about this adventure and when things go wrong, that's when the adventure begins. If we were to take this tiny car across the world and run into mechanical difficulties, we would have no hope finding spares for such a rare compact car. We would have better luck with good old-fashioned carburetors, something that requires a hammer to mend rather than a degree in automotive electricals.

The next morning, I woke up and thought I'd just have one more look before work, I had thought about it all night, passed on my worried to Caroline and listed the positives and negatives about taking it. The list of negatives was high but I tried to have the most neutral approach towards it I could.

I loaded up the webpage for one last look to see 'This item is no longer available'. A sigh of relief shot through me, I really didn't want to disappoint Lee, this just saved probably the first argument of the trip. I was just about to step out the door to work when I had a terrible thought, *"he didn't."* I grabbed my phone and text him *"please say that that wasn't you" with* a screenshot of the eBay page.

After a few minutes I could have cried when I read his reply. *"I couldn't help myself..."*

Chapter 2 - Couldn't give a Scooby!

658cc Mate!
"I know but it looks like it would be a great choice"
43bhp!
"That's the same as your last motorbike that was quick enough"
I've never even heard of one!
"Me neither I think it's really rare, 14 registered in England I think"
WHAT!
I couldn't take it, I just told Lee I would message him at the weekend and that I was not convinced at all, he sent me a long message back with information about it and reassurance, but I knew at the end of the day it would be me fixing it, researching it and sourcing parts. It would just make the preparations and the trip 100 times harder. But most of all I was upset because I never even agreed on the car. From the very first time I looked at it, it was a no from me. I just felt that my opinion had been ignored.
I was furious, stepping out the door to work, I read one final text.
"I'm going to pick it up at the weekend then after Christmas I'll come visit you, if you aren't 100% convinced by the time I have to go home, we won't take it and I'll sell It on. I just didn't want to miss out on it."
Hallelujah. That was the Lee Marriott I knew!

I calmed myself down and made an agreement with myself that I would give the car the fairest trial I could. I looked at positive reviews and even an episode of Fifth Gear (The old rival of Top Gear, for those of you who aren't old enough to remember) where it was challenged against two other tiny cars in a test where surprisingly it did extremely well. Whilst all this was happening, Lee had taken it to a Subaru garage that had been recommended for it to have a full once over, they checked everything from the oil levels and tracking to the fuel injection system and the drum brakes before passing with flying colors.

It had been well looked after which was great news, the bad news was that after the mechanic completed the check, he took a photo of it and told Lee that it was the rarest car he has had in his garage.

Sigh.

"No, No, No Alastair, you promised yourself that you would be neutral and do your best to fall in love with this car".

I decided that was it, I had to see the car for myself, give it a drive and speak to Lee about the worries I had.

Lee drove up to Blackpool (Lancashire), about 8 hours from Deal (Kent) on a cold evening in November, we ordered more pizza, drank fine ales and looked over the car as much as we could but sadly the black and night and the car being smaller than an Austin mini, even up close I couldn't see much.

Lee said to me very calmly, *"Drive it tomorrow, lets rag the shit out of it mate, throw it into every gear, take it off road if we can, if it's not the right car, we won't take it, it's our choice not just mine."*

It was good to hear him say that again and I really did respect him so much for sticking to his word, but the smile he had on his face was very strange, he was almost positive that he could persuade me to take it, it really must be a cracking car I thought.

It was.
The next day I insured myself to drive it fully comprehensive through the snow-covered roads of the Trough of Bowland. It drove superb, In and out of 4-wheel drive we slid it around each corner. We took it in turns to throw the car around as much as we could trying to break it, but it just didn't budge. Every test that we did, it passed with flying colors; the Subaru Vivio truly is a fantastic car.
Stopping to help some girls who had gotten lost, we hoped they were stuck so we could try our first rescue mission, pulling them out the snow in such a tiny car, but sadly they were fine, they had just pulled over to take a selfie in the snow.
Heading back home I was set on it, the car was fantastic. I wanted this tiny car to be our chariot to Mongolia. I just needed to read up on and get my head around fixing a fuel injection engine and the problems that we could face. Being much more suited to carburetor engines, I had some reading to do.
We set a plan for the rest of the weekend, we would head back to my house, drink a lot of tea and route plan for the rest of the day, then we would look at spares for the car and have the final decision on if this was to be our rally car, tomorrow. Lee was so confident that he booked a bus home for Monday morning leaving me with the car to sort, service and learn from whilst he was away. We kept to our promise and that evening and spoke nothing about the car, our focus was on the route and pre planning.

The route was decided quickly, we didn't have enough time to get the Iranian visa and there was no way we were heading through Russia the whole time on the northern route, so it was decided, we would take the 'Central Route.' From Blackpool, heading to Dover, and crossing the channel before entering France, Belgium, Germany, Czech Republic, Slovakia, Hungary, Romania, Bulgaria, Turkey, Georgia and Azerbaijan then crossing the Caspian Sea via ferry. Then into Turkmenistan, Uzbekistan, Tajikistan, Kyrgyzstan, Kazakhstan, Russia, Mongolia and back into Russia to the finish line in Ulan-Ude. It all seemed so easy on paper; little did we know what we had really gotten ourselves into and the scale of the whole adventure.

It was time to look for spares, it seemed that not only I hadn't heard of the Subaru Vivio, it turns out most of the internet were unsure also.
eBay? No.
Amazon? No.
Auto Trader? No.
Facebook Marketplace? No.
Weird foreign websites? No.
Westockallcarparts.com? No.
Ifwecantgetitnooneelsecan.com? Okay, maybe I'm fibbing about that last one.
Impossible, it was literally impossible; I even looked at finding another Vivio just to take of what we needed as a sort of donor car but with only 14 registered in England and 6 of them being on the road in a road worthy state, it was impossible.

I joined the Vivio forums, but no one got back to me with any parts or useful information, only their anger that we were planning on taking a rare car to Mongolia.

Funny side note, the person who Lee bought the little Scooby from said *"I'm glad a young chap like you has taken an interest in this little car, one buyer tried offering me half its value and they wished to drive it to Mongolia"*.

Lee just sniggered and handed over the money.

By the end of the day my love for the car had gone. I couldn't take a car to Mongolia, 10,000 miles away from home with no spares, no knowledge but my own about fixing it and just no belief that there was anyone out there who could help.

"Lee, we can take the car if you really want but, I can't guarantee I can fix it"

to my surprise he agreed.

"Its okay, we'll find something else"

I could tell that he was more heartbroken than me; his heart and soul had been poured into this car. However deep down inside we both knew that this adventure would be challenging by testing our friendship on every corner, battling illness, battling tiredness and fatigue. Having a car with us that was impossible to find parts for would just be silly.

We hugged it out.

Two grown men stood by a living room window, holding each other close. We were so upset knowing that this wasn't the car for the journey and that we had to start again with a much more restricted timescale.

The launch day was getting closer and closer but we still had nothing.

Lee would have loved to take that car more than anything, thank you Lee for respecting my opinion, thank you for being patient and understanding, I really admire you for that.

Chapter 3 – Money, Sponsors and Legends

Lee was about to board a plane to the States to start his next
contract, but a buzzing on his phone with an eBay link from
me showing him either more VW Polo Bread-Van's or the old
Nissan Micra K10 always kept disrupting him.
I had agreed the last time we spoke that I would find the car
for the job. I'd ensure it was perfect before purchasing, I'd
make sure that spares were out there, I'd make sure that I
would be knowledgeable of its entirety to ensure
breakdowns were uncommon and quick to be repaired. But
mainly I promised him I would buy a car that we would both
not only enjoy but also keep the challenge alive. We were not
going to go with anything young, we wanted something with
a bit of age, common around the world with interchangeable
parts.
There it was. Newly listed, under 1.2l, well known make, well
known model, over 1000 of them still on the UK roads and
more around the world, could it be the perfect car?
eBay item number: 182991515961.

Mk3 Ford Fiesta 1.1i Quartz 5 speed

Good Service History, 54k miles

Only Selling to fund putting my Mk2 fiesta on the road

Great little car drives spot on!

Tidy for its age but does have a few scratches on paintwork.

Long MOT 1 October 2018 4 good tyres and recent tracking

Can deliver at extra cost

Car is in Ivybridge

Devon PL21

It looked average, scratched, tiny, unsuitable, everything we needed for the perfect Mongol Rally car!

I sent the listing to Lee saying to forget all the others, this tiny, old ford fiesta would do the job. I went on to inform him how it would still be challenging but easier on time and our wallets. For a start it was a carburetor model so I knew I could fix anything like that at the roadside, it had no electrics installed except for the bare minimum, with no power steering, no air conditioning, no electric windows not even a clock! I went into keyboard warrior mode with lee, typing away about how this car was perfect; he replied with, "*looks good.*"

I was hoping for a little more, but that was good enough for me. I messaged the seller about the car asking every question I could think of and how much it would be to deliver all the way to Blackpool (around 300 miles away). He replied to all my questions, he was extremely enthusiastic and friendly, but he wasn't in the mood for a three-hundred-mile road trip in a tiny car then a train ride home, especially because the train would cost him over £100 and he was only getting £550 for the car. I thought it was game over; this was until I got a text late that evening.

"I'll tell you what Alastair, I'll borrow my brothers trailer and hitch it to the back of my land rover, I'll drive it 150 miles north to Birmingham and you get a lift 150 miles south to Birmingham and drive it home. I won't ask for any petrol or delivery money, I'll just be happy to see it go to someone as enthusiastic about old fords like I am."

"deal, see you on Saturday at 5pm" I replied.

Wait.

I've committed to the car, I didn't even ask Lee, I haven't given it a health check, nothing! Everything I promised I would do for lee, I didn't.

I made an agreement with myself that I would get everything checked over once it was in my possession, take a lot of time with the car, test drive and jack it up before handing over the cash. Then if I agreed to have it, I would get it looked at straight away.

Saturday came very quickly, I had persuaded my friends Andy and Nathan to give me a lift and help me give it a check over before buying, we drove to Birmingham once Andy had finished work and met up with the seller.

There it was on the back of this trailer slowly being taken off, it was dark, but it was completely as described, nothing missing, everything seemed fine. I got in the car and took it took it for a test drive. After about half an hour I returned with only one fault, the clutch was a bit heavy. Grabbing a torch, I took the time to look under it, but it was so cold and damp I didn't even give it a glance. I needed to get the car home and look at it in the daytime.

The deal was done, I shook hands, singed the new keeper slip on the V5 and I was off driving it home, for 150 miles it cruised at 80mph all the way home, no knocks, beats or problems, I smiled at Nathan and knew I had picked a cracking car.

I didn't tell Lee, not for a few weeks. I had a mechanic look at it and he gave me a small list of faults, it was nothing too major at all, back box is rusted, rear wheel bearing has slight play and a few other things. I asked if I should bother getting them done and his reply was 'if its only got 10,000 miles left in it, I'd just leave it.

INFO: I would like to say at this point I took his word for it and it was the best bit of advice for the entire rally, I didn't fix the exhaust and I didn't even bother looking at why the rear wheel had a slight angle on it. You will find as you read on the terrible, expensive problems we had due to this, but for now I'll keep you on your toes.

After months of scrolling through the deepest and darkest parts of the Internet and three car heartbreaks, we had finally found the car for the rally! We were going to take a 1995 Ford Fiesta from England to Mongolia.
With the car sitting on a neighbor's driveway *(Thanks Jackie)* The task to get sponsors was underway. I was extremely lucky at this point because my partner Caroline is the most talented graphic designer I have ever seen, she whipped up a perfect logo and created some snazzy letterhead paper, I found some large companies online who I thought *"Great these will be fantastic if we got one of these guys on our car"*
So I created about twenty emails on the letter headed paper, saved them as a PDF and sent them away. Within a week I had heard back from no one but within a month I had a reply from three!
No. No. Not interested.
Brilliant!
Looks like my writing had let me down, I needed a way to inform these businesses what a charity rally from England to Mongolia would do for their business.
"Wait, what can it do for their business?"
I realized soon it wouldn't be much until Caroline said to me *"Publicity! That's all people want this day and age, if you get their logo on the side of your car and photograph it around*

the world in 100's of locations and get the local and national press involved everyone would be jumping at the chance."
So that's exactly what I did.

On a cold February morning at 6am I drove to Leyland to pick up Andrew, a colleague of mine who creates and edits amazing promotional videos. Along with another colleague called Brendon who had just started a Drone business, *(Pixel Sky Drones, Check them out!)* I had begged them a week before to create a film for me explaining all about my adventure that I could give to potential business sponsors, as repayment to them I would put their business on the car, they were happy to help and I can honestly say that without them I wouldn't have been so lucky with sponsors as I was. We filmed a short promotional video with the most high-tech drone over a viaduct in Yorkshire piloted by Brendon, along with brilliant fast paces shots from Andrew with his camera, the snow came in slowly in the distance as we recorded as much as we possibly could in the time we had. It was all edited together that evening and sent to me first thing the next morning.

Being a Lancashire lad, I decided that I wanted to try work with more local companies and businesses, making the car more of a community effort more than just my own. I sent a short email to a local graphics company with an explanation of my trip, my charities and the link to the video, crossed my fingers and waited.

Within half an hour they had read the email, watched the video and given me a call.

"Hello Alastair, its Blackpool Van Signs here, we watched your video and we really want to help your adventure happen, how about we make you the offer of covering your car in full graphics of the businesses and local companies you get as

sponsors along with having our logo on there a few times and all we ask in return is you get us in the local paper as an official sponsor."

I couldn't believe my luck.

The video had worked.

Within half an hour I had bagged my first sponsor, not only that but a graphics company who were willing to offer so much for so little. Not only were they so generous but also, they were the nicest most down to earth guys ever.

Once I had them on board, nothing was stopping us, everyone wanted to be involved, we asked for a contribution to our trip and a donation to our charities from each of our sponsors, In return we would get them printed on out T-shirts and sponsorship coats, their logo would be on the car and we would get as many photos as we could of their logo around the world.

I would just like to take this moment to say thank you to our amazing sponsors.

Blackpool Van Signs
Baler Services Limited
Pixel Sky Drones
Barrage esports
Darkveil Paranormal
M&B Logistics
Pied Piper Educational Resources
Marriott Eco Projects

In your own unique way, you made this rally happen, from the bottom of our hearts. Thank you.

With all these sponsors on board the planning for the trip was extremely enjoyable again, we had gotten bogged down with all the car negativity and we needed this win. With three months to go we had a car, all our sponsors and an amazing design for the car that Caroline and Blackpool Van Signs created. I hadn't spoken to Lee for a while. I was worried I was doing too much without his input and at the same time I was concerned that I hadn't heard anything from him about visa dates, applications and travel itinerary. Little did I know, I shouldn't have worried at all, the first contact we had just a few days later he sent me numerous excel sheets for everything, visa start and finish times, a guide to every location we were going and their road conditions, information about what to do and not to do in certain countries, where petrol was illegal, information about government, whatever I hadn't done, he had.

It was obvious he had poured his heart and soul into this trip just like I had, he had worked extremely hard using all the downtime he had on the ship to get onto his managers computer to research. What a man!

Lee finished his final contract and almost instantly headed to Blackpool, this time he was driving a 3L jag, I would love to tell you the story about how he decided on the Jag however I heard it so many times on the trip that if I was to write it out now, I would probably kill myself.

That weekend we took the Fiesta around the Lake District up to my caravan just outside of Penrith, testing it on every corner, up every hill, anything we possibly could to break it. It passed every test, I wanted to prove to Lee I had thought of everything and addressed everything I could, just as we had agreed.

We stopped at a local scrapyard we happened to stumble across randomly where we grabbed two spare wheels and tyres for a great price of £15 each. A few weeks after I even ended up going back too to buy the roof rack off a totaled Citroën Berlingo that my boss Keith, shortened and welded for me one weekend before finding a way to Frankenstein it to fit the fiesta, he did a cracking job!

Lee was happy, I was happy, we finally had our car. We both agreed, shook hands before beginning our endless visa applications.

Now I won't bore you about how long our visas took or how many times we thought we had left things too late, but what I will say is that if you are planning to take part in the Mongol Rally, apply for the visas as soon as you can. Luckily Lee's work saved us, so we had all ours sent off on time and returned just before the start, however we did hear some horror stories from other teams about late visas and some who were setting off without a Mongolian visa!

Chapter 4 – Not long now eh lads?

The Adventurists had changed the start line this year from Goodwood racetrack to *"somewhere west of Prague"*. That was literally how they told us, we were told nothing about what was to come, only expect a launch like never before in their new country the D.P.G.R.A (Democratic People's Glorious Republic of Adventurism) and my goodness did they deliver! But we will get to all of that later.

This meant that both Caroline and Mica couldn't come with us to say goodbye and wave us off the start line, this was upsetting for all, but I really do believe that it saved quite a lot of heartbreak.

With the rally only a few weeks away we planned two launch parties of our own, one in Blackpool the night before I was to start the drive down south and one in Deal, Kent next to Dover with Lee's chums before we crossed the channel.

We had volunteered to become the 'Convoy Leaders' for leaving the UK this meant that we would try and get as many rally teams to meet up with us and drive to the start line. The adventurists had asked us to do it a while back and sent us a briefcase of goodies as a thank you, they said *"Use a tracker to tell everyone where you are, meet up with all the teams you can and on your way to the start line, gridlock as many cities as you can, the idea may fall on its arse, but if it does just make the most of it."*

After a lot of planning from myself and Lee we sorted out the final Idea on how to start the convoy, with a week to spare we posted on the official Facebook page: *"Meet outside 'Blackpool Pleasure Beach' at 9am the morning of the 11th, team AFK will be there as the convoy leaders to lead the charge down to Prague."*

We had no idea if anyone was going to turn up, but it didn't matter, we had a plan, a set off date and we were ready to start our adventure.

I took the car to Blackpool Van Signs and dropped it off just before I headed off to work, the lads there were fantastic and with the help of Caroline they had created a fantastic design for the car, I kept looking at the vector file and then back at the car thinking 'My car will never look like that'.

I left them with the keys and went off to work, I remember sitting at my desk just itching to head back to them and watch them at work, watch my little rust bucket of a fiesta be transformed into a rally car, I mean that's every little boy's dream, right?

I got the phone call to go and pick it up and just ran out of work. Without telling my boss, I just started running.

Once I got there, my car was outside, glistening in the sun when my jaw hit the floor. It was incredible.

They had done the most fantastic job, I don't know what I expected it to look like but my god those lads created a work of art. Everything was perfect.

All our charities were listed; the sponsor's logos were down the side and, on the bonnet, along with our Facebook and twitter page. Then I saw the map on the back window. Caroline had designed an amazing map with our route sketched out on it, it was printed on some high quality vinyl that meant you couldn't see in the car due to the huge map however you could see out of the car as clear as usual.

It was at this point realization kicked in. it meant that everything was complete. I had to go and do what I set out to

do, not only due to the promises I had made to the charities and sponsors, but the promises I made to 16-year-old me who used to dream of entering the Mongol Rally.
"I will do this adventure one day."
That day was finally here.

Lee drove up with his partner Mica in his beautiful Jag. That's right Lee has a Jaguar, mainly because he liked to say *"I've got a Jag"* in the style of Jeremy Clarkson. (I really didn't need to tell you any of that, however he told absolutely everybody on the rally, so I thought I'd continue the trend) As soon as he arrived, we emptied out his Jag of all the gear he had acquired and then we emptied out the Fiesta of all the gear I had collected, oh my, it was a lot of gear. We had originally agreed to take as little as we could, keeping the weight down mainly but this also meant we could possibly pick up things on the way and save a bit of petrol. Instantly this went out of the window, almost everything got packed. car spares, cloths, camping equipment, random hats, everything and anything including a camping toilet that I said to Lee *"we are not taking this, we will never use it"* but after a bit of persuasion on lee's end, it was packed. The only thing we had left to get was food, we had agreed that we would always have a large box filled with food stored in the boot and at any time if we took anything out, we would replace it as soon as we could. A brilliant system to stick too as the last thing we wanted was to be stuck in the Turkmenistan Desert or Southern Mongolian without any food. We had also agreed that we would keep as much water on us as we possibly could, we had heard some horror stories of past teams running out of water and having to resort to drinking tap water, that's a huge NO NO when you're going through the 'Stans' unless you want a stomach pump or to be squatting over a hole for a week.

After a lovely meal at a local Thai restaurant called SUDA THAI in Poulton (*SUDA PLEASE SEND ME FREE MEAL VOUCHERS*) we sat there completely full. For the final time we reassured our partners that we wouldn't take unnecessary risks and that we would try not to do anything stupid.

Lee seemed very happy to be hearing me say this, I'm sure deep down he had a few worries that I would go off doing crazy, silly things like the Alastair he knew at university.

I heard him do a breath of relief. It was time to let him know about a little secret myself and Caroline were hiding.

"The reason why I'm not talking any risks is because Caroline and I are expecting."

I showed him our 12-week baby scan and after the congratulations and celebrations we both knew that we had the other ones back throughout this adventure. We were both getting married as soon as we got back from the rally and at the end of the day our health and welfare of our families came first. We clinked glasses, *"To life's adventure."*

The following day we rammed as much food and water into the car as we could and got our sponsor shirts out ready for the Blackpool launch party. I had invited friends and sponsors around to my tiny house for a party, however it clashed with the World Cup match where England were knocked out! However about 40 people turned up to pass on their best wishes. Endless jokes were made as the alcohol flowed, photographs were taken with me and Lee around the car with friends, family and sponsors because this was the last time they would ever see the car, no matter how the rally would end for us, they would never see it again. It was to be recycled straight after the rally.

Lee was a little quiet at the party, but I think it was all down to nerves.

Bottles of sparkling wine littered the garden as the smell of cigars wafted inside the house. The car paint pens came out, giving everyone the opportunity to write on the boot of our car, *"Keep it friendly"* I was endlessly shouting and making sure that no-one wrote any foul language on the car as we had arranged to meet our charity on the way down to Dover the following day, I couldn't have any profanities written on it for them, not only would it have been embarrassing, but they also work with many children, so it would have been highly inappropriate.

It was fantastic to be surrounded by so much support; we had a few group photos around the car then started the ignition for all the kids. Not to hear the roar of the engine as the 1.1l was measly and embarrassing. It was to show off the accessories I had installed. I had gone a little wiring mad a few months before the rally, by installing 100-amp wire from the battery to the dashboard where it met a large master fuse and accessory switch, then it went into an additional fuse box and from there to the accessories. All this was nicely displayed on some blue Perspex. It wasn't the best-looking job, but it was safe and secure. Interesting fact: it turned out compared to other rally mods, it was the best-looking job.

We had a Loudspeaker wired in that was just incredible, I'd urge everybody to take one, it allowed us to play music, speak and play the loudest pre-installed sirens I have ever heard, it was amusing to do in every country to make people jump or just as a friendly passing hello on the road. I had also wired in a 50-inch LED bar that was installed on the front of the roof rack, we thought it was a little overkill at first, but it certainly came in handy on the trip. Next was the 12v cigarette lighter socket, I had to install this because the car didn't come with one installed, this came in handy for charging every phone, camera battery and eventually our Bluetooth speaker. Finally, the last thing installed was the CB Radio. I loved it, when in convoy we always had one CB radio user at the front (usually us) and then one at the back so if there was an unexpected breakdown, corrupt police or a wrong turn, it meant everyone could keep in contact. Some people did use hand held walkie-talkies but they were very unreliable and usually lost within the first week.

My estate was woken up with sirens, flashing lights and cheers just before midnight as the guests gave one last blast of the siren before heading home, wishing us luck as they left.
I went to bed holding the love of my life. I was nervous, I really wasn't looking forward to saying goodbye to her and the kids the next morning at all. After a few hours of just lying there in each other's arms, I contemplated everything that had been and everything that was to come before peacefully falling asleep.
Lee and I were meeting at 9am at the Pleasure Beach car park to see if anyone would join us for the first leg of the convoy down to Dover.

Prepped and Ready
Photograph by George Hargreaves.

Chapter 5 - Days 1-3 – The Creation of Convoi Exceptionnel

I said goodbye to my two beautiful children, passed them over to their Nanny and proceed to drive down the depressing looking Blackpool promenade. It was a gloomy day and I had a day driving solo all the way down to Dover. I had Caroline following me to the Pleasure Beach so she could say her final goodbyes before heading to work and had arranged with Lee to meet me there also as I didn't want a crowded house whilst saying goodbye to my children. I was down, cold and nerves were starting to build.

I wasn't expecting any teams to join us in Blackpool, we had already received many messages saying teams would either meet us at the port of Dover or a few miles from the start line. I wasn't anywhere near as pumped to set off as I thought I would be until I was at the traffic lights almost directly outside the Blackpool Tower and I laughed at a car coming towards me, it was a Fiat Panda 4x4 raised up with huge wheels, it looked so stupid with 'Mr. Lee's Chippy' written all over it. Surely it couldn't be?

I watched as it drove past me going the opposite way and saw the sticker as clear as ever on the side 'MONGOL RALLY 2018'.

Pumped is an understatement, we had someone join us, they were a little lost on day one as they were going in completely the wrong direction, but I knew they would find us eventually. The plan had actually paid off, we had a someone at least. as I continued down the promenade, I looked down a side street to see what looked like a black Clio with Astroturf on the roof supporting two gnomes. *"It must be another team"* I said to myself. Who else would do that to their car?

I had arrived outside Blackpool Pleasure Beach at exactly 9am to a completely empty car park, I was happy and excited about what was to come. Knowing that somehow our silly plan had worked, we had at least one team with us down to dover and then we would join many more on the ferry the next morning.

Shortly after Lee and Mica turned up followed by the Fiat Panda I had seen earlier, they were called 'Global Nomads' and their team was based in Manchester. They had decided to join us in Blackpool because they had 'no plans or any idea how to get to the start'. *"we will follow you for a few days"* they said. I wasn't shocked because they somehow got lost when looking for 'The Pepsi Max Big One ride' and Its so big, its unmissable! We were then very shocked to find out that the local paper had turned up to get our picture, the Adventurists had spoken to them about our Blackpool launch and they sent a reporter, we all posed for photographs as we waited for the mysterious 'Gnome' car I'd seen earlier. Then the reporter asked who was from Blackpool and could he have a short interview, I explained to him that it isn't about 'who was from Blackpool' it was about the adventure, that there were many teams all trying to get to Mongolia in tiny cars.

I thought he had understood, that was until a few days later when I was sent the entire article that pretty much only mentioned me, who I was, where I worked and the name of my children. I didn't even tell him most of that information but somehow, he seemed to have it, reporters eh? all the same they just want the juiciest story. But at least I got a mention in about Blackpool Van Signs and a few other sponsors! I was worried I wouldn't have been able to deliver on my promise.

It was close to 10am and with no sign of any other team, we decided to get on the road, we had planned to meet our charity SpecialEffect at their HQ just outside of Oxford between One o'clock and two, so there we were, with no time to lose.

It was time. Time to set off on an adventure I had dreamed about for years, time to start the few hundred miles of a ten-thousand-mile journey with my best friend Lee and a crappy old ford fiesta that was already making squeaking noises. But first, before I push on east, it was time to say goodbye. It was so hard to say goodbye to my partner in crime, my enabler in mischief, Caroline. Especially because at that time she was growing our next baby inside her. It was hard to say goodbye, the words just wouldn't leave our mouths, but we knew it was now or never. We plucked up the courage to say goodbye whilst we both tried to hide the forming tears around our eyes, we then embraced into the biggest snog before I got in the car, roared the tiny engine, played the siren on full and with my best friend behind me and global nomads taking up the rear we set off on our Mongol Rally. The M55 out of Blackpool was just a complete blur, I was so happy to be on this adventure with my best mate, but It was so upset to be leaving my family for 6 weeks.

I was cruising at about 75 mph with the radio on loud, just trying to take into account the morning and what the journey ahead would bring. I had completely lost the Panda and Jag they were nowhere behind me, but we had a schedule to stay on if we were to meet SpecialEffect. I had a lot to learn about convoying at this point, so I pulled over just past Stoke and gave Lee a call. Turns out they were miles behind, the top speed of the Panda was 60mph when 'pushing it' they could only really cruse at 50mph. I found it amazing that such a modern car could only move so quick, a car 10 years younger than ours with all its modifications couldn't take the weight of two blokes and all of their gear, when a 1995 Ford Fiesta was doing just great. About 45 minutes later they turned up, I could tell that Lee was a little upset that I'd left them behind, but it most definitely wasn't intentional, nevertheless we were back up and running. we hit the usual roadworks that are expected in England and made it to SpecialEffect about an hour and a half later than planned.

SpecialEffect are incredible.
They are the most amazing charity. I feel so fortunate and grateful that I have had the chance to meet everyone behind the magic. If you are thinking about doing the Mongol Rally but you don't have a charity in mind to support, I urge you to find a local, independent charity that needs your help and support, we found exactly that with SpecialEffect. I know that every penny that myself and Lee raised has gone into changing the life of someone with a physical disability. What they do is, they give the fun and inclusion back to those with physical disabilities by creating a way for them to play videogames. By using technology ranging from modified joypads to eye-control, they are finding a way for people to play to the very best of their abilities. But they aren't just doing it for fun. By levelling the playing field, they are bringing families and friends together and having a profoundly positive impact on therapy, confidence and rehabilitation.

I mean, how cool is that?

Whilst we were there, we met the entire team and had a tour of their amazing office and working space, it was so inviting, comfortable and looked like a fantastic place to work. After a round of tea and biscuits, we went outside to get pictures with them all stood around our car. although our car barely looked impressive, the trip we were heading out on within it made the adventure ahead look even more of a challenge. After a lot of photos, we were taken on a tour of the building and then we were asked the most amazing question.

"Would you like to come and play some Eye-Control dirt rally?"

We couldn't believe it, Myself and Lee headed through to a room with Mica filming our every move to find a bag of goodies and a card with our name on next to the Dirt Rally PC. I mean, we were meant to be doing everything we could to help them, but they seemed to be pulling out all of the cards to help us more. It was at this point I knew that I had to support SpecialEffect throughout my life, they looked after me as much as I wanted to help them, I could see how they were genuinely exited and happy to have us on board. Their goodies were welcomed, crisps, sweets and game memorabilia were handed over before the PC was fires up for a few stages of eye control Dirt Rally.

It was incredible, Lee went first, he found it hard at first as you have to keep your head completely still and just move your eyes, the mouse is calibrated to follow your gaze and that's what points the car around the corners (with a little built in auto assist) Lee scored an excellent lap time, then I followed and just beat him by less than a second, I couldn't believe it!

but my celebration was short lived when Mica thrashed us both, she was a natural. Her time was a new laptop record if I remember correctly. We were then showed modified Joypads, controllers and large buttons that were other options of modified controllers they had used with previous clients. We learnt so much, it was truly inspiring and inspirational.

If you would like to hear more about them, get yourself over to www.specialeffect.org.uk.

It was time to hit the road again, Global Nomads had waited in the local town of Chipping Norton, gotten themselves some lunch and were ready to head off again. They were a cracking bunch and it was fantastic to re-join them for the last stretch past London and over to Dover. It turned out that we were setting off the same day that Donald Trump was heading to England to congratulate the UK on Brexit. we passed political rally upon rally, blocked roads and police barriers all protesting his visit, it was rather funny driving through the middle of them in a logo covered Ford Fiesta and looking at their extremely confused faces. I remember seeing a child pointing at me and shouting, *'Top Gear, Look its James May"*. Fuming.

Within a couple of hours, we had completed the busy London ring road and it was smooth sailing through Kent, I was thinking about the road and how lucky I was to be on smooth tarmac, yes England sucks for its traffic jams and roadworks, but on its major roads its smooth tarmac for hundreds of miles. I couldn't stop thinking about how long I would have left on roads this smooth and what country would give us the first 'bad road', *"Georgia or Azerbaijan recon."* (Fact: I have never been so wrong)

Then finally there it was, over the motorway hills we saw them, the beautiful white cliffs, the stunning castle of Dover and a Banksy painting showing the hardships of Brexit.

We had made it through day one.

One day down, at least forty more to go.

We left Global Nomads at the port as they were yet to buy a ferry ticket and had a hostel booked already, we were running a little late to Lee's Leaving party or as I liked to call it 'The Alastair and Lee have Brexit party'. I drove the car straight down the drive to be greeted by Lee's family and friends, I was instantly handed a beer and taken over to the buffet table.

Lee's mother and father are just incredible, they are two of the most generous people I have ever met, extremely hospitable and brilliant party hosts, if you don't have a beer or some food in your hand, they will solve that problem. Lee greeted his friends and showed them around the car while Peter (Lee's father) came over to me and gave me a short quiz about the adventure, I could tell he wasn't doing it maliciously, he was just worried for us both, *"I've taken cars apart all of my life, engines, transmissions, everything and I wouldn't dare take on this adventure, now you are either mad or you really know what you're doing. Lee said you have taken the engine apart and re-built it?"*

"Sure did, took a while but we got there in the end" I replied.

"Also, you have had it checked over professionally and no one can see any problems".

"Of course, the only little snag is the exhaust needs a new backbox or a good old bit of welding, I didn't see the point in in doing it as its only going to rip off halfway through Turkmenistan.

He asked about ignition, the benefit of carburetor over fuel injections, I answered as well as I could, I would never have called myself a mechanic as I much prefer the title 'Chief of general bodge jobs and anything to keep the car moving.' It wasn't that he was trying to catch me out or find a question I couldn't answer, he was just worried for his son and his friend.

Quiz over, drinks flowed and the pen came out to write on the car, I couldn't believe it when I saw 'Sponsored by Brian Cox-sucker' on the bonnet, penned by one of our sponsors, nonetheless. I had made sure all my friends had been sensible, but when I took my eyes off the car for a few seconds it had profanities written on it, nevertheless It was soon rubbed off and replaced with some words of support. It didn't seem like long before guests started to head home, I looked at my watch to find out it was just about to hit midnight. I went over to Lee and said, *"Tomorrow we leave English soil on an adventure to Mongolia, we could last a few days or we could make it to the end, I don't know. but what I do know is, were going to give it a bloody good go!"*

We sat waiting in line to board the 9.30am ferry, no teams had been spied as of yet, but thanks to the Facebook and WhatsApp groups we knew we wouldn't be alone on this ferry, passing a few checkpoints we had our tickets in hand as we drove to the huge parking area before boarding, we were in row Q that seemed to be ages out of the way compared to where your everyday tourists were having to stop. passing all the holiday makers we then passed a flurry of lorries to join the back of row Q.

Now we understood why row Q was so important, parked in front was a whole row of cars all supporting 'Mongol Rally 2018'

Nissan Micra's, a Ford Fiesta MK4 (Spare parts yay!), a tiny caravan and a very familiar looking Renault Clio were all parked in front. The Cleo was familiar because its roof was covered in fake grass and upon the grass were two garden gnomes, one with its pants down that mooned everyone who happened to be behind them.

We introduced ourselves to everyone in front we had, Team Rally McRally Face, Team Don't Smell my Shoes, Team Cunning stunts, Team Two Fake Yank's and A Scott and a few more right at the top of the waiting area. Everyone who takes part in the Mongol Rally, no matter what age, gender or race seem to have the automatic 'click', knowing that everyone else around you are about to partake in the same, stupid, travel around the globe.

Let me tell you a little about some of these teams.

Team: Don't smell my Shoes (DSMS)
Three boulderers called Adam, Danny and Oli from Winchester, driving a silver, blue and red 1994 Nissan Micra covered in climbing holds. Their roof rack if fully packed with two spare tyres strapped to the rear and their 4th driver 'Edgar the Eagle' strapped to the front. Their car is covered with sponsors, messages of good luck and a little gravestone ready for when Oli gets eaten along the way.

Team: Two fake Yanks and a Scot (Gnomes)
Jessie and Russell, brother and sister from just outside of Edmonton in Canada had teamed together with a crazy Scottish lass called Hattie, after meeting each other online,

they formed a team and purchased a more modern looking black Renault Cleo with all the luxuries, such as power steering, electric windows and the beloved Air conditioning. they had painted the bonnet pink thrown their sponsor 'Tunnocks Caramel' on the side, covered their roof in fake grass and not forgetting their two garden gnomes perched on top. They had no mechanical knowledge at all but a fantastic attitude towards the adventure!

Team: Cunning Stunts (CS)
Richie, Baz and James. A marine, a world class DJ and James. In their Ford Fiesta Mk4 supporting a jam-packed roof rack attached with bolts through the roof and a novelty horn, they plan to use POWER at every opportunity to get them out of tricky situations. With plenty of spares and a very good knowledge of extreme bodge jobs, they are confident on tackling the famous Pamir highway in Tajikistan, The Darvaza gas crater and the nonexistent roads of Mongolia.

Team Rally McRally face: (RMcRF)
Two friends (Carmel and Kate) who searched the internet and found a bloke (Gareth) and a 23-year-old car (Nissan Micra). Once the team bonded over their love of drinking and knowing nothing about cars it was time to get ready. Pimp the car to look like gay pride on acid with a Syrian charity sticker on the side. Yes, they were ready to head towards Russia through countries known for their gay rights, love of women drivers and white cars. Hopefully the luck of Irish, Welsh and English would be on their side, and Russia would have stopped bombing Syria by the time they arrive as time was the only thing they had on their side.

After boarding the ferry, we all made it up to the top outside deck to wave goodbye to England, a place that neither of us wanted to see for a few months because if we did that would have meant our rally would have ended early and badly. DSMS were all supporting an ugly tank top and a selection of groomed mustaches, Oli with the classic goatee and Adam and Danny supporting the porn star and handlebar mustache. Myself and Lee were in our perfect white softshell jackets covered in our sponsors that Caroline had designed and made for us. Lee and I had tried to set up a 'gaming theme' before we set off to match the charity, Lee had purchased a few gaming related t-shirts and Mica his significant other had printed some T-shirts with myself and Lee as Pixelated characters with 'Choose your player' written above it. We also had a Mario and Luigi hat that were given to us from SpecialEffect but that was about as far as our gaming theme had gone.

We left England and crossed the channel, Team AFK had officially Brexit.

"Pint?" I said to lee.

"Pint" he replied.

Everyone was a little unsure of what their plans were but we were all extremely eager to convoy, meeting at the bar for a quick one, we agreed to meet in the first 'pull over' point we could find after we had left the port of Calais, then we would head as close to Frankfurt in Germany as we possibly could.

Jumping back into the cars we started our engines and go ready to burn some rubber on European soil; the ferry staff knew that we were all together so did his very best to keep us all together. once the ramp clunked into the bank of the

French port, we set off and instantly split up. absolutely no one had a clue of where to go, Lee had a plan however, SIREN!

we left the port with the siren on full, everyone heard where we were and headed that way, we suddenly became leaders of a 5-car convoy.

Now I don't know if you (the reader) have ever been in a convoy before, but as soon as you create a convoy, as soon as that final car slips into place at the back and all you can see behind your mirrors are terrible cars driven by adventurists such as yourself, you go from 0 to 100, everything completely changes. you just feel happy, giddy, 100% alive. It worked for about 30 seconds.

As Lee pulled our car into a lay by, DSMS, RMcRF, and CS pulled in but Gnomes drove straight past. We had other teams behind that too but they were just completely lost. Lee tried flagging others down by standing at the lay-bys entrance, flailing wildly. But no other teams saw us.

Chatting at the side of the road was a good laugh, we were just passing the time and getting to know each other, talking about our chosen cars. Adam from DSMS popped open the bonnet of his Micra and told us about a few problems he was facing. *"When we go uphill, it just loses power and I have to keep pumping the accelerator to make it move"* that and I *think there is a leak in our coolant"*

Tap.

Tap.

Crack, *"shit I've just poked a hole right through our coolant"* Duct tape out, bodge job one complete.

"Does anyone else need petrol?"

Arriving at the petrol station, we somehow managed to completely gridlock the area, each of us at different pump, unable to read the instructions and the first time for all of us to have to use a 'pay before pump'. for those who have never used on of those before, you have to estimate how much petrol you need, go inside, pay for it then come out and pump it. if you get it wrong and need more you start the whole process again, if you get it wrong and do too much, you overfill, waste all of your money and the system wins. however, if you get it correct you automatically get a Doctorate of Mechanics because no one has ever managed to get it dead on.

Everyone needed petrol, then everyone needed to use the toilet, the toilet took euros and no one had any change it was just vile. we ended up just parking where we could and using the nearest tree as a piss stop. We had previously planned to stop at every large service station, hoping to grow the convoy, but you find that when you are in convoy things take four times as long to do as they would by yourselves, toilet breaks, coffee grabs and fueling up take so long but once you are back on the road, the miles are eaten up easily.

We were heading as close to Frankfurt in Germany as we could this evening as this was the halfway point between Calais and Prague, if we managed to get there tonight it would mean that we could do the same mileage tomorrow to arrive in Prague a night before the launch. The Gnomes had finally re-grouped with us as we put our feet to the floor trying to make good time into Germany.

The drive to Frankfurt was beautiful, we passed through France, Belgium and into Germany, it was getting late, but spirits were high as the mileage was racked up, we were only near the end of day two and we were close to hitting our first thousand miles, that and we had conquered 4 countries so far. The WhatsApp was pinging every now and again from messages from home, once again wishing us luck but it was mostly from other teams ahead of us or behind us asking for advice or saying where they were staying that evening if anyone wanted to join them.

"Where we staying tonight mate?" Lee asked.

"anywhere, let's get where we're going and just find a patch of grass mate". I could tell Lee wanted to be as relaxed as me for a spot of wild camping, but It was still early days, once we had done it the once, I'm sure he would have been up for the idea.

We eventually pulled over at a motorway KFC around 10pm, everyone is so happy for some warm cooked food rather than cold petrol station crisps and energy drink. Me, being a vegetarian couldn't think of anything worse than KFC, but the convoy was happy, so I didn't speak up.

"Oh everyone, listen to this". said Kate *"I've just spoken to another team and they are at a campsite 30 miles away, it's close to empty and they have a key to the gate, they will just let us all in when we turn up and we can pay in the morning".* Jackpot.

We arrived just before midnight, the campsite was on the beautiful river Main, it was down a narrow track that could have been easily missed but thanks to a conveniently placed car crash we slowed down and spotted the sign.

We arrived at the gate and messaged the team.

30 minutes later we still had no reply,

1am came around sooner than we thought and we came to the realization we were not getting in, everyone was tired and just wanted a few hours kip but no one knew what to do.

"Right, let's just stay outside the gate", I said. *"There is a small patch of grass here we can all squeeze on, the only problem is we have to park tactically to make sure there is enough room"*. suddenly the convoy hive mind kicked in. we all knew what needed to be done, a game of car Tetris kicked off until we were packed completely clear of everything and the tents were up on the tiny patch of park grass that at 01:30am was still full of cyclists and mopeds in the busy city.

We woke early, mainly because we shouldn't have been camping where we were and the sound of morning commuters struggling to get down a footpath blocked by tents made them shout. With the cars packed and loaded ready to charge to Prague, then who should make an appearance but the team with the keys who were to let us in last night.

"oh, sorry we didn't check our phones, that and we only really meant it as a last resort, didn't expect all of you to turn up. If you are still here in an hour, we'll convoy with you."

It's not in rally spirit but I'm happy to say we left them behind.

I was looking around when I saw that throughout the night we had been joined by another car, a stunning, classic, Austin Mini. Team Mini Adventures.

Team: Mini Adventure (MiniAd)
James and his co-driver that can't drive Jade! driving a beautiful Austin Mini, the roof rack off a ford transit van bolted on top completely full, sporting a set of off road tyres on 12 inch wheels, jerry cans and a roof tent that folded down at the back. James had taken pride over his mini doing everything he could within budget to get it ready for the

adventure, whilst Jade brilliantly stood and watched. She had taken her driving test a week before the rally and completely fluffed it, her plan was to drive once they had left Europe, or at least James would hope, he couldn't drive the entire way completely by himself, could he? …. or COULD HE.

Everyone was ready to get to Prague, our convoy had an extra member that looked even more ridiculous than all of our cars, I thought I was mad to be taking a 1995 Ford Fiesta but to see an 83' Austin Mini whose parts are nonexistent outside of England, you had to hand it to James and Jade, their rally wasn't based on *"what happens if we break down".* It was *"what happens when we break down."*
Lee was back in the driver's seat, I was once again in charge of navigation and music, navigation was a big role, not just for us, but being convoy leaders, it meant if we went the wrong way, so did the other five cars behind us. luckily throughout Europe almost everywhere is signposted and you know to just 'keep heading east'. The sweeping bends and autobahns were just bliss, we were leading and MiniAd were taking up the rear, not only due to its speed but more because they had a CB radio like us. Not many others on the rally did but I'd say it was one of the most useful bits of tech on the trip, especially in convoy. Using the CB, we could constantly keep an ear on everyone, any issues or problems with anyone meant we could all pull over and sort them together, rather than splitting up or losing a valuable member of the convoy. throughout Europe WhatsApp and co-drivers can sort this but once everyone loses data come Turkey/Georgia, phones are thrown out and CB's are in. Every now and again we would be informed that DSMS had dropped back while driving up hill, losing power and revs,

56

close to cutting out but then somehow managing to keep the revs high before cutting out completely.

Pulling over for petrol we snapped a few photos of all the cars taking up every pump at the station, they all had their weird and wonderful tweaks and differences that made them unique.

At some point during the beautiful journey through the sweeping German countryside Adam from DSMS decides he needs to take piss. Being far from nowhere and with no service station in sight DSMS make the unfortunate decision for Adam to go 'in transit'.

Finding an empty 2 litre bottle in the front passenger seat Adam tries to achieve an effective angle before quickly realizing that sitting down is hampering his efforts. Heading into the back of the car (with Oli) Adam finds that he can aim properly if he kneels on the back seats while looking out of the rear window. And so, he begins to rapidly fill a 2 litre bottle, he really needed to go. Midway through this, while they all become increasingly concerned about the capacity of the bottle and with Oli currently lamenting his proximity to Adam, a German family decides to come up behind them and ride close enough to figure out that the man locking eyes with them from the back of the Micra is not family appropriate at the time. In between their hysterical laughter Adam shouts *"They're backing off, I think they know"*.

An hour or so later, spotting a McDonalds we went for lunch only to spend 90% of the time there complaining about how good European McDonald's is compared to UK. They have such a better selection and you can pretty much customize everything, then to top it all off TABLE SERVICE. This was rather normal to the Canadians Jessie and Russell, but for us, it was luxury. More photos were taken outside, we lined up the cars in the car park, put around five cameras on timer and got snaps from all angles.

Phone numbers were swapped, and the Convoy WhatsApp created, I finally jumped into the driver's seat and for the first time ever, set off on the wrong side of the road.

It wasn't bad at all, I don't know why I worried, the straights were just normal, the motorway was just normal, the roundabouts *"OH MY LORD HOW DOES THIS WITCHCRAFT WORK."*

I may have drifted onto the wrong side of the road a couple of times, nothing too dangerous but Lee did have to shout every now and again.

We overtook a convoy of huge lorries, *"There's the real deal Lee"* I said, about 6 of them in a row all pimped up with extra lights and CB radios, they were ready for a trip across the world, they were so huge compared to the tiny cars we were attempting the same if not more dangerous route in. Then on the back of the lead lorry was a stretched-out banner, a yellow background with 'CONVOI EXCEPTIONNEL'. written upon it. We had no idea what it meant, but it just sounded great.

WhatsApp pinged, it was James and Jade saying they had booked a Hotel,

Ping.

James, Baz and Richie, *"yeah, booked it, were in too"*.

within seconds everyone had booked a hotel in Prague, *"Book it Lee."*

"Already on it", he replied.

Teamwork, that's what me and Lee always had.

"We have reserved you a room guys, you guys were busy driving and navigating so we wanted to make sure there was room for you" said Kate from RMcRF.

Woah, the Convoy was just incredible, everyone was looking out for one another. This was just a taste of what was to come. everyone on the rally works together, if you see a team broken down you pull over to help, if your close to a town where a team left their passports, you drive a 60-mile detour to pick it up. You just help when and where you can, as you never know when they may just be helping you.

Arriving in Prague, we parked in the secure car park, went up to our rooms for a quick shower and dressed to impress, a night out in Prague was on the cards. I called the girls back home and told them we were 20 miles from the Starting line, it felt insane that I had driven further than I had ever driven before but I still wasn't at the starting line. WhatsApp pinged once more, and we met up with the group in the lobby.

"We really need a name for this WhatsApp group, it's just a list of names and I don't even know who's in what car".

Ritchie from Cunning Stunts, *"Did anyone see what was written on the back of those lor...."*

cutting him off, a chorus of *"CONVOI EXCEPTIONNEL".*

Chapter 6 - Days 4-5 - Welcome to the Mongol Rally 2018

Today was the day we headed to the start line, Lee had been planning a meetup about 20 miles from there, a sort of Mega Convoy. He had sent out a Facebook message to everyone who had signed up saying.

"Meeting point TOMORROW MORNING! 40 mins from the Start Line, we shall meet 9:30-11:00! Set off at 11am from the last spot of Western luxuries and be as noisy and grid-locky as possible to reach the Start Line gates at Noon. Be there and join the Convoi Exceptionnel! Skandinávská, 155 00 Praha 13, Czechia."

A few people had shown their interest but not many had confirmed, we set off about an hour before the rest of Convoi Exceptionnel so we could gab final supplies and lock down the meeting point early. Once we arrived, there were two cars there, we were grateful that a few had arrived, but it was still early. more could come! We chose an obvious empty area near the entrance, and beckoned the others over. We shopped in Tesco's and grabbed as much as we needed, left the store and were greeted by the most incredible sight. Around 20 rally cars had pulled up, engines roaring, sirens wailing and horns echoed around the complex. It was fantastic, shaking everyone's hand and asking everyone's team name seemed to take an eternity all this whilst more and more cars arrived, including the most amazing 'VW Poo' a Polo with its roof cut off. Convoi Exceptionnel turned up ready to move, so messaged The Adventurists. *"34 Cars in convoy, you will hear us before you see us, see you soon. Convoi Exceptionnel."*

Lee had put a lot of planning and prep into setting all of this up, it was only fair to let him drive the huge convoy to the start. after a victory lap completely gridlocking the entire complex, we set off on a back-road route to the start line, passing as many towns and villages as possible. the feeling was truly incredible. We were still completely oblivious to what we were about to face at the launch party, we just knew where to go and that it was an extremely dangerous place that we entered at our own risk.
The convoy roared through Prague, through smaller towns and villages who were rudely awoken having no idea what was going on before we turned down the last main road. sirens on, engines roaring we had made it to the Launch site. the D.P.G.R.A. (The Democratic People's Glorious Republic of Adventurism)
Hundreds of cars were all spread out on a huge festival site made from junk, large wooden structures covered in steampunk theming towered over the tree's, burnt out cars, hybrid vehicles and rickety shacks littered the entire grounds. It was a complete health and safety nightmare. But it looked fantastic. Actors had been hired to stop your car occasionally and act out a very corrupt border guard interrogation, pretty much setting us up for the future. We carried on driving around passing car after car, each team supporting their own crazy themes and brilliant sponsors. Once out the cars the tent was up within second, mainly down to only packing a 2 second tent, *(which I would totally recommend, everyone was against them at first but by the end of the rally they wished they had brought them).*

The sun was blazing hot, it was the middle of July and it just so happened the summer of 2018 was the driest in years, forest, bush and field fires were at an all-time high. we had planned to cook on our stove but due to a naked flame ban all over the grounds, festival food it was.

We headed over to the site center to register our team, find some food and more importantly, the bar. Checking out the cars, shaking hands with newly formed friends we made it to registration, we signed a document or two, collected our t-shirt's and the launch site currency of 'bottle caps' before heading to the bar. We passed a Mongolian yurt, some incredible smelling street food, a casino, cool earth's charity hut and passed under a large wooden bridge structure with 'Mongol Rally 2018' spelt out in junk strapped too it, on top was a set of mixing desks and a DJ blasting out music.

To be surrounded by hundreds of people about to set off on the adventure of a lifetime, all exited showing off their cars was incredible enough, but for the adventurists to pull out all the stops, find a brilliant location, filling it with endless things to do and all night entertainment, we couldn't have asked for more.

Still in search for the bar, we headed up and over the hill to a rather built up area near the Launch gate, it was fantastic to see, knowing that at mid-day tomorrow we were going to speed through it and have officially started the Mongol rally, The bar was right next to it, perfect! along with a tea room, a food stall that sold dried bugs and insects and a shooting range.

Wait, what?

A full-on Shooting Range?

Jam packed with handguns, rifles and enough ammunition to take on the British army, we loaded ourselves up and shot some tin cans. everything was completely free, you just paid in the bottle caps given to you at the start, what happens if you start running low? either drink more beer and collect the caps or go to the casino and double your remaining caps.

I would like to take this opportunity to say that some teams never turned up to the launch and others slated it saying it was a waste of time. I want you to know that they were foolish and wrong. It was incredible. It's up to you to make your Mongol Rally adventure your own. If you throw yourself into the adventure and give it your all, you will have the most amazing time. If you think 'that won't be fun' or 'boring' then it will be. If you break down in the middle of nowhere and instead of laughing about the situation you are in and sorting out the problem, you get angry with your teammates and cry into your last pot noodle. you are going to have one terrible time.
"The difference between adventure and ordeal is ATTITUDE" - Written by Natalie (Dan's partner) on the car of DSMS.

After firing as many clips as we could into tin cans, targets and dummies we grabbed food and headed back to the main area for the launch ceremony. hundreds of participants flooded area fueled by booze and excitement. The adventurists were up on the platform, microphone in hand we were asked.
"Please Kneel for the D.P.G.R.A National Anthem"
We knelt down on the warm ground.
a few minutes passed, muttering commenced,
"Who the fuck hired this guy"
Still kneeling a few more minutes passed.
"Right, fuck it, sack the DJ"

The DJ was removed from the booth, a few seconds passed and the National anthem began.

Patriotic music begins.
"Look around you, our entire planet is known and monitored, mapped by hand, by plane and satellite. Our world seems controlled and predictable, but humans need the thrill of discovery, children love to play hide and seek but we fear to venture without technologies tether. We have forgotten we need adventure, we need to get lost, we need to get stranded, we need to live by our wits or we will lose them. Evolution has made us this way, we are wired to survive, designed to explore otherwise we die. The Mongol Rally is not another health and safety course, this is an adventure"

The celebrations begin, cheering could be heard from all over. We were introduced to members of the team and given information and facts about this year's rally, Cool earth spoke about how raising money for them was really making a difference in the rainforest. Turkmenistan's British embassy had sent a representative who told us all about the place but that all went in one ear and out the other, all I remember hearing was *"try not to hit a camel"*.
A small auction began in aid of raising a little bit more for Cool Earth. Bids were thrown around, usually the winning bidder was a completely drunk bloke whose team were tricking him into bidding, but they didn't care, and all money promised was eventually paid. We were then told about some stickers we had been given during registration. It was a sticker of Her Majesty, the Queen of England pulling her face with a large angry frown whilst above her it read 'SHAME'.

They had been given out to everyone and the plan was to find the team/car that had put in next to no effort with the rally by either breaking the rules, using a modern car, getting no sponsors and not taking the time to make their car look silly. All the cars we had seen so far were brilliant, I'm sure I'd have struggled to use this sticker.

The Adventurists took us on a mini tour of the site showing us the 'Fight Swamp' that was pretty much a huge puddle of dirt and water that two people would jump into and try to remove the socks of the opponent, whoever's socks were pulled off first were the looser.

then we passed the D.G.P.R.A museum where we were asked that before we set off the following morning we could leave an item in there to be auctioned on eBay to raise more money for Cool Earth, a brilliant idea, but we never found out if it paid off.

The tour ended in the 'Funk Bunker' a huge underground bunker fully kitted out with a stage, LED moving head lights, a fully PA setup and a live band, the music began and the tour ended. The funk bunker was an all-night music extravaganza where after the bands at 1am DJ's would play all night to take you into the early hours of the next day.

It was getting late, almost 2am, many beers had been drank and the legal limit of alcohol allowed before driving in the Czech Republic is 0%, I returned to the car to find James and Jade from MiniAd had removed their tent from the top of the mini because a lovely group of hornets had taken refuge in one of his jerry cans, I squeezed into my car without being stung to leave a voicemail on Caroline's phone to the girls to listen to when they woke. *"We made it"* I said, *"were at the start line and tomorrow at noon we will be off, we have made loads of friends and were thinking of convoying for a few days over to the Romanian beach party! thank you for believing in me, thank you for letting me go on this adventure, I love you all so much but right now I need sleep! I've lost Lee, I think he is SKA dancing in the Funk bunker! (Don't ask) Sleep well my girls, Goodnight, I love you!"*

I returned to the tent to find Oli and Adam from DSMS and Hattie from Gnomes sat having a quiet beer, I say quiet, we were camped by a petrol generator that powered a couple of LED lights so why the generator had to be so loud, I have no idea. nevertheless, the idea of quiet was short lived when Jessie (Gnomes) and Danny (DSMS) turned up, Danny was drunk and only wearing his boxers, that and a thick layer of black mud. Adam calmly said *"you have been in the fight swamp haven't you"* sounding like a disappointed father. But before Oli had the chance to say anything, Danny had leaped onto him, covering him in mud. Then, as if it was any sort of apology offered him a singular baby wipe. I hadn't laughed so hard in a long time. After a shot or two of Peppermint Vodka from MiniAd I was exhausted, the long drives, celebrations and alcohol had beaten me.

I woke early to the sound of snoring Lee, left the boiling hot tent and headed to the car for some fresh clothes, toothbrush and phone power bank. At the car I met James and Jade again, they were happy because overnight the hornets had been removed by the landlord's association of Adventurists and it was interesting to see that parked a few cars down from us was a rally car covered in flying ants, almost infested. Everyone was feeling hungover, I could tell it was a fragile morning for all when James from CS was walking in a zombie like way to his car, followed by Danny from DSMS wearing a tank top and sunglasses at 8am in the shade. Everyone addressed each other quietly and shared stories of the following evening until all hell broke loose. A 16 person Czech brass and woodwind band fired up next to us along with one of the Adventurists armed with a megaphone. *"Get up Shit-heads, get to the centre, we have entertainment before you set off, you have 30 minutes till it all starts".*

Lee had followed the band to the car, I could tell that the wakeup call had worsened his hangover, just like it did with us. However, I could also see the excitement on his face. When I originally told Lee about the Mongol Rally and forced him to watch endless rally videos, I could see the excitement in his eyes, the idea of an adventure of this scale to be possible outside of Euro Truck Simulator 2 was a dream come true for us both. This excitement had never left him, but had been buried under a small amount of worry and fear of the unknown. I could tell that Lee had his courage back, his can-do, positive thinking and problem-solving attitude had kicked back into gear working at 110%. The first few days to the launch party had given us both a taster of what was to come of the next six weeks and I knew that we were both completely ready to drive though those launch gates and give this rally all we could give it. But first, entertainment.

What's better? a Fiat Panda or a Nissan Micra? There is only one way to find out, FIGHT.

The adventurists had informed us that the most used cars each year are the Panda and the Micra, many of them had completed and even more had met their deaths on the terrible terrain. To see which was best they got everyone who had brought a Micra to stand on the left and everyone with a Panda on the right. A huge game of tug of war formed in front, after a little wrestle to and from, the Micra came out 1st. But that was a test of the drives, not a test of the car. *"I want that Micra and that Panda over there to drive their cars here"* the crowd followed the Adventurists instructions and moved for the cars. once in place they explained the next game.

Note: I would like to say at this point, if this happened to my car I would have been devastated and I truly felt for the teams whose car were chosen after viewing the aftermath of the game.

"How many people can we fit on and in them... GET ON THOSE CARS"

It was like a scene from 'Dawn of the Dead'. Watching the hungover teams pile in and on the cars, as if a tasty human snack was hidden inside. I'm sure at this point The Adventurists realised the mistake they had made but they had no control over what was happening. They began shouting for people to get down or out of them, but no one would listen. The cars were full, the roof, bonnet and boot of each of them were just peeking out from between the flesh of other teams. Tires were bulging, suspension had collapsed, roofs, bonnets and boots had been dented, windows had cracked and the cars just looked wrecked. I know that The Adventurists hadn't meant for that to happen, if it happened to me, I'd have been devastated, the rally would have been close to over and I wouldn't have known what to tell my sponsors and friends. Kicking them into gear the drivers got them started and out of the way. *(Fact: Adventurists paid for the repairs and both teams made it to the finish line.)*

"follow me everyone" Shouted the host.

We followed him up and over the hill where some entertainment had been provided next too some breakfast stalls, we watched a man described as 'The World's Strongest Man' pick people up with his teeth before some awards came out. There were three categories...

Most money raised by a single team.

Most money raised by a single team for 'Cool Earth'.

and 'Shame - The team with the least effort/worst car.

It was fantastic to hear how other teams had raised so much money for some of the worthiest charities, everyone had done amazing and not one team had failed to reach the minimum donation target. however, it didn't feel fantastic to hear about the team who had done the least effort. An Australian team who had purchased a brand-new Nissan Qashqai. Although it was a turbocharged 1.2 (according to the V5) is was a huge car. it had only the rally stickers on it with no attempt of any 'Mongol Mods'. It had huge wheels with off road tyres on, a roof rack with nothing in it because they didn't actually need one and to top it off, everything fit so comfortably inside. It was a shame and it had been shamed well, everyone had covered it with their shame stickers, including me and Lee.

They were invited up to the stage to 'Explain themselves' where they let us know that their rally plans were a bit of a rush, but had managed to raise a huge amount for charities, they were obviously in the money. Everyone was furious, the shame chant began and they were given a huge 'old school' cathode television that had been painted gold, they were told they had to take it all the way to Mongolia as a punishment. They didn't need shaming anymore, they were just a shame to themselves, they were not going to

breakdown on this adventure nor were they throwing themselves into the challenge they simply had a comfortable boring ride all the way to the finish line. I felt sorry for them, because the places and people they would miss are what makes the Mongol Rally truly unique. *(I would like you to know that not long after they removed all the stickers, dumped the TV and avoided other ralliers. SHAME)*
"NOW GET BACK TO YOUR CARS AND LET'S GET YOU ALL ON YOUR WAY!"
Everyone raced back to their cars, pure excitement filled the air, a chorus of car doors being slammed, car horns and megaphones scared all the birds in central Europe causing an early migration, engines fired up and then like every adventure starts, stand still traffic.
We waited for about an hour in a huge line of other rally cars, talking to the Convoi around us and sitting on the roof of our car in the hot sun just waiting for our moment, we had lost Mini Adventures as their little car snuck past to the front but the rest of the convoy remained close.
Lee stayed on the roof of the car as we drove around the entire site until we made it to the start. Spotting The Adventurists and they slowed us to a stop as Kevin who is in charge of the Mongol Rally shook our hands and thanked us both for starting the Convoi and Lee personally for organizing a fantastic meetup the previous day.
"It's the AFK boys, get your GoPro on, were doing the launch again"
Lee fumbled to get the GoPro on, record was hit, a quick 360 of the location was filmed. *"Everyone, let me hear those engines roar!"* with myself in the captain's seat I set the revs as high as I possibly could, hearing the limiter struggle. *"Get ready everyone, In five, four, three ...."* I couldn't stop smiling,

I had dreamt of this moment for at least the past 10 years. *"two, one..."* the until I heard the most amazing words, my dream had come true.
"WELCOME TO THE MONGOL RALLY 2018!!".

Chapter 7 - Days 5-7 - Don't forget your Vinaigrette

I threw the handbrake down, lifted the clutch and we were away. Fire blasted from the effect machines lined up down the road. As I sped off down the little lanes with the siren on full, flashing the LED bar and music playing loud, 3rd gear, 4th gear, I was using the last bit of the site as a miniature rally track, I turned to my best friend. Shit.
"LEE'S STILL ON THE ROOF"
Without thinking I slammed on almost forcing him over the roof and bonnet of the car. Lee jumped off the car, into the passenger seat and slammed the door. I expected a bit of a telling off but Lee must have been enjoying himself so much that the smile on his face remained as 'Flight of the Valkyries' turned up to full blast. Waving at other teams, Adventurist Staff and spectators we left the site, down a few roads and pulled over to re-group Convoi-Exceptionnel.
The plan was to head to Bratislava in Slovakia, but on the way head to a place called Sedlec Ossuary also known as 'The Church of Bones'. It was just outside of Prague, a little outside the way but we were told it shouldn't be missed.
DSMS, CS, RMcRF and Gnomes were with us, James and Jade from MiniAd had just messaged the Convoi to let us know they were at a Petrol station just north of our location, they had rushed off because they were running on fumes and didn't want to be left behind.
We often found that with the mini, the tiny petrol tank meant it needed a lot of fill-ups. James had the idea of always carrying a couple of Jerry cans, but when you filled them up it added weight to the front of the car, extra drag and he ended up using more fuel than usual, nevertheless I'm sure

we would be grateful of a few extra stops here and there to stretch our legs and see some sights. We passed the petrol station and in true Convoi formation the mini joined the slip road and slotted perfectly at the back of us all, it was a beautiful sight. Pushing on we got to the Church of Bones, Sedlec Ossuary is nothing spectacular in the outside. It is a small chapel located in the town of Sedlec, in the suburbs of Kutna Hora, in the Czech Republic. You would think that it is just an average old medieval gothic church.

As you enter the Sedlec Ossuary though, you will soon realize why it is one of the most amazing and unique churches in the world. The Sedlec Ossuary is artistically decorated by more than 40,000 human skeletons. One of the most fascinating artistic works inside the Sedlec Ossuary is the big chandelier of bones that lies in its centre. The immense chandelier contains at least one of every human bone.

It's honestly an amazing place, the atmosphere is a little strange and you feel a little guilty about taking photos, but once you have gotten past that and read into the history of the place, is fantastic. It all goes back to 1278 when the King of Bohemia sent the abbot of the Sedlec Cistercian Monastery to Jerusalem. When the abbot came back, he brought with himself a jar of soil from the Golgotha, that was known as the *"Holy Soil"*. Soon people from all over the places desired to be buried in Sedlec, thus the cemetery there had to be expanded. In the 15th century a Gothic church was built near the cemetery and its basement was used as an ossuary. The bones stayed there for centuries till 1870 when a woodcarver named Frantisek Rint was appointed to place the bones in order. The result was impressively shocking. If you are doing the rally and passing

Prague it's honestly a place not to be missed. I took a few photos and after a lovely man told me that in every photo you take of yourself in the church, at least 10,000 other people are in the photo.

Just Wow.

Like all tourist traps however, it ended in a gift shop, I slagged it off a little too Lee.

"Sick of these gift shops popping up everywhere, you can't just enjoy a place anymore without having souvenirs thrown at you". I said.

"I know mate, it's a world gone mad" He ironically replied, whilst purchasing a fridge magnet.

Heading outside the rain of the Czech republic started to beat down hard on the ground, we spoke to MiniAd who let us know they had to be in Bratislava that evening because the following day Jade had to be in Budapest to get on a plane and fly back for graduation.

"We best get going then."

Prague is Beautiful, but it was time to enter Slovakia, waving goodbye to the Czech Republic we entered Slovakia and immediately pulled over at the border due to the WhatsApp group going crazy.

At this point in my life my daily phone was a Frankenstein iPhone 5 in which I had taken apart hundreds of times and even done a quick screen replacement on the night before the rally when I snapped it when giving Lee a hug. *The things we do for love eh.* I tried to open WhatsApp but it was safer to just pull over and see what all the fuss was about.

"We need to buy a Vinaigrette, or we will get stopped and fined for not having one" said Kate.

"A what?" Ritchie from CS said with a chuckle.

Then suddenly James from CS piped up, *"I don't see how a salad dressing is going to help us through a country"*. We all went into fits of giggles, she had meant a vignette, a vignette is a small payment of road tax for tourists when they wish to drive on a country's road, it's cheap enough to buy but the hard part is trying to find somewhere that sells them. by purchasing a sticker to go in your window for around 12 euros you're just covering yourself so that when you get pulled over you don't get a hefty fine. *(which happened to a lot of ralliers, before and after us, the highest one was for 300 Euros, because they were caught by the same policeman three times over five days. strange huh?)* Nevertheless, we managed to get one quite easily, after many salad dressing and sauce puns we were back on the road bound for Bratislava. I had also found a sign that read in a different language 'Have you seen this cat' with a picture of a ginger and white cat, peeling it off the wall carefully I stuck it to the back of the car whilst no one was looking. Music was on full and for a little while we played karaoke for James and Jade down the CB radio, every now and again we would get a blast of 'Lazy town - Cooking by the book' back from them or a cheesy hit from S Club 7, Jade didn't know how to drive, but she sure knew how to DJ.

I shouted at them *"Have you seen a ginger and white cat around here? Look at the back of our car."* the convoy had all noticed it by this point and were tooting and laughing at the poster. speeding up to talk to us we were constantly shouting *"Look for our cat, we lost it about one hundred miles back."*

It was getting late but Kate and the team from RMcRF had googled and found a campsite just the other side of

Bratislava, she sent the pin to me and Lee and a course was plotted.

"James and Jade, we have sent you the directions for the campsite just in case you get stick at some lights". Lee said down the CB.

"James?"

He wasn't in range, he wasn't behind us at all, where was he? We arrived at the campsite along with the rest of Convoi Exceptionnel but sadly missing the mini, *"he isn't replying to any of the WhatsApp messages and it was getting dark."* We continued to put our tents up and get the stoves on, Gnomes were struggling with their stove, Russell had used one before but no luck. Our stove on the other hand was ready, I had purchased it a few months before and taken some safety innards out making it a Jetboil. This pretty much meant that it was four times as powerful and boiled 2 liters of water in under 3 minutes, which is fantastic for an outdoor stove. That combined with our two second tent meant the only thing that slowed us down were our camping beds. I was ready to just use my foam rollout however Lee had persuaded me to try out the camp bed he purchased for me. I have to admit it, he was right. They were comfy and well worth it, I'd recommend one to anyone doing the rally, it gets you off the cold damp floor and gives you a little more comfort, however do take a foam roll matt to use when you're doing the endless car fixes, it's a lot easier to lay down on one of those rather than gravel.

A loud bang and a clunky engine could be heard in the distance. It was a misfiring car and oh my did it sound British. James and Jade had caught up to us and the mini didn't look well at all. Tracking out of alignment and a misfiring engine, James pulled it into the car park, jacked up the front and began the much-needed work. I helped where I could but if James was to have this fixed by the morning, It was going to be a long night.

Heat filled the tent as ultimate dry mouth woke me up, I was gasping for a drink. like a seal going onto land I shunted myself in my sleeping bag out of the tent, only to find Hattie and Jessie already up wondering what on earth I was doing. Leaving my sleeping bag and drinking a full bottle of Evian I saw that the Mini's front tyres were straight again and the bonnet was down, James had done a sterling job and even managed to get himself a couple of hours sleep.
We showered, packed away the campsite and loaded the cars, Jade had to be in Budapest by 12 to catch her flight at 3pm. with it being 9am, we had plenty of time.
We left the campsite and joined the motorway that followed the beautiful Danube River, it was a very peaceful drive resting at a beautiful 50mph, we waved other rally drivers as they passed, it was annoying to see the speed they were going at times, we could easy hit 80mph in our car but the Mini at the back of the convoy had no chance. Convoi Exceptionnel stayed together as much as we possibly could It was brilliant to have each other's backs and it also gave everyone a morale boost when the group worked together. Cunning stunts began overtaking, undertaking and having bit of fun on the motorway, Russell from Gnomes joined in but DSMS didn't have the acceleration, their car was constantly struggling and getting close to cutting out. We were half an hour from Budapest when we hit the busy city traffic. 12pm hit and we were still in standstill, the CB was quiet as no one wanted to break the news to Jade. With little made progress over the next hour it took a long time until

we came to the airport turn off, I picked up the CB to break radio silence *"what's the plan? its 13.30"*.

James replied with *"Her gate will be closed by the time were there, looks like were pushing on"*.

Jade never spoke but I promised her that we would have a Graduation at some point on the trip, be it at the Transfagarasan Highway or on the Turkmenistan Ferry, we would find the time to celebrate.

Pushing on past the traffic we reached clear roads and opened the throttle. Lee had worked out if we made it into Romania that evening, we could do the Transfagarasan Highway the next day. Lee was extremely excited to do it as Top gear had once called it 'The best driving road, In the world.' so the push on was a good idea. Entering Romania, we made sure we got a salad dressing vinaigrette for the cars and watched as the motorway disappeared.

It was just gone.

We could see where it should have been but it just wasn't there. Road closed signs and overgrown road was all that lead ahead of us, we were diverted onto a smaller A-road completely covered in potholes. Passing tiny villages stricken with poverty it was almost as if we had travelled back in time. Romania is a beautiful place, stunning hilltop views and as thousands of stray dogs for you to make friends with, the only thing that lets it down is the amount of litter. It's everywhere. nobody cares for bins; the woodlands and mountain roads would be perfect if it wasn't for the litter scattered throughout them.

I realised I had raced ahead a little so pulled over to allow everyone time to catch up and stretch my legs a little. I instantly regretted my choice when I pulled into a rubbish filled lay by. Stepped out of the car only to be attacked by

100's of flies, they seemed only to be interested in my face and it was just vile. I wafted them away as much as I could, jumped back in the car and then proceeded to slap myself in the face to kill little bastards. It was like the scene in Wicker man when Nicholas Cage gets killed by bees. (Oops Spoiler alert) Lee couldn't believe it and was extremely grateful that I went fist meaning he didn't have to face the same fate.

I grabbed my phone to warn the others but it was too late, DSMS had pulled up behind, Oli and Danny got out of their car and started to walk towards ours. Seconds later they were wafting their faces and running back to the car. After that we didn't give anyone else the chance to stop as soon as they pulled in, we edged forwards as if to say 'we aren't stopping' that I believed may have annoyed the other members of the convoy, but I'm sure they would thank me later.

We drove until the sun started to go down, other rally teams had joined the Convoy throughout the day. Forgetting about the poster on the back of the car they would drive next to us shouting *"I think I saw your cat a few thousand miles back there"* The poster was a lot more entertaining than I imagined. Some teams had then sped off getting bored at our cruising speed of 55mph but Team: Over 9000 stuck with us for a short while until we pulled over in the town of Zam. DSMS were completely out of petrol, luckily having a half filled jerrycan with them I spied for a safe place to pull over. We were running low ourselves but with no sign of a petrol station in miles we pulled over at the top of the main road this small town. It was extremely quiet except for the occasional sound of lorries passing. This was the main route to Deva due to the earlier motorway closure, The locals grateful that their once quiet town was now swarming with cars, especially the owners a small corner shop at the top of the hill who had come outside to say hello. I'm sure not every day a convoy of six terrible looking tiny cars covered in sponsors park outside your shop.

It was raining, a full day's pothole filled drive had made everyone just feel drained, with the sun going down and nowhere to stay the mood was getting lower by the second. After filling up the Micra, Adam from DSMS stood on the top of his car, waited for a lorry and signaled him to beep his horn.

The lorry driver was happy to oblige and tooted his overly loud horn. What followed was truly incredible. As the sound echoed around the town, lorry after lorry followed suit and whilst passing our parked convoy, *"HONK HONK"* bellowed from everyone who passed. Families ran out of their houses to see what the fuss was about. when they realised it was just a bunch of tourists making every passing vehicle scream I thought they would be angry, but no. Everyone seemed excited and interested in what was going on. Spirits were instantly lifted, it was exactly what we needed. Kate from RMcRF comes over with a brilliant plan. *"There is a campsite on the other side of Deva, I've just rang ahead to another team who are already there and the owners are going to wait for us to arrive."* It was brilliant to hear, I was all for wild camping as much as possible but the litter infested woods did not look appealing at all. *"Even better there is a restaurant nearby called Grizzly, they serve food till 10 but I could ring ahead and persuade them to stay open."* Kate worked her magic and the table was booked. She was a brilliant mother figure not only for her team but the entire convoy.

Back before the rally started, I believed it would be endless stove cooked noodles and camping in the woods, not hotels and campsites galore. but I'm sure there would be a lot more time for that in the journey yet to come.

Cars filled up with drops from Jerrycans, most of us were in our reserves when we set off in search for a Petrol station, we pulled out, went around one corner and there it was. We had literally pulled over 300 yards away from the station to fill up with jerry cans when around this one blind corner was our savior. We filled up quickly and set off ready for a good meal and a nice spot to camp.

Thuds constantly came from underneath the car as we managed to hit almost every pothole on the road. It was so dark and with the rain was falling hard it meant we couldn't see anything at all except for the rear lights of the car in front. Trying to take it slow we ended up with locals doing the most dangerous overtakes and riding up our arses so much that we ended up having to speed up just to avoid an accident.

The lights of Deva appeared in the distance, I started to relax.

"POT HOLE" shouted Lee.

We could finally see them again in the dimly lit streetlights of the town.

Driving into Deva we parked in an extremely unsecured car park, two homeless men tried to explain that the car park was theirs and for only twenty USD we could have parked there for an hour. Completely ignoring them, we headed over to the restaurant for some brilliant food.

I couldn't eat.

I don't know what it was, but I just couldn't. The thought of eating just made me feel sick, I was nervous and upset but I didn't know why. I checked my phone to read a text from Caroline.

"You are doing brilliantly my handsome man We are following you every morning when we wake up and at night before I put the girls to bed, you have covered so much ground and I couldn't be any prouder. I hope you are somewhere safe and warm, we love you so much. Goodnight my king."

I smiled, replied with how much I loved them all and felt my stomach untwist as I began to scoff all my food down.

After a few drinks it was just after midnight and time to find the campsite, driving down the dark roads we slowed when we saw a woman in the middle of the road. She was stood just off a roundabout in only her underwear. Next to her was a large man hanging out of his parked car smoking and gesturing at us trying to get us to 'sample his goods.' We drove around and chuckled, as did DSMS however Cunning Stunts were so interested in what was going on, Ritchie forgot to turn and nearly took the woman out.

It was late, we were tired but we found the campsite, woke the owner up and he showed us around. We were eager to pitch tents and get to sleep but the tour lasted about twenty minutes with an average of ten steps. He just really wanted to practice his English but I was so tied, I hardly paid attention.

Tents up,

Beds up.

Heads down.

Another day on the rally had come to an end.

Waking up on a rainy, foggy day a few sighs were heard around the campsite, not only because we were to get soaking wet packing everything away but also because today was the day, we planned to tackle the Transfagarasan Highway. It was meant to be the most glorious drive in the stunning sun however we didn't have high hopes with this weather. Lee was most disappointed however he was still 100% up for giving it a good go.

Mornings on the Rally were unusual, everyone seemed to always be unusually quiet, I mentioned to Lee that we were the same in the car, we would snap at each other in the mornings a little and then after lunch we would feel fine again, it was unusual but no one really had anything to say to each other. *"We should have a coffee every morning before we set off, sugar, warmth and caffeine will help us start the day."* He agreed and our quest for a coffee began. Lee took to the wheel and we left Deva, the roads we had tackled the previous night in the dark were much less scary in the light. Potholes were visible and locals seemed to have slowed down. We managed to get to the north road of the Transfagarasan very early, stopping for petrol, coffee, crisps, energy drink and 'something that looked weird that we had never seen before.' We seemed to have started this tradition from France, we would find something strange in every petrol station that 'we didn't get in England', buy it, try it and rate it. This time it was 'HELL' an energy drink sponsored by Bruce Willis; we downed our cans of hell followed by double shot coffee. we were ready for the Transfagarasan.

Convoi Exceptionnel were all excited. Except for DSMS, they had a huge problem with their revs slipping when going uphill and their coolant had started to leak. *"We must bid you good day sir on your quest"* Adam said in his Lord of the Rings style Side quest voice. DSMS had agreed to give it a miss, by fixing their car now and not pushing it up Transfagarasan, it would mean that their minor issue would be fixed before anything major happened. It was a sad goodbye, Oli, Adam and Danny were fantastic Lads, I just hoped that we would be seeing them again soon.

GoPro's were mounted on the front of Ours, Cunning stunts and Rally Mc Rally Face's cars, bladders were emptied and the beautiful mountain range in the distance was calling us. Following the stunning road with the Convoi behind us, we cheered on cyclists and runners who were about to tackle the beast just like us. Going around the first sweeping bend we knew our cars would struggle but the road was going to be worth it.
Lee drove for quite a while, it was a little foggy and the rain was still coming down, but he didn't care. I can only describe the way Lee drives as 'technical', he loved tapping the break at the exact time, accelerating through the corner and opening her up on the straights. He thought about every corner and hill in advance in order to achieve the smoothest ride like a professional driver. It would have been fantastic to have done this road from the comfort of his Jag, but for now a Ford Fiesta would have to do. We stopped in convoy for every photo opportunity we could, view after view, Group photo after group photo. Well, I say group. Hattie from Gnomes was too tired today, she didn't want to get out really, she just slumped on the back seats of her car and slept whilst Russel did all the driving. She came out of the car occasionally but only for a quick snap, bathroom break then straight back to bed. It seemed very unusual for such a bonny Scottish lass. Lee continued as we got higher into the mountains, passing the cable cars and day tourists until we were extremely close to the top. *"One last group photo"* was shared over the WhatsApp group so we pulled over.

Baz (CS) got out of the car and got out a beautiful camera, mounted it on the tripod, placed it on the roof rack of his car and lined up the shot.

Hattie slowly climbed out the car and the photo was taken. We looked down at the beautiful road we had come from to see a few busses holding everyone up. *"we need to go now so were not stuck behind them"* said Lee.

He was right, no one wanted to do this stunning road stuck behind sightseeing busses. Everyone piled in the car, Lee offered the driver's seat to me and we were away.

I set off wheel spinning in the gravel, not because of the power of the car, but because of loose road and steep hills. we passed through the tunnel at the top and I came out to the most beautiful, clearest sun light of the day. Lee had driven all morning in the rain and fog, but as soon as It was my turn the sun shone through the clouds and the views were as clear as ever. I could see Lee was upset, that and we were finally going downhill on such a beautiful day, but after a promise to him that I'd only do half and he could do the rest, he was happy.

I looked in the rear view to see the convoy, we were one team short.

Cunning stunts were not with us, I had to pull over.

"one more photo now the suns out" I said to everyone as they piled out. *"we need to wait for those Cunning Bastards as well"*. Snapping away we were eventually joined by them. *"Get a little lost did we"*, I joked. *"Nah we just needed a piss."* said Richie. I could tell something wasn't right here but I wasn't one to intrude.

It turned out that Baz had jumped in the car with all excitement and forgotten about his camera on the roof, they had turned around to grab it from the road only to watch one of the busses drive over it, completely destroying it in the process.

Joined by Hattie the last photo was taken before our decent. Snaking down the most beautiful road full of the smoothest tarmac I had ever driven on was such a blast, the Transfagarasan truly is a stunning road, I would recommend it to anyone, just don't take a car too powerful and know your skill level, plenty of opportunity to kill yourself on it for sure. Half an hour passed and I decided to swap with Lee, pulling over we were one short again. Gnomes. They were right behind us all the way but the views, being so eye-catching means that the last thing you want to do is look back in your rear view to a banger of a Renault Clio. I soon realized had chosen the worst place to stop because of a sign that read 'Do not stop here, watch out for bears.' I mean, bears are one thing but the reputation I would have had for leaving a member of the convoy behind would be another. Waiting for what felt like a very long time, I was about to get in the car and turn back until at the last second, they arrived. Joining at the back of the convoy they all got out the car quick.

"We had to pull over, we finally realised why Hattie was so tired". said Jessie.

"It stinks of gasoline in the back, we didn't notice because we had the windows open in the front" Russel added.

Checking over their car, we grabbed Hattie and made sure she was out the car breathing clear air, that and drinking a whole lot of water. I looked around the car to see what the problem was but I couldn't find it, looking underneath I could see dents and holes in their exhaust but nothing to make such a strong smell. Whatever it was, it wasn't fixable at the roadside. Especially one that supposedly was crawling with bears.

Kate (RMcRF) offered Hattie a seat in their car for the remainder of the day whilst Russell and Jessie sat in the front with the sunroof open and windows down. *"If you feel light headed whilst driving, you pull over immediately."*

After another hour we had finished the Transfagarasan Highway and what a road it was. But where to next? We had only planned up to now. Maps out, phones out, it was time to plan the next part of the adventure.

"Bran Castle or Bucharest?" Lee shouted.

Bran Castle is a huge castle situated on the border between Transylvania and Wallachia, commonly known as Dracula's Castle. Even though there is no evidence to support this, people believe it really was the home of Dracula. I instantly said yes to this, what a fantastic idea. We had a slight deadline because in a few days we had to be in Vama Veche for the Romanian Beach Party that The Adventurists were putting on. Looking at the map I saw that Bran Castle was the opposite way to where we wanted to go. *"Please it sounds fantastic and I think we will all love it"* I asked the Convoy. *"But we could push to Bucharest and get a cheap but wonderful hotel"* said Richie. I could tell in the eyes of everyone there that I had already lost, after two days camping everyone was ready for a shower and a nice bed. Richie being one cracking bloke came to me afterwards and said *"I'm sorry about that mate, it's out of the way and for what I hear, it's a complete tourist trap."* I was a little upset but having managed to get everyone to come to the Church of Bones with me so let this one slip and agreed it was best to head to Bucharest.

We drove in the beautiful sun for hours, stopping for lunch at a huge ALDI in the middle of what felt like the 19th century. We hadn't booked anywhere to stay that evening, Kate had booked into a hotel and she passed on the details to the convoy. Myself and Lee were enjoying our lunch of warm crusty bread so much that by the time we had gone to book, there were no rooms left.

Bollocks.

Kate rang up the hotel to see if she could use her powers of charm and persuasion on the owners. *"We don't care about a room, if they have land, we will pitch up our tent"* I said. *"Or even floor space, we have camp beds"*. Lee added, we just wanted to keep the convoy together as much as we could. After a short phone call Kate told us not to worry, we were in for a surprise.

Pushing on we arrived in Bucharest and after around two hours of rush hour traffic and terrifying city traffic we made it to the hotel, well, I say hotel. Two huge gates in the middle of the city completely covered in Graffiti. Where the bloody hell had she managed to book.

After a few loud knocks and a long press of the buzzer, the gate opened, Rally Mc Rally Face drove in first followed by Cunning Stunts as those two were the only ones to actually have a booking there. I parked up and wandered over to the gate. I was completely taken back by a small but well looked after hotel with a large pool and a beautiful garden, the owner came over and shook my hand *"you come inside, bring your car, you park on the pool"*.

"Sorry, for a moment then I thought you said to park on the pool" I replied.

"Yes, park on pool, come inside, I get my camera, take pictures of your good cars and I bring you beer and Wi-Fi password."
When you think of the Mongol Rally you really do think of desert tracks and sandy tents. Here we were in a beautiful hotel being looked after like royalty. I did as I was asked and drove the car in, due to limited space I had to drive up a curb and navigate around the grids by the pool. Sadly it was completely empty from water as it had just been cleaned, it was a shame but you can't win them all.
"Wi-Fi here, beer here, You are all in top floor Villa, I take photographs and then show you to your rooms".
After a few snaps we were taken up to our rooms, it was no Caesars palace style of Villa, but it was hot showers, clean sheets, own rooms and a place to charge up all of our gear. The kindness of strangers surprises us again.
"Alastair you have to come and see this" Jessie shouted up the stairs. I came down wondering what the noise was all about to be shown to the garden where a ginger and white cat that was completely identical to the poster on our car stood. I couldn't believe it. I snapped some photos of the cat and its missing poster. Of course, I knew it wasn't the same cat but to find one completely identical was hilarious.
"International pet rescue can now be ticked off the list of things I didn't expect to do on the rally."

I called Caroline and the girls back home whilst sipping a cold beer in the lounge, Lee was calling Mica up in the bedroom. For some reason on the entire trip we never rang our partners in front of each other, I think it was all down to feelings. We both wanted to say how we felt and exactly what our experience of the rally had been so far, but neither of us wanted to express our true feelings or doubts in front of the other. It wasn't as if we had bad things to say about the other, it was more we didn't want to voice our concerns whilst the other remained in the room.

With everyone showered and our hotel owner taking care of our washing, It was time for food and time to explore the wonders of Bucharest.

Other rally teams were scattered about the city in random hotels and hostels they had found online, I hoped for the return of DSMS too as they couldn't be too far behind us. WhatsApp came out and a meeting point was made with those close by. Octoberfest a bar in Old Town Bucharest was the place to be that evening, Ubers were called and once again we were shocked at the price, we worked it out that it was costing us around 75 pence for a 15-minute drive. How they made a profit on this, I have no idea. We were in no rush to head out as cold beer and Wi-Fi on the terrace was truly amazing. We even took the time to work out how many thousand miles we had left to the finish line and that if we booked a cheap uber it would have only cost us £900 in total to hire one, however doubtful any of them would be up for the job and visas would be a big problem. Nevertheless, plan B was there!

The short drive showed us Bucharest and how its nightlife truly thrives, cheap party goers and stag-dos were all in action. It was annoying to see a stag-do and hear an accent from 'just down the road.' For them they were a few hours plane ride away from home, for us it was a 7-day intense drive.

The Oktoberfest bar seemed really cool, myself and the rest of Cunning Stunts arrived first, Grabbing a large table outside, Baz took the opportunity to grab the waitress quickly and order four pints of local beer, within seconds they were here and the drinks begin to flow. A cold beer on a warm night after a long, beautiful drive really was the best way to end a perfect day. Other teams had started turning up looking a little worse for wear than we were.

"Hey lads, good to see you, how's your day been? We went to Bran Castle, what a shithole, complete tourist trap, then our hotel gave our room away at a really nice place with a pool"

Richie held up his pint, clinked it against mine and we both nodded knowing full well we dodged a bullet from not going to the castle and that our luxury apartment in our hotel was most probably theirs at first. Baz ordered them pints and they joined the table. Joined by Lee and the rest of what remained of Convoi Exceptionnel, there wasn't enough seats but our large crowd were in high spirits. Baz called the waitress over and she refused to serve anyone who was stood up. We couldn't believe it. Only those who were sat down could be served. Squeezing onto tables and benches everyone managed to get a seat but the waitress was having none of it, we took it in turns to speak to her thinking the language barrier was a problem but she seemed annoyed, stomping off she soon returned with 6 pints that she gave only to my table. we tried to hand them out to others, but she literally pulled the pint glasses from their mouths and handed them back.

"Oh well, more for me then" Ritchie commented.

The waitress refused to serve anyone from this point, another lady came over, took our order of what was around 16 pints of local beer and the Convoi was re-fueled once again. We have no idea what we did to annoy this waitress, she probably thought we were just another stag do!

After too much beer we had completely ran out of money and time, it was around 1am and a chorus of *"chips, kebabs and miscellaneous meat"* echoed the table. We found a takeaway but all being out of local currency we...
Oh, wait.
This wasn't just any old takeaway; it was a takeaway with a Bureau-de-change inside. *"If we had one of these in England, I'd be fat and skint"* shouted Ritchie who had probably been three pints ahead of us all by this point. Ordering the only vegetarian option on the menu, I settled for 'chip kebab'.
I returned to the hotel with Lee, James and Baz soon after, leaving Kate, Ritchie and the others to drink the town dry.

Stood in the hotel room with the window wide open, I looked out into the darkness. I could hear all the crickets, cats and traffic, It was warm, I was full and I couldn't have been happier. I missed my family so much but I was on the adventure I had dreamed of for so many years. It was the end of the first week and it made me think back to everyone who made this adventure possible for me, the sponsors, family, friends, just everyone. I was in debt to so many yet the only way to pay them back was to have fun and enjoy myself. If I did that every day, in the good times and the bad, as long as I made the most of my trip and threw myself into the adventure. I knew the debt would be settled with the smile on my face and the stories I would tell when I get home.

Chapter 8 - Days 8-10 - Traveling to Turkey

We all woke early and packed the cars. Every morning was a complete struggle to get everything loaded up, as soon as we had pulled out our personal rucksacks and the tech box (just a clear big box that all electronics went in) the rest of the car's contents seemed to cave in on itself. When it then came to putting things back in, an entire re-pack was in order. We had planned to sort it out but still had not found the time. Lee reversed the car off the swimming pool and turned it round in the tiny gap between the other cars. We had a short drive ahead of us today to a place called Vama Veche (Romania) where The Adventurists were putting on a party on the sandy beach of The Black Sea. I couldn't wait, a lunchtime finish, a warm sandy beach and a beautiful sea to dip into followed by as much alcohol as I could drink!
I took the captains seat in the car as I needed a little more experience of city driving in a place where having a license is optional. Lee took navigation and we were on our way, I edged out of the hotel car park.
SLAM
I hit the brakes as just as we were about to leave our good friends DSMS turned up. Convoi Exceptionnel was almost complete again, we were just missing our good friends James and Jade from MiniAd.
"Cigarette or a coffee before we leave Sir's?" someone shouted.
Hugging Oli, Dan and Adam we all greeted them with open arms. *"It's good to be with you again chaps".*
After a rushed cigarette and some freshly brewed coffee, attempt two. I edged out slowly and onto the road, it was

busy with nowhere to wait or pull in, turning down the road I found a gap just big enough to squeeze into whilst I waited for the rest of the convoy, After pulling in, I looked behind to see I was parked on Tram tracks with a Tram about to run up the arse of the car. Flooring it we were out of danger and out of sight from the rest of the convoy. I wasn't doing very well at this 'driving in a busy city' but by complete luck, somehow we all seemed to meet up and once again the convoy was complete, we drove south east leaving the city, every now and again we would stop at the lights for the cars next to us to spark up conversation. *"Good luck my friends"* or *"You, where are you going?"* were some of my favorites, occasionally people would see our stickers and license plates and we would hear *"It didn't come home!"* This was in relation to the world cup, the day before we set off on the trip England had been knocked out of the world cup, anyone who was a football fan on the trip liked to remind us about this.

Leaving the city, the roads worsened until we got onto the motorway, we all needed petrol so we pulled in to the next station where were extremely lucky because at this point Emma from Team: This Is Gonna Yurt who I had been speaking to before the rally, gave us the heads up on the 'Official Mongol Rally 2018 Facebook Page' that the way we were going there was a bridge that you HAD to pay to cross BEFORE you went on it, either that or their camera's would catch you and you would be paying out a large fine. It's wrong that somewhere with such bad pot holes and such friendly people that they try catch you out and take as much money off you as they can.

I queued up in the long que at the petrol station, purchased a ticket and we were on our way (Thanks again Emma) I even managed to pass the info onto another rally team who just pulled in as we were about to leave. We were starting to see other ralliers more often from this point as we were all heading to the same spot in Romania, from there everyone would branch out across the world with some taking the northern route through Russia all the way and others like us heading more central/southern. The beach party is a sort of farewell party to European grounds and a welcoming to either an Asian or Russian beginning to the trip.

The road was boring. Mainly because it was flat, straight and smooth. The weather was dull as rain attempted to fall and the beautiful landscape of Romania was hidden by low clouds. We weren't on the motorway for much longer before the toll bridge arrived, driving straight though we saw it was completely unmanned but the signs for CCTV were everywhere, even though we couldn't see any, we didn't want to think that we had queued and paid for its use for absolutely nothing. As we drove evermore southeast to the coastline, I thought that I had never seen such a flat landscape, most of Northern Romania were stunning hills and magnificent views across valleys. But as we headed more towards the coast and the border of Bulgaria, It was incredibly flat, on a fine day I bet you could have see for miles.

I was feeling tired, Lee swapped with me and took the wheel allowing me to nap, I fell asleep with my head resting against the passenger window completely conked out. An hour passed and I awoke to the smell of emissions, in stand still traffic, with the sun shining in my face, it was so warm. My

eyes began to focus as I dropped my sunglasses over my eyes completely dazed. I looked out of the window.
It was beautiful.
The cloudy, dull, flat looking side of Romania was gone! We were in beach party central!
I'd only been asleep an hour and the entire landscape had changed completely. Checking my phone, the Convoy had been looking at places to camp on the beach and by serching booking.com They had found a really cool looking site with tents already set up with Hawaiian looking roofs over the top to protect them from the wind. It looked like a private oasis, seeing free parking only sweetened the deal. Knowing that close to one thousand ralliers were about to turn up, we booked it as quickly as we could.

Arriving in Vama Veche was very surreal, the dull northern landscape of Romania had turned into a raving hotspot with everyone walking around in sand filled flip flops as the sun melted the ice cream out of every tourist's hand. We got a lot of attention in the main tourist area, this worried us slightly as our campsite was extremely close and a lot of attention isn't always what you wanted.
My first glimpse of the black sea came as a shock, it was beautiful. For a completely landlocked sea it was surprisingly clear, as the sun reflected off the water and into our eyes.
"Get me to the campsite and get me in that sea"
I shouted over our loudspeaker system to the rest of the convoy.
Seeing Cunning stunts and DSMS put their thumbs up with approval, I made Lee step on it.
"Turn Right,

Turn Left,
You have arrived at your destination"
we heard from our Maps.Me Navigation App.
Then there it was, Paradise.

Well, it may have been if your name was 'Hope', age 18 and
this was your first budget holiday without mum and dad.
The music from the club next door was LOUD. The toilets
were situated a short walk away and the stench made your
eyes sting, the tents had seen better days and the secure
parking was non-existent.
The only plus side to it all was the company we had and the
beautiful sea view in front.
I re-read the adventurists email about the beach party, it was
sent to us months ago, way before we set off and at that
point it felt so far away, I only read a little bit. I wish I had
taken more notice when it read *"book in at our official
campsite in Varma Veche, Sandalandaland. with secure
parking and cheap pitching for your tent."*
Bollocks.
We drove out cars round there to find so many teams parked
up, their tents up and beers in hand. It was so tempting to
pay again for camping and move our gear over there but as
Hattie (Gnomes) said quite clearly *"Were going to get so
drunk tonight, I don't care where we sleep".* That said it all.
We all agreed to park our cars there securely (witch we
negotiated to get it for free) and took only a sleeping bag
over to the tents we were in, about a ten-minute walk away.
This meant if anything was stolen from inside, it wouldn't be
anything of value.
With the thought of a dip in the black sea etched into our
minds we quickly changed and ran for the beach.

Almost all of us ran into the refreshing, cold water. It was glorious. Our convoy was like a newly formed family. The laughs and jokes were incredible, we were purposely splashing each other and diving under the water, popping back up trying to scare the shit out of each other pretending to be sharks before making Adam dodge rocks we threw at him like a real live version of space invaders.

Lee took a while before he joined us, he was helping Kate blow up her giant pizza slice lilo, it took him about fifteen minutes before needing a rest due to how light headed he was. It wasn't until he finished, a local pointed over to a free to use compressor, less than fifteen meters from here he sat. Thinking back, it's amazing to see how our five teams from all around the world who had only met just over a week ago had gone from complete strangers to the most amazing of friends.

We swam quite far out, I did my best as I couldn't swim well at all, Adam and Danny had to save me a few times but gave me some helpful tips to stop my head from going under. Eventually the storm clouds from earlier in the day had caught us up, as we went to leave the sea the rain began, but this didn't dampen the mood at all. Sat in the rain up to our shoulders in the still sea, swaying in the warmth of the water as the waves rocked us gently, it looked as if someone had spilt a massive bean-bag over the Black Sea as the water droplets glistened whilst bouncing into the air above the shimmering surface.

Jessie (Gnomes) was sat in the water close to the sand, joining her she said *"I didn't expect to be doing things like this on the rally."*

None of us could have agreed more, the rally is surprising in many ways, you don't get out of your car often, but when you do, my god do you make the most of it.

Looking out to sea we couldn't believe what we saw, just above the water enjoying the empty water.

Dolphins.

Exactly where we had just been swimming, a pod of dolphins swam past, it was so beautiful to watch such large elegant mammals splash around in a natural environment. I only wished we were still out there in the heat and the rain with them swimming around, but it was time to get out, it was time to start drinking.

A quick trip back to Sandalalala (whatever it was called) for some food ended in quite a few beers before meeting up with Emma and her Aussie friends. *"Try this drink Alastair, it's called Tuica, its 84% and its Romania's version of Moonshine"*

The shot entered my mouth and slid slowly down my throat, the burning sensation went from the lips, to the back of my mouth and straight into my stomach. I could feel my body screaming at me *"Why did you just do that to yourself!"* but I paid no attention and tried to show little emotion towards the disgusting taste.

"That was vile."

The official party was just a little further down the road, without delay we all headed down to see what The Adventurists could surprise us with this time. We were greeted to a huge bonfire on the beach, burning away in the sand, the music was loud and the alcohol was flowing. Everyone was in such a fantastic mood as horror stories from the road so far were passed around. Hearing about the three wheeled Reliant Robin setting on fire in the middle of the motorway was an upsetting tale. Everyone is extremely supporting to all other teams, it's what we call 'Rally Spirit'. Helping those in need when you can is a must because you will never know when you may need them to help you in the future, karma really is always with you.

Beer after beer the night got darker and darker until the only thing illuminating the beach was the large roaring fire and a few dull lights from the club, I had lost the convoy but had mingled and made a few new friends as I offered out a few cigarettes and showed off my sleeve tattoo to a few locals.

After a while I drunkenly stumbled outside the club where I found an MK2 Ford Fiesta parked directly outside, It was completely covered in stickers, some Mongol Rally, another Budapest rally, Mongol Rally 2016, absolutely loads!

The owner was stood next to it, he was an absolute Viking. Tall, heavily built with a long ginger beard, rough looking ginger hair and a fur style outfit, to top it all off he had a large knife in one hand and the leg of an animal in another, slowly cutting bits off, he offered chunks of flesh to the ralliers around him. I was hesitant to approach at first but a burst of courage from the Romanian moonshine pushed me over to him, he was called Vidar Øksendal and he is probably the coolest person I have ever met.

Extremely generous he offered food and drink to those who came over to say hello, he spoke about all of the rallies he had done before and you could tell in the calmness of his voice that he wasn't scared of anything that lay ahead of him. His roof rack on his car was empty which was unusual for a rally car, when I asked him why, he unfolded it and set up a mosquito net. *"It's where I sleep, under the stars, as close to nature as I can be."*

He was a badass.

No doubt.

A naturally born traveler and good friend to all. (Vidar Øksendal if you ever read this, I salute you my good sir!)

I had spotted Hattie (Gnomes) in the corner of my eye and said my goodbyes to Vidar, I headed over to find the rest of the convoy stood around the slowly burning out fire one the beach, it needed wood and fast. This huge bonfire hadn't lasted long, but luckily a few other ralliers looked around with us only to find a huge piece of driftwood, it was perfect and extremely heavy. Dragging it through the sand was tough but through determination we all got it onto the fire, it started to burn away as drunken ralliers decided to take their shoes off and walk along it whilst it burnt away, cheers could be heard every time someone crossed it successfully followed by a few screams from those who just hadn't made it and needed a helping hand across.

Suddenly the entirety of the staff from the bar ran out and dragged it off the fire, the owner looked furious and in broken English he said *"Decoration is very expensive."*

Looking back at the wood we could see it had been carved, shaped and sculpted to be the wacky shape it was. It was probably worth a fortune.

Whoops.

Shots were consumed, washed down with beer by the stein. However, like all good parties it soon came to a close. What a fantastic night it had been, *"those Adventurous blokes had done it again."*

Waking up in the tent on the beach, fully clothed and not in my sleeping bag was the sign of a good night.

It was early but with the sun shining down off the beautiful sea into my eyes, I came to my senses quickly and slowly got out of the tent. Boiling hot, dry to the bone feeling like a raisin, I took of most of my cloths until just in my underwear and waddled gently into the sea.

It was fantastic.

My hangover was almost nonexistent after ten minutes in the refreshing water, I could tell that Lee was feeling fragile but the crazy upbeat music from the nearby club had finally ended. One by one everyone crawled out of their tent, Russell and Jessie were feeling good but when Hattie appeared from out of her tent, we all knew it would be a bad day for her.

We had completely lost Cunning Stunts and RallyMcRallyFace this morning so our convoy of five had gone down to three, AFK, Gnomes and DSMS. We tried all the usual ways of contacting them, messenger, WhatsApp and carrier pigeon but no luck, with time slipping away, if we were to get to the Turkish border today, we had to set off now.

I took the first shift driving, knowing Lee wouldn't be up for it just yet and that there was a border crossing into Bulgaria very soon. Sooner than we thought actually, I pulled out of the campsite and onto the main road, within seconds there it was. A quick border change and another Vinaigrette in the car we were soon winding through the sunny roads of Bulgaria. Following the coast all the way round with every now and again being pushed back in land into the beautiful Bulgarian hills, smooth roads and stunning views. Occasionally you would get a glimpse of the next town coming up but somehow we would never go through one, the road always winded us around them, this wasn't an issue as the countryside was so stunning, but it was an issue when it came down to looking for a spot of lunch.

Pulling over intermittently for photos, videos and wee breaks we decided to push on till late afternoon to eat. We passed 'Sunny Beach' which we quickly renamed to 'Tourist Trap Shithole'. Due to the number of run-down clubs and green water waterparks. We passed through Burgas where we saw a terrible car accident, it really brought us back to earth with the dangers of the journey ahead. Especially when we found out about a few Ralliers who had crashed their car earlier in the day and ended up in a very bad way. Until we finally reached the golden arches! Turkey.

No, wait, McDonalds. Sorry.

Pulling in for fuel, we spotted the sign that no raillery could ever resist 'Free WIFI', me and Lee didn't really care much for it as we had free data roaming in Europe but until the two Canadians got a Sim Card, this is the best they could get. After a quick re-fuel we were back on the road, Lee's phone was blasting out the motivational tunes as we pushed to get to the Turkish border, we said goodbye to the Black sea as the road took us more inland to the border, Emma from 'So Good it Yurt's' messaged me telling me they had just got there. They set off a good few hours before us, so we had a bit of catching up to do. It was a shame we had to rush through Bulgaria so quickly, there was so much we missed however with the gateway to Asia just down the road we couldn't resist pushing on.

Lee took the pilot's seat and cruised us through what was left of Bulgaria, I'm quite sure I fell asleep at one point, I was thinking how at this point on the trip you can just fall asleep in the car, but soon we would be facing off road sections and unbearable road conditions that sleep would be almost impossible to catch up on, So I took the liberty to have a little snooze when I was woken by Lee.

"Were close to the border my good man, you need to take the wheel soon."

Before he took a slight wrong turning down a dead-end road in a quiet village. It was the perfect time to swap over once again. I got out of the car, DSMS and Gnomes all did the same just to grab some food or water from the boot, then I looked up to a telegraph pole at the end of the street.

At the top was the biggest birds nest I had ever seen, it overflowed the top of the telegraph pole like the top of a belisha beacon, structurally It was completely solid, this was proved when a huge stalk landed on top and began walking around. I couldn't believe it, all the locals didn't seem to care, it was normal for them, but for us to see such a huge bird nesting in the middle of civilization was just so strange. *"I wonder what Lancashire County Council would think of that"* I joked.

"Ali, how long has the back wheel been like that" Lee asked calmly.

I turned to see what he was talking about to be greeted with our rear driver's side wheel pointing inwards slightly on a camber.

"Oh Bollocks"

I instantly went over to the car, wrapped my arms around the wheel and gave it a wobble, it sure wasn't happy.

Lee didn't have much mechanical knowledge before setting off on the trip, so whenever a problem arose, I spoke through it as clear as I could to help him understand.

Looking around I put the reason down to a broken bearing,

although I hadn't heard any grinding lately, though I had just been asleep.

"Once we are in Turkey, we can get the wheel off and take a look, it's okay to drive on, whilst we wait at the border we can re-distribute the weight in the back to help it."

Lee was fantastic, he understands things very well and isn't afraid to ask questions or challenge anything, he takes in information well and learns very quickly. With this said, he was confident and happy to move on. Which was good as I didn't think the stork would come back with a Mk3 Fiesta Bearing no matter how much we gave it.

I was meant to be taking it easy but with the smooth road and the winding bends we were at the border in less than an hour.

A huge sign above our heads that read 'Türkiye' provided an excellent opportunity for photos and the queue itself gave an excellent opportunity to speak to some of the locals returning from a trip to Europe or a guard of no man's land supporting an AK47 like it was nothing.

It was close to 8pm and the sun had just started heading over the hills. *"Won't be long now lads, we could be in Istanbul by midnight tonight If you guys wanted to push on"* said Adam.

The idea made sense, we would be ahead of schedule and it meant first thing in the morning me and Lee could go to a garage.

"Sounds like a plan," both me and Lee chorused.

The plan was shattered instantly as by the time we got to the front of the queue it was close to 9.30pm and we still hadn't sorted out car insurance. This was the first country we had entered outside of Europe so from now on, car insurance had to be purchased at every border. Parking up I saw Emma's car and other cars parked up who set off hours before us. Something didn't seem right. *"Why are they still here?!"*

We met everyone at the Insurance hut, before I could ask anyone why they were still there, Emma headed over with the bad news. *"The insurance system is down, its being rebooted at midnight, he can still do insurance but he is moving at an average of one car an hour sending car documents to a mate at another border using WhatsApp, looks like you are in for a long wait"*

She was right.

10pm hit and we still hadn't moved, the man in the booth was just on his phone with the window shut, to make it worse it had just started raining and there was no cover. I got speaking to a cracking guy called Chris who was doing the rally solo on a motorbike, a Suzuki Intruder 125cc if I remember correctly. He had been there since 2pm that afternoon and had to watch as other ralliers arrived after him and left before him. This was because the insurance hut couldn't process bikes at all until the system was back up and running, I felt for him, he had nowhere dry to stay and his gear on the bike was getting wetter by the second.

He covered his bike with tarp we found at the roadside and joined me at my car, he couldn't take his eyes off the can of cola I was drinking.

"You have supplies with you right? food and drink?" I asked.
"I only had enough for lunch, wasn't expecting this delay".
Within seconds I bombarded him with water, cola, biscuits and fruit. I'd never seen a man so happy!

11.45pm was greeted with good news, we had gotten to the front of the que and within seconds the system had come back online.

we gave him 30 of the queen's English pound because he had no clue of the exchange rate, other teams before us had been paying in dollars costing them about $80. We were certainly getting a bargain.

The deal was struck and we headed to our cars to wait for the convoy.

12.30am and we were away.

"Race you to Istanbul" I said to Danny, Oli and Adam.

"Turkey Awaits" they replied.

I drove through the night until 3am where we stopped for food at a roadside cafe that just had chunks of meat in a broth for sale, we ordered 8 portions for the meat eaters along with the beautiful delicacy that is rice and bread for me.

Sitting there to the chorus of crickets, wide awake after a meal and a few cigarettes we used our last bit of Bulgarian data to book into a hostel in the centre of Istanbul.

Finally, a bed was in sight.

Chapter 9 - Days 10-12 - "Smells like a Destruction Derby"

I didn't sleep at all. The hostel we had booked was rather full meaning I was put in a room by myself with complete strangers who snored, argued and shouted in whatever language they spoke all night long. At one point some bloke tried starting a fight with me as 'I was in his bed' when really, he wasn't even in this room, he was the next floor up. At first light I packed up my gear and headed out to the car, I felt miserable. I had to scout around the streets for a second before I stepped out the Hostel because as we were driving down the narrow streets of old Istanbul in the early hours the street the Hostel was on was crawling with dogs, barking and howling. One had even chewed the tire off another rally car until it had bust. With the coast clear I took some time to check over our rear wheel problem, it didn't seem good, the wheel was rocking slightly but not from the point you would expect it too if a bearing had broken. Also, the drive into the early hours of the morning gave me the chance to test out the car, no knocks or noises could be heard.

Slowly the rest of the convoy started to wake, I had to go into Lee's room and wake him up personally as it was getting close to 9am and we had to find a mechanic before we could move on any further today.

"You look for mechanic" I heard from the Hostel owner. *"I know many Ford mechanic, follow me I take you there."*
Brilliant.
He rang up the mechanic and told me to follow him there.
I had gone from not knowing where to start, to having booked into a mechanic within seconds. I went to nudge Lee

again who had fallen back to sleep and told him we needed to move NOW.

Eventually he was up and out of bed, clothes on, bags packed and loaded into the car, I then turned to the convoy and said something I was dreading the entire time. *"We are going to have to leave you to find a mechanic, we don't know what the problem is yet but don't wait for us, go ahead, we will catch up."*

DSMS were planning on staying for a day in Istanbul to see the sights, so they didn't mind and we assured them we would get Wi-Fi and speak to them if we were to stay another night due to car troubles.

Gnomes were a little more unsure, they had relied on us and the convoy to lead them this far and I think their plan was to follow us the rest of the way, they were torn between staying, pushing ahead or coming with us.

"We don't know what the outcome will be, but we plan on being at the Turkish/Georgian border in four days' time, we can always meet there if we don't see each other along the way" Lee said.

He was completely right.

The car was ready to go and the Hostel owner was getting impatient. We said our goodbyes, for the first time since the Ferry until we were on our own.

Following the hostel owner though the snake like streets of Istanbul, he tore through the streets at breakneck pace, nipping in and out of lanes, between busses and jumping stop signs. He thought himself quite the race driver, but not a very good one judging by the number of scrapes all over his car. We had to follow him at all costs or find ourselves lost without a mechanic. (This guy could have learnt a few things

from this book about convoy driving, but it wasn't published back then.) Eventually we pulled up to a garage, no luck.
He waved us around the corner to another garage who came out to take photos but not offer much support, they seemed to just wobble the tyre, find a picture of a part on their phone and do the international sign for money.
rubs his thumb against his index and middle finger
Eventually though Lee's translator Apps and some broken English he gives us an address on the other side of Istanbul, a kind of car graveyard and repair centre.
It was our only choice, we had to just keep looking.
The Hostel owner got into his car and drove off quickly, he had clearly had enough and couldn't be bothered with us anymore so we did the only thing we could and headed to the closest matching address that Maps.me had to offer.
After an hour searching, I ended up driving the car into some sort of abandoned shopping mall with a half tarmac, half dirty marble floor. Where each shop had been converted from retail to garage, this meant that there was absolutely no ventilation at all. It was completely packed with cars billowing out smoke, welding torches on high, smokers sparking up and grinders flying with sparks. The noise was insane, it was just like a chop shop you see in films.
A lad about the same age as us came over, he didn't speak a word of English but by his actions he showed us we were in the right place.
I don't know what it was, but this guy was just completely genuine from the first second, like lost sheep, me and Lee had driven into this place and anyone could have taken advantage of us, but this guy shook our hands, greeted us with a big white teeth smile and signaled me to put the car up on the ramp.

Getting out of the car another lad joined us with water, cigarettes and chai tea. Shook our hands and took us into the small garage, it was extremely easy to tell that these two lads were brothers and the bloke who was now under our rally car having a look around with a zippo lighter and a hammer was their father.

With broken English and google translate in hand we communicate very well with the two lads, The map we had printed on the back of the car window helped so much, they could see the scale of our adventure, where we had come from and where we were heading too. Their eyes opened wide in shock that we were doing the journey in such a tiny, overloaded, old car.

Their father came out from under the car and signaled for me to take a look, my mood was great and I was in high hopes that we were with a bunch of genuine people offering their help, I took a look under the car and...

"...Oh Fuck."

"That's a game changer that one mate" I said to Lee.

He joined me underneath the car.

"Oh Shit, can it be fixed"

The problem was obvious to anyone, it wouldn't matter if you had been working with cars your entire life or if you had no idea about them at all, a GIANT crack and hole in your rear axle causing the wheel to be bend in due to the weight is a huge problem.

I turned around to see the older gentleman with a huge flat metal bar in one hand, a welder's mask in the other and a huge smile across his face. We were in safe hands and I was confident that we would have it resolved soon.

Lee went to withdraw cash to pay them and had HUGE problems asking for a bank or ATM on a Sunday. Thankfully a little boy who knew a tiny bit of English came to the rescue. I stayed with the car, drank tea, smoked cigarettes next to some of the most flammable materials I had ever seen in my life and sat near a desk fan to get a slight breeze on my face. It was over 35 degrees Celsius outside and inside this sweaty converted shopping mall/garage/chop shop it was easily in the 40's.

One of the lads came over and sat with me, he enjoyed showing me pictures of his life, his wife and daughter were very beautiful, they lived in a small flat around the corner and this was his first job since leaving his three years military service in Syria.

Syria!

I couldn't believe it, a man whose eyes widened in horror when he saw our map was showing me pictures in his regimental uniform in a completely destroyed country. In my eyes he was the crazy one, but over there, military service is a requirement not a choice. I showed him pictures of Caroline and the girls back home and he patted me on the back, it doesn't matter what language you speak, emotions speak a thousand words and he could tell I missed them dearly.

Lee arrived back with cash, sweets, water and his usual sausage roll.

Lee has this amazing trick that no matter where he is in the world, he can always find somewhere that sells a bloody sausage roll. Whilst he ate, I checked out the car, he had done a cracking job with very good braces where it had snapped, It looked strong and a few bashes with a hammer showed us that it was. I asked him to do the other side to save heartbreak in the future of it happening on the rear left. He cracked on as the lads popped the bonnet and topped up our oil, checked the battery and took a look at some of the weird and wonderful gear we had with us. Everyone seemed to enjoy the CB radio, loudspeaker and LED bar, these were mods that were rarely seen on any Turkish car.

The car was welded, dropped off the ramp and driven off by Lee with the siren on, LED bar shining bright and a great mood all around.

"Right, now for payment, let's try not get fleeced here mate, but good work deserves a good wage" I said to Lee.

I was referring to the horror stories from other ralliers where they keep hold of your keys or fiddle with parts to stop your car from going anywhere until you have paid up. 'Ne Kadar' (How much?) was written on Lee's phone and we waited to head the inevitable.

"Erm…. Fifty"

I looked at Lee, *"… Dollars?"* … That's not bad at all.

"No, my friends, Lira"

50 Lira at that point was close to the equivalent of £15 and I can honestly say that whilst we were there I smoked and drank over that amount. I could not believe our luck. We gave them a little extra and had a toast for the road. With no Wi-Fi or internet anywhere around we didn't know what to do, there was no point going back to the Hostel as everyone would have left by then, it was getting close to 1pm and we just made the decision to crack on, get out of Istanbul and see where we can get to that evening. We could either catch up or wait for the rest of the convoy if needed.

Meanwhile,

DSMS wandered the grand bazaar and picked one of the millions of identical shops to buy some tea from. This turned out to be very fortunate because the shop owner found Hattie (Gnomes) to be rather lovely and declared himself to be her new boyfriend. Hattie blushed her reciprocation and acceptance of the proposal. He also popped some free chocolates, little green things that looked like exotic eggs into all their mouths and I mean actually put them in their mouths. What a great guy. Then finding a rooftop bar with a good view of the coast and two gigantic Mosques. Each had their own speaker system for the hourly prayers and in order to not talk over one another took it in turns to sing their prayers. This quickly turned into an epic rap battle with Red mosque absolutely slaying blue mosque.

Back to the AFK Lads!
I took the first shift for driving; I drove for about 3 hours but only managed around 20 miles as that's how long it took to get out of Istanbul.
Its absolute carnage!
The motorway is completely gridlocked at all times and to top it all off its full of families trying to make a few coins by selling water, flowers, pretzels and nuts. Once the traffic cleared up, we had to pull over to use the bathroom and freshen up. After this, Lee took over driving, I didn't get much sleep and it was starting to affect my driving.
I fell asleep for a short time but woke up with the sun shining on my face down a beautiful, smooth, clear motorway.
I had decided to spend £6 on all you can eat data for the day in Turkey, I wanted to let the convoy know about our troubles and how we would hopefully meet up with them

again soon. I also wanted to let Caroline know what happened.

As I was about to WhatsApp call a rainstorm hit that slowed the traffic right down, With the Turkish drivers being rather unpredictable I waited and helped Lee with vision. It was a huge rainstorm, one that makes visibility close to nothing and your wipers do absolutely nothing, a few times I had to throw my head out of the window just to make sure we were safe.

As quick as it had started, it ended.

We were greeted once again by the sun and to celebrate not dying, the radio was turned up full and 'The Book of Mormon - Original Broadway Cast' was belted around the northern hills of Turkey. after a while I turned the radio down to speak to Lee. *"Do you ever have Deja vu but instead of seeing something you smell it?"*

I could tell he was extremely confused.

"Like a smell that transports you somewhere you have been but you can't figure out where it is?"

I could see that I was finally explaining myself instead of talking complete shit. (I do that very often) *"Well, I can smell a Destruction Derby, I used to go to Stock car racing in Silverdale near me and it smells like that."*

"Oh yeah, I know what you mean" he said. *"I've had it before with a few things, I once... wait."*

Pause.

Lee glanced over to me.

"Do you mean like, a kind of burning rubber smell?" he asked.

"Yeah that's the one, it smells like that." I replied.

Note: With the heat of the car, Lack of sleep and service station food keeping us on the ball, I think we both regret how long it took us to work this one out. We both felt like complete Idiots afterwards.

Lee looked around in the mirrors to see the lorry behind us flashing us like crazy and white smoke began to billow from the rear driver's side tyre where we just had the axle welded. Luckily, Lee being the absolute legend he is, he spotted a service station about a quarter of a mile up the road and he cruised it in there brilliantly with the help of the lorry slowing down traffic behind us. We both felt sick, this was classed as our first full on breakdown. The truck behind us turned his hazard beacons on and controlled the traffic behind us as we slowed to a crawl down the hard shoulder. Once we were in the service station, I left the car and before checking out the damage, I gave Lee a good, friendly whack on the back and said well done for keeping control and calm. I feel as if I was driving at this point it could have been very different, I don't think I'd have been as calm or tried to coast it into the services, but Lee did and it made this situation safer and 100% easier than it could have been.

The damage was exactly what I expected, the guys in Istanbul had done an amazing job repairing the axel where it had weakened, but now because that section was so strong, the next weakest point had given in, a lot further down the axel just behind the brake drum.

I got the jack out and began jacking up the car however with every turn of the spindle, I started to hear the crunching of metal. Nothing I could have done at the roadside would have fixed this.

"We need a tow truck and another welder" I announced to myself.

Lee didn't say a word, he walked off towards the services whilst I had a prod abound the axel and began weight shedding in the boot, trying to re-distribute the contents so that when we finally had a solution, it wouldn't cause further damage.

Lee came back and my god he came back in style.

Cash in his hands, *"I got this out for the tow truck cost,"*

Security guy by his side *"this guy knows someone with a truck and he is setting off now, he will be about 20 minutes."*

Oh and *"Here is some food from in there."*

That my good friends, is problem solving.

That my good friends, is friendship.

That my good friends, is Lee Marriott.

Before I'd finished re-packing the tow truck had already arrived, it was getting dull and the rain was making a reappearance so I was rather grateful. Handing the video camera to Lee I asked him to blog what happened as he could describe it best being the driver. Whilst he did that, I let Caroline know back home it was a tough day but we were doing what we could to get it fixed and keep on going.

It was time to message the convoy too, let them know to push on and if we ever get it fixed, if it's even fixable, we would hopefully meet up with them again one day. It was a hard text to send, I dropped a pin to them to show them our live location letting them know how far we had gotten, put my phone on silent and focused on what was in front of me. The car was filmed as it was dragged onto the back of the truck, we jumped in the front and we were away.

To where? unknown.

Who with? unknown.

For what? unknow.

A short drive took us to Hendeck a good-sized town about 220km east from Istanbul and thankfully still in the right direction. We really had chosen a great place to break down. The sun was slowly setting as both me and Lee were trying to figure out what we were going to do, but after a short debate we realised there was nothing we could do until we knew where the driver was taking us.

We arrived at a garage, still open at 7.30pm on a Sunday, Jacking the car up he bent the wheel back straight and made a buzzing sound to signal a welder. What I didn't expect next was he got in the car, started the engine and just drove off in it.

Everything was in the car, passports, documents, food, cloths, literally our entire lives and some Turkish bloke had taken it for a spin. We were on a huge industrial estate filled with garages, some looking modern others looking derelict, the sound of wild dogs and engine revving broke the silence of the landscape. Then we saw the headlights of a car coming towards us. *"Thank god, he's back"* I thought. As the car got closer I realised, it didn't have a roof rack, its headlights were curved and on the top were two garden gnomes.

Wait.

GARDEN GNOMES!

Team Two Fake Yanks and a Scott were here, but How?

"Hey guys, need a lift" said Russell with a huge smile on his face. We were so excited to see them, it was fantastic to have some help and support with us at such a shitty time. Jessie and Hattie ran out and I instantly threw my arms around them, *"How on earth did you find us"* said Lee.

"You dropped your location on WhatsApp, we have been following you for the past two hours" Hattie said, as if it was completely obvious. If anything, it was genius.

I was so happy to see them, to have their support with us meant that my worries of this evening had completely disappeared.

"Where's your car" Jessie asked as he looked around the garage. SHIT THE CAR! We had no idea where it was still or what was going on, so we had to split into groups and search, it was like old school Scooby doo! eventually Shaggy and Scooby (Lee and Russell) found the car and I was called over in haste. Running over as quick as I could thinking there was a huge problem I realised that Lee had shouted as they were about to start welding. I instantly noticed the negative on the battery was still connected. At that point I had no hope whatsoever.

It was at this point Jessie, Russell and Hattie caught up to us, Hattie smiled at then both before speaking. *"We want you both to know that if this is the end of the rally for your car, then we will happily steal your roof rack, put all of our equipment on the roof and take you with us. We were thinking about it on the drive here. We would love to have you with us."*
I was instantly touched, I couldn't speak. Their generosity was truly amazing. Eventually I found my words and thanked them for their kind offer, I just wasn't ready to throw in the towel on our car yet.

An hour passed and the welding was complete, we changed a wheel to one of the spares on our roof as the amount of tread we had burnt away driving with it running against the shock absorber was astonishing and even more incredible, the tyre hadn't burst.

We all felt good, I looked at the weld and it really wasn't the best, but for now it would have to do.

Then the worst thing happened. We were completely fleeced.

The owner of the garage must have thought we were loaded when he asked for $400 American dollars. Not a chance, we didn't even have that on us (We may have done hidden in the car, but he was never to know) We argued, the same weld we got for 50 Lira was now costing us 400 dollars. But he has us and there was no escaping, we managed to negotiate down to 300 Lira for the fix and about 60 Lira for the truck.

This in pounds works out at about £56.

Fuck it, we just paid him, got in the car and drove out of sight. I didn't care anymore, I was tired and I wanted to get a good night's sleep before taking a look at his shitty job the next morning. If we needed a new axle or a re-weld, that would be tomorrow's problem.

It was dark, we didn't know anything about the place where we were, thankfully the data I had bought earlier came in handy.

"There are two hotels in this town, they are 12 miles away in opposite directions and they are both 5-star Ramada Hotels."
This was quite a shock to us all that somewhere in this strange, slightly rundown, ghost town sort of town was a five-star hotel, let alone two. We all deserved a little comfort and agreed to head to the closest Ramada, but if we saw something else or camping along the way.

We saw nothing.

It was too dark, we were all exhausted and it was about to hit midnight. We pulled up to the Ramada and I hatched a plan. *"I'll go inside and just talk it down as best as we can, once I get a price, I'll come outside and let you know and we can make a decision from there."*

I sprayed some deodorant and put on a fresh t-shirt, as if that was going to do anything. *"Here goes nothing."*

The man at the desk spoke wonderful English and was very happy to practice with me, I asked the price and it wasn't the best, I mean it wasn't bad, they were looking for 150 dollars for 5 people. That really isn't bad, but we needed it a lot cheaper. Jessie and Russell were on a strict budget and Lee wanted to spend as little as possible if he could on the trip as he would be returning home jobless.

I told him about the day we had, I told him all about the amounts we had spent and how upsetting it had been but still not really budging. I showed him the rally cars through the window but still nothing.

"I take your passport, try something on computer."

I didn't know what he meant at all, but I passed over my passport, he typed for a while but then stopped abruptly. With a look of confusion on his face he looked at my passport, then at the clock on the wall behind him, then back at the passport, then back at the clock, he waited, looking at the clock until the seconds counted up to midnight. Finally, he caught my eye and said *"5 people, one night sixty dollars and have a happy birthday."*

Gob smacked.

With everything that had been going on the past few days, I had completely forgotten I had a birthday coming up. Smiling from cheek to cheek I signaled to the others to grab their gear, it was good news. *"They wanted $150, but I got them down to $60 that's $12.40 each"* I announced. *"That and they took pity as it's my birthday."*

I was instantly showered with hugs and celebrations as everyone dropped their bags. My upset, worried mood had been completely lifted and I was ready for a night in a comfy bed.

I woke in a cold, comfortable bed, it was day 11 and the rally already felt like it had been going for months, I loved the life on the road, forever finding new places, new challenges and new friends.

Breakfast was included in the price of the room so heading down we went down for a very strange breakfast that consisted of meats, mushrooms and a pineapple. Thankfully I wasn't hungry. In the lift on the way down to breakfast I remembered what happened the day before, I felt sick and anxious again. Over the table with Lee, Russel, Jessie and Hattie, I spoke about the day we had ahead and what a good plan would be. I knew that Gnomes were happy with sticking with us all the way to Baku, where we would split and hopefully meet them in Uzbekistan. This was all down to the Canadian visa process in Turkmenistan, they were unable to enter so would have to skip it out.

"Right, so the plan is... Me and Lee will empty our car, repack and weight-shed, I'll jack up the car and have a look underneath to see how confident I am with the weld. Then we can decide where we want to push onto today or if we take it easy."

Everyone was in agreement, Lee also researched plan B for the car as he google searched 'How to scrap a car in Turkey.' The chances of this holding all the way to Mongolia were not good, it would be easier and cheaper for us to scrap it now instead of paying out over four thousand pounds in Asia.

"While you do that, we are going to teach Jessie stick shift"
Hattie announced. This looked like the first time she had
heard this as well.

I couldn't believe she had gone 11 days and 2762 miles
without driving yet, but I had no time to help, I had to
concentrate on the task in hand.

The car was empty within a few minutes and we were
exhausted, I regretted not moving the car into the shade
before starting, 9am Turkish sun is a killer. The car was
jacked and I checked the weld, prodding, hitting and testing
the strength at every point.

*"Well, it seems okay, but there is a hole about the size of a 5
pence coin that has been missed, I honestly think it will be
okay until we hit the bumpy stuff, but if we push on today,
before we hit Georgia we should get someone to weld a little
more and cover it in hammarite."*

CRUNCH!

Jessie had just tried swapping from 1st to 2nd gear without
the use of the clutch.

SCREECH!

Then slammed on the breaks as she narrowly missed hitting
a car at the junction.

Lee and I started reloading the car trying to distribute the
weight a lot more, adding more to the front of the roof rack
and the front of the car. A few things were thrown away. A
camping BBQ that Lee was very fond of was one of them.
Looking in the car I could see that something that should
have gone ages ago was still there.

"Can we get rid of this bloody camping toilet." I shouted.

*"No! when you need it in the middle of the desert because you
have the unbearable shits, you will be glad it's there."* I mean I

could see his argument, but he was forgetting one major flaw.

"So, you expect me to get the shits, use the bucket toilet then wash it out, scrub it with chemical cleaner and put it back in the car? It will stink of either shit or blue loo chemicals the entire way to Mongolia and I don't really want to be reminded of the rally every time I smell a freshly bleached toilet."

The argument continued however I eventually gave in; the camping toilet was light and it was proving useful to store another things in.

Once Jessie had the hang of stick shift, we set off east though Turkey in the glorious sunshine, we had planned to head to the Cappadocia Hot Air Balloons for my birthday but with the Axel the way it was, it just didn't feel worth it at all. Lee was very flexible and was happy to go with whatever I chose, I had all morning to think it over but the risk wasn't worth it, I would rather get the axel looked at sooner and meet up with the rest of the Convoy rather than chance it heading south and out of the way.

"Samsun it is mate."

Samsun is on the north coast of Turkey and a whopping 577 kilometers away from our beautiful Ramada in Hendeck. I thought If we aimed for there as our destination of the day and looked out for a promising mechanic along the way that would be our best bet, keeping us on schedule and in the right direction.

The E80 is a beautiful road, its smooth and full of sunning views, mountains, villages and fields of grapes give you so much for a long ass game of eye spy. The weather forever changed, burning sun one moment then a downpour the next, 200 kilometers down the sickly feeling from my stomach was finally starting to bugger off, the weld was strong and the car was doing perfectly. To celebrate the moment Lee decided to put on 'The Book of Mormon Soundtrack' again and we spent the entirety of the next hour singing our hearts out to every word of every song.

You can take the technician out of the theatre but you can't take the theatre out of the technician.

WhatsApp popped up, it was Emma, *"We are in Samsun, booked a campsite on the water and we have reserved you a spot, if you make it, we will see you tonight. Happy Birthday Ali."*

Decision made. We would push to Samsun.

Fueling up, I got talking to a few bikers, three of them with their modified bikes, no English was spoken by any of them but the map on the back of the car spoke all about our adventure.

The paint pens came out and they proceeded to write all over our car in Turkish, we had no idea what was written but had our fingers crossed it wouldn't cause trouble.

When it came to saying goodbye, we handed over a handful of Mongol Rally stickers for their motorbikes, shook their hands and waved goodbye. Seconds later they were on the Motorway with us, they were driving extremely aggressively and looked like they wanted us to pull over, break checking, surrounding us and a few kicks to the bodywork, we floored it and never looked back. *"Alastair, stop making friends with people, it always gets us in trouble."*

We pushed to Samsun and arrived at 9pm, we were looking for a campsite directly in the middle of the town. Eventually pulling up to some huge gates, we found it and were allowed in by a very friendly, fluently English-speaking campsite owner. *"Your friends are over there, park just here, tents go*

over there, I also have been told you had had car trouble so I will book you into my friends shop tomorrow morning."
Absolute Bliss and thank you Emma!
This is Gonna Yurt and a few other teams had made friends with a caravan owner nearby, greeted with a free beer and a warm welcome from them I was told it was Emma's birthday tomorrow and that we were running low on beer. All being hungry, a quick run around Samsun for food and alcohol was in order. Lee and Gnomes all went to a kebab house, but the awkward vegetarian over here wasn't as luck to get warm food. Spying a cake shop, I entered to see some huge fantastic chocolate cakes. The man behind the counter spoke no English but a woman next to him decided she would translate.
"Hello, I'm looking for something small with no meat" I said calmly.
"What celebration" she muttered back.
"Well, it's mine and a friend's birthday, but I'm not here for..."
"Congratulations" she spoke in Turkish to the man for a moment before he pulled out a giant chocolate cake and placed it on the counter. He then pulled out 5 candles and stuck them into the top.
"I'm not here for that, I just want somethi-" I said before I was interrupted again. *"Where are you from?"* the lady asked.
"England, I drove her from England in a very small car, it's taken me 11 days." I managed to say just before they both applauded and smiled. She shook my hand, followed by the gentleman, he then put the cake away, went around the back and grabbed an even bigger cake, he then replaced the candles and slid it towards me on the counter.
"I cannot believe you have driven so far, so far to be here at our little shop to have a cake on your birthday."

I was tired and hungry. I couldn't be bothered explaining to them that I was driving to Mongolia and their shop was the only appealing looking place on the street that didn't sell meat in broth. That and they really seemed delighted.

I wonder how much all this is, I thought.

Never mind, the woman saw me pull out my wallet, grabbed it, took out all of my Lira, she then counted some out as she placed the remaining back in my wallet and pushed it back to me.

"Looks like we're eating cake tonight."

I couldn't really complain however because it looked amazing and when I counted the Lira in my wallet it only cost 30.

"THAT CAKE ONLY COST ME £4.42 AND ITS HUGE."

When we arrived back at the campsite, the candles were lit, we drank the remaining beers we had and sang happy birthday to me and Emma, after a while I headed to the tent alone to read my birthday card that Caroline had made me before I set off on this adventure. It was beautiful, thoughtful and heart hitting, how I didn't cry, I have no idea.

I awoke to the usual dry mouth of hot weather camping, undid the zip of the tent to see the campsite owner a few feet away waiting for us to wake up. He had already booked us into his friends' garage and very kindly given us his address. Emma's team had already gone and Jessie was sat in the porch of her tent, applying suntan lotion with a clear hangover from the previous night.

"You think we can make the border today?" I asked.

"I don't think I can make it to the car."

I couldn't stop laughing, but I eventually helped her up and into the shade.

Lee started moving.

"Think we can make the border today Lee?"

"I think we give it a bloody good go, after we find this mechanic that is."

Yes Lee! that's the motivation we needed today.

I could tell that over the past few days, Lee had gone completely of his comfort zone, but instead of finding his way back in there, he challenged himself. Instead of letting things break him, he was motivating himself to get the job done. It was extremely satisfying to see and I knew that this attitude would help us in the future if anything went tits up! Samsun to the border of Turkey/Georgia was a 577 km drive that would take at least 8 hours. So, with no time to lose we said our goodbyes to the stunning campsite on the coast and after an hour searching around a completely destroyed industrial estate, we found our mechanic.

WhatsApp buzzed to show a text from the campsite owner, "wait in the cafe my friends, he will be there soon."

A spot of breakfast sounded good to me and after 2 Coffees and a cola each our mechanic arrived.

I called the campsite owner who translated our problem. Within seconds he had checked our car and signaled me to drive him a few streets away.

When we got there, we were greeted by a crowd, all offering their help and support. One man looked under the car and smiled before saying, "bad weld, I am to make good."

We all felt extremely relaxed around everyone and knew we were in good hands, I was shocked to see that the mechanic did exactly what I expected. The hole was welded up and the Hammarite paint came out.

"Good shout Ali, you said they would do that." Lee said cheerfully. I was proud but I gulped slightly as that was a full

on bodge job and random guess. Asking how much, we were laughed at before my money was pushed back into my wallet. *I then asked about the coffee and cola we had just drank. "Jessie tried to pay but they said no and gave us 50 cups of instant coffee for free to take with us"* Russell said.

This my friends, is the Mongol Rally. One moment you can be getting completely screwed by someone and the next you will see the kindness and generosity of those who are genuine and really wish to help. What I thought would take all morning, took less than an hour. I checked out his work and it was just perfect, my faith was completely restored in the car and completely restored in the kindness of strangers. Thank you Turkey, you have been wonderful.

We needed supplies if we were to spend the entire day driving once again just to make good time. It turned out we were making brilliant time and driving the equivalent of Glasgow to Dover every day this meant we needed water, sugar and energy to keep us on point. We illegally parked outside a shop and left Russell and Lee in charge of waiting with the cars. I grabbed water, fruit juice, crisps, chocolate, fruit, bread, cheese and ham. Fed and watered it was time for Fuel.

We had a good system where each day either me or Lee would fill up for the entire day, if we stopped twice or three times it didn't matter. Eventually the other one gets a good deal or a bad deal. It was Lee's turn so I wandered away from the petrol station for a cigarette, I watched as man shouted and screamed at me whilst running towards me with a sand bucket about to throw the entire contents over me. I was so far away, about half the distance of a football pitch away, but to this benzin station assistant, not far enough. Just before the sand left the bucket I had to dive out of the way and stub the cigarette out on the floor.

With Gnomes in Convoy we followed the same long northern road we had been traveling down for the past three days. This time we followed the coast with the sea on our left heading east, It was an even better, well maintained road that you could really get up to speed on, however for some reason they decided to put traffic lights every 5 miles that took about ten minutes to change. What we expected to be an 8-hour day was looking more like 12 hours. We passed Ordu, it was a beautiful looking town filled with more modernized looking buildings, car dealerships and the odd McDonalds. After smelling the oriental food surrounding the car, Lunch felt like an excellent idea so I pulled over where I could. *"What are the odds."*

I had pulled over right in front of a Mongol Rally car, I didn't even notice it when I pulled over but there it was outside an excellent looking cafe. *"looks like a good place to stop to me."* Gnomes agreed. Cokes, water and Fanta was instantly ordered along with 4 dishes of meatballs and the vegetarian option, salad.

Unless you swap cars, you don't spend that much time with other people, usually just the evening and morning with your company discussing what you all did in your cars, what you both may have seen out of the window and what you all plan on doing tomorrow, so time together with food and drink having a good old chinwag is always fantastic.

The other team came over (whom I have no idea of their team name and I never saw them ever again) and asked if we had any Lira because they were short for their tab. So, if you are ever to read this and know it was you, you my good friends owe me £3.27. With Gnomes and Lee tucking into their Meatballs I waited for my salad. The waiter seemed to just stand there, awkwardly next to us and smile. Occasionally pointing at cans of Fanta, cola and energy drink to see if we wanted anymore. My salad came out just after everyone had finished. *"better eat it before it gets warm."* After being overcharged and leaving us with little cash in our pockets we put our foot to the floor and drove the remainder of the day and into the night. Stopping for petrol when we needed to and picking up energy drinks at every chance, although the day wasn't very eventful, just taking in the sights of the northern Turkish coast is just breathtaking.

Even with the sun down, Turkey in mid-July is boiling hot. As we drove past a few ralliers also making a break to the border we managed to take a few pictures and pass them sweets though their car window as we sped past but no one wanted to stop, we all wanted to make it to the border. We passed Trabzon, Rise and Batumi, all of them being the largest towns on the Turkish north coast before finally we were close to the border. Stopping for petrol one last time we filled up with the finish line for the day in sight. We paid up quickly in such a rush to get into the next country, instead of a receipt we were all given baby wipes, the stench coming from our uncovered bodies covered in crisp crumbs and spilt cola must not have been appealing for anyone. In a rush to get this border over and done with we pulled out onto the main road and there it was a huge que of lorries ahead, but no waiting for us! We drove down the side of them through tunnel after tunnel until we came out the other side to a huge sign. *'Turkish Border Control, Welcome to Georgia.'* We drove to the gate with such a smile, hooting and laughing only to be shown the que of cars to our left, it was huge. I drove and drove and drove past car after car, I saw 'Team: Jurassic Tart' who were another team from Blackpool. *"How long you been here lads?"*

"Alastair, Lee, Good to see you both. It's been four hours but were so close to the front." We drove over a mile around the corner to the back of the que, passing other ralliers as they cheered, laughed and joked about the wait. We had made good time as some of these ralliers had been days ahead of us on the Facebook page.

Getting out the car, we had a celebratory beer and took it in shifts to sleep. We met with Team Reisefreiheit 2.0, the two Germans who we had passed sweets too though their window as we both sped through Trabzon, so at least some new company brightened the mood. The queue moved so slowly; many people simply pushed their cars instead of wasting petrol switching it on. Also, we figured it was less of an offence to be drinking beer and only pushing our cars as we waited in line. A police car then pulled up alongside us and beckoned Lee to their window. Holding the beer can behind his back he approached with a worried look. It was rather fortunate that they just wanted to practice their English, ask where we were from and what our team name was. They had been enjoying the sight of many wacky cars as ralliers began to appear on their patch, brightening their day up from the usual locals and trucks.

Four hours and twenty minutes later I was at the front of the que, sat alone in the car trying not to fall asleep. Lee had to go through the passenger gate and would meet me on the other side, the same applied to Hattie, she was behind in the same tired state as I whilst Jessie and Russell went through by themselves.

1st checkpoint was completed quickly, with just a quick look at my passport, the car V5 and a browse into the car. 2nd checkpoint I was out of the car getting a few stamps on my passport on the Georgian side, another quick look though the car and I was back in with the engine ticking over in another queue. 3rd and final checkpoint, a woman at a barrier with a huge smile. I drove up to her booth and an alarm screeched through the border, over the loudspeaker system she shouted *'Turkish fines, you pay here, you pay now! You need to slow down!."* I had obviously been caught speeding on one of the cameras that littered the north coast. I was escorted to the booth where I handed my things over in the order, she snapped at me. *"PASSPORT, INSURANCE, CAR PASSPORT, CAR LICENCE PASSPORT & FINE or SOUVENIR FROM ENGLAND".* Handing them all over and a fresh £1 coin along with a Mongol Rally sticker, she stamped everything, the barrier was raised and we were out of Turkey.

I had officially entered Georgia. Ew er!

I met Lee, Jessie and Russell on the other side, who were sat outside a strip club with a beer and sausage roll in hand. Yes, he found another sausage roll in the strangest of places. and was Immediately informed by all that we needed to get Insurance about 15 miles down the road as everyone claiming to sell it here was a scam.

"Looks like we are going here then."

I had completely woken up after the border alarms and I was so happy to be in Georgia, the generosity of Turkey had been fantastic, but we needed to make progress. If progress was driving all night into the unknown to buy insurance then progress it was. The Germans also follows us down a potholed road filled with stray dogs, we ventured away from the border and into the dark, quiet, run down coastal town of Batumi. It was 3am at this point and we spent till 3.30 looking for this bloody insurance hut that we eventually found in the middle of a car park. We paid for a slip we couldn't read and tried some hostels in the local area, nothing. everywhere was either nonexistent according to our map or full. Camping it was!

I ended up in the driver's seat of Gnome's car as they were all extremely exhausted from a full day driving and their problem with fumes inside the car, never really got fixed. Another hour passed as we drove into the dark unknown countryside of Georgia until eventually, I found what could have been a perfect, flat camping spot. I got out, climbed to the top of a small hill and peered over the side. *"It's a no"*. I announced to the Convoy. Lee was getting tired and grouchy, we all were but he shouted back. *"Why? why is it a no? if its flat and we can put a tent there let's just do it"* he shouted. *"Well it's certainly flat mate, but there is one thing that would definitely put you off staying here for the night!"* I replied with just as much anger. *"Oh, really what's that!!?"* Then, in perfect timing, I turned and shouted, *"THIS"*. At this point a huge train went zooming past, the noise was unbearable and whilst it passed, so just for a laugh I continued shouting *"IS THIS OKAY MATE? WANT TO PUT THE TENTS UP RIGHT HERE DO WE? WELL BE MY GUEST"* but not in anger, we all erupted into giggles, the timing of the train in the middle of the argument was too funny not to laugh, as I carried on shouting Lee could just see my mouth move but hear nothing over the noise of the train. We both had to hug it out before getting back to the cars. The comic timing had completely lightened the mood and gave us all a much-needed boost. Eventually finding a spot to put the tents up we all finally got the sleep we all desperately needed. We were on the south east coast of the Black sea (West coast of Georgia) It was strange to think that not many days before we were on the beach in Romania, on completely the opposite side, we had come so far. If we were to get to Mongolia, we had a long way still to go.

Chapter 10 - Days 13 -15 - "You are a month early Oli"

11am was a good, suitable time to wake up, yesterday had
been such a long day so catching up on much needed rest
was definitely the first tick off the task list. But we needed to
be in Baku Azerbaijan as soon as we possibly could! Why? all
will be revealed soon.
Being so close to the Black sea it would have been rude to
not go in for one final dip. Trunks on, towel ready and off we
went. On our return we realised that we had actually
camped on a campsite, though all the darkness, the one
random flat field by the side of the road that we just
happened to drive onto was a camping ground, it was
hilarious up until the free nights camping we just had cost us
Georgian Lari, to top it all off, none of us had any. Thankfully
we managed to pay in dollars, three times the price of what
it would have been in local currency. Brilliant start to
Georgia eh?
Trying not to let anything phase us, we said goodbye to our
good friends in the German Peugeot and gave them many
free cups of coffee from that strange garage cafe in Samsun.
Two of Convoi Exceptionnel were back on the road and
heading east to the capital of Georgia, Tbilisi. The first part of
the day started with driving through the outer country lanes,
passing very old houses built with local wood and driving on
the half stone half mud, dirty roads. It was definitely a
change from the smooth tarmac road all the way through
Turkey however every now and again something
ridiculously Russian would appear, such as a building or
monument, it was strange to us to be seeing Russian
inspired monuments, even though we were so close to the

southern Russian border, It would be weeks before we were to enter it, if we ever make it that far that was.

Eventually we found ourselves on a motorway, well, it was more of a dual carriageway, raised up on a banking with the odd turn off. It was completely empty, only a few cars passed every hour so this led to a lot of mischief.

With the Mario and Luigi hats on, both myself and Lee pelted banana skins at the Gnomes windows shouting *"Wahoo"* in the voice of Mario, they got us back with whatever they had to hand, crisps, empty bottles, everything they possibly could that wasn't nailed down or treasured. I'd just like to remind you all this is with the windows open, hanging halfway out on a slippery Georgian road going 70mph.

We had one banana left and an idea to throw it through the small gap in their window. I edged the car close to gnomes, as Lee pulled his arm back ready to throw it. It was at this point he retreated as we saw Hattie, armed with the biggest watermelon we had ever seen. It supported a crudely drawn face as they shunted to their left and threw it directly at us. It missed our bonnet, swiped the side of the car and went under the rear wheel, exactly where we had just been welded. It was extremely dangerous but where laws and health and safety don't matter and a tourist is a local celebrity, you can get away with anything.

Every now and again we would be passed by a car driving so quick they were an instant blur, coming of the main road and heading into small towns the local driving got no better, speeding, beeping, cutting people up and driving with a car packed with ten people. Nobody cared for any sort of road safety and almost everything that passed was completely overloaded. Roof racks piled up with sofas, chairs and mattresses, all balanced on the top of a tiny Russian car.

Indicators were a luxury and very rarely used, you had to know exactly where you were going at all times to predict the manic driving of the person in front, behind and the bloke ten cars back who thinks the pavement is acceptable to drive upon. It really is that bad, it really is that dangerous. This was the worst driving we had experienced so far and I congratulate all ralliers who have made it through Georgia without a bump just like us.

Lunchtime came and left as we pushed on, eating crappy food we had left in the car. It wasn't until around 16:00 that we finally stopped to freshen up and get some food.

 Just to be sure I checked the rear axle and nothing had moved at all, it was holding strong against road conditions and flying watermelons well. Tyres were next, I looked around them all for any problems in tread, punctures or rim dents. All clear.

"Erm, Gnomes, when was the last time you checked your tyres" I asked.

"England?" I heard shouted in the wind as they walked into the roadside cafe.

Their rear tyres were in great condition but they looked to be about 14-inch rims, their front tyres were what looked like 12-inch rims and had completely no tread on them at all. completely bold, perfectly flat all over. I couldn't believe they had been driving on them and not noticed any sort of difference. One side even had all the metal mesh hanging out, one good hit and they were gone.

"Right you need to put your spare on this one, the other can wait a little longer."

I turned to see them looking around at each other with a guilty look and then It clicked, they had no spare.

"You will have to be careful, break early, if it rains you need to either pull over or be hesitant on the breaks." The worry had started to kick in and I was bombarded with 'what if' questions.

"Let's crack on to Tbilisi and if we see a tyre shop along the way, I'll pull over and start haggling, Deal?"

Deal.

We had been recommended a hostel in the centre of Tbilisi by our German friends in Team Reisefreiheit 2.0, Hostel Fabrica, so that was our destination for the day. It was only about an hour away and we were managing to keep good pace.

WE SPOKE TO SOON.

As soon as we hit the outskirts we were stuck in traffic, not because it was busy but because everyone drove like utter wankers. It was so dangerous but with both mine and Lee's eyes fixed to the road we made it safely to the hostel. It was huge, an old, converter, modernized warehouse with everything we could need, WI-FI, washing machines, alcohol, beds and all at an affordable price.

The only thing that let this place down was that everyone who was booked into the Hostel was a 'Gap-year Wanker' as we liked to call them. Usually 18-25 with hippie trousers, a peace tattoo and their journey had no end, they were forever searching for enlightenment and the perfect shag.

But instead of trying to beat them, it was best to join them, to try and blend in after our much-needed showers we put on our best Gap year wanker cloths and enjoyed a relaxing evening of food, drink and cloth washing. Mongol Rally life eh? you cannot beat it.

At one point I took the time to head out front to smoke where I met an Englishman with his fully kitted out 4x4.

"Hello" he said. *"Isn't she a beauty! For three years I've been kitting her out to take me all the way to Turkmenistan, I can't believe it's made it so far"*

At this point I knew the perfect reply.

"You see that Ford Fiesta down there with the roof rack? Its taken me three months to kit her out and its taking me all the way to Mongolia!"

The man instantly turned to me with a red, anger filled face. *"oh, well... FUCK OFF"* he said as he jumped into the 4x4 to sulk. *"See you in Turkmenistan mate!"*

Our phones buzzed in the convoy group chat, it was DSMS. *"We will be in Tbilisi tonight, we have booked a hostel if you guys want to book into the same, then we can go out for drinks."* I was ecstatic, DSMS had caught up to us and we would be reunited with them soon. I let them know where we were, that we had eaten and with the exhaustion of driving the past few days we would meet them tomorrow at a tyre shop we had recommended to us. Then we would all lead the charge into Azerbaijan.

We were one whole day ahead of schedule. Lee's planning was fantastic and gave us the opportunity for breakdowns and sightseeing. Along with the opportunity to push on when we needed too. This was all down to visa times. You had to get your visas correct, just one mistake, one misprint or miss entered detail could mean the difference of completing the rally or being denied entry into the next country. Little did we know; we were about to get a reminder of why it's important to always double check your visas.

Up, showered, dressed, packed, car loaded, fueled up and away. That's how most says started now. No time for anything else, it was best to get on the road as early as possible and do a quick pit stop for coffee and supplies once you were out of the main town. We did exactly this and pulled in at a tyre shop, I showed the owners the problem on the Gnomes car and they went away in search of a replacement.

My god did they try and fleece us, I had to negotiate like crazy, for two tires they wanted 110 lari, that's £30 and a great deal in England, but it's a pretty crap one in Georgia.

I got them down to 60 lari for two part worn tyres, spotting a brand-new set hidden at the back I made a sill offer of 80 lari and it was accepted.

I couldn't believe it; I had managed to get two new tyres for their car for a whopping amount of £26 fitted.

I heard the roar of a rally car and turned to greet our good friends of DSMS.

Wait.

What!

It was Global Nomads, the chaps who met us on the official convoy start line two weeks ago in Blackpool. We hadn't seen them since day one, here we were in the middle of Georgia at the strangest backstreet tire shop and they somehow manage to find us. We celebrated with shots of vodka, purchased for us by the chaps at the tire shop. We told them we had a long journey ahead and alcohol isn't the best idea, but we were easily persuaded.

DSMS arrived and another celebrational shot of vodka was necked back as we hugged and celebrated the arrival of our long-lost convoy. Drunk on pure excitement we made our way to the Georgia Azerbaijan border driving like total maniacs, or in Georgian, normal. Adam drove the mighty Micra, indicating left and turning right, weaving in and out of

traffic, honking as soon as the traffic light hit amber.
Absolute knob heads we were.

Lee was piloting our fiesta around cars to try take over them
in the rush to the border but proving unsuccessful he waited
till they were stuck at the lights, drove around them and sat
on their front bumper in front of the stop line. Adam began
nudging our car revving hard and honking. Lee, like the
locals decided to then ignore the lights and sat still as they
turned green. We were all in fits of laughter much to the
local's dismay. Gnomes watched in horror and didn't want to
join in so we decided to use what we had left of our fruit and
throw it at their car as they dodged every grape and banana.
Before we knew it, we were at the border, we had managed
to cross Georgia in just over a day.

Me and Lee went through first smoothly and into the holding
pen also known as 'no man's land' the tiny bit of land
between borders. Gnomes next followed by DSMS but we
had a problem.

Oli had made a mistake on his visa and it didn't start for a
month, we all felt sick. This could have meant a huge
problem for him, however eventually he was allowed into no
man's land with a shrug of the shoulders from the border
guard he was escorted over to the Azerbaijan border where
a few smiles and handshakes were exchanged before he
came back over to the tree where we had decided to take
shade from the sweltering sun. *"I have no idea what just
happened but If I'm here, I must be okay."* he said to the group
with slight worry in his tone.

After an hour of slowly moving closer to the gates, we were
finally at the front. There are two ques usually at borders. At
big borders there is one line for lorries and another for cars
(Turkey/Georgia for example) Simple! At smaller borders

like this its locals (Those from Azerbaijan) and tourists. Just as simple! Or maybe not if you're a Georgian bloke with a small penis. If you are just that you just go in the smaller que and when at the front you argue and argue until you get your own way, If you still don't get your own way you threaten everyone and ask to see the person in charge. Once he comes out, if he is having none of it you pretend you are part of a huge organization and that you know his boss and continually say "Do you know who I am." Failing that, if none of the above works you wheelspin back into Georgia.

Heading through the gates I drove over the inspection pit and began the long document process including getting stamps for me and the car and eventually insurance. It was quite simple and after a small bribe for no reason whatsoever (he just asked me for another dollar) and a quick draw on the car with paint pens, the guards were happy and I met Lee on the other side.

Gnomes joined us soon after and then finally the Micra from DSMS joined us.

"wait, where is Oli?" Lee asked.

It turns out his visa was not okay and he was completely stuck in no man's land and there was nothing we could do to help him.

The reason why we couldn't go and help him was because if we went back into no man's land, we would then have to re-enter Azerbaijan and in doing so, we would all need another visa. We were completely stuck, only time would tell Oli's fate.

After an hour or so a guard allowed Adam to go back into the border hut and speak with him, on his return he told us an update. *"Good but shit news lads. Oli has gone on their*

*computer and purchased a new fast track visa for $100, the
shit news is that it takes 3 hours to come though."*
That wasn't bad at all, we were all okay with waiting as there
was a small shack on the other side and shade under a tree,
we weren't going to leave him on his own all night.
Sitting under the tree drinking warm cola, I brought out the
dice and four cups giving me the opportunity to teach
everyone how to play liar's dice, this was an instant hit and
helped the next few hours go past just a tiny bit quicker.
5pm soon came around and still no sign of Oli.
6pm.
7pm.
8pm.
9pm and there he was, on the other side. Finally.
but not everything was as good as it seemed.
*"They have allowed me over to get food, drink and my sleeping
bag from you all. This border closes at 10pm and if it's not
through then, I have to wait till its open in the morning. So,
looks like I'm camping in no man's land."*
We gave him all the food he could carry including an
emergency tin of peaches, a battery pack for his phone and
his belongings to last him a night, watched him walk back
into Georgia and waited till 10pm hit. Darkness was upon us
all and the gates were locked from the inside.
"What's the plan then?" I had to ask, we had completely lost a
day and there was nowhere to stay.
*"You guys push onto Baku, we will meet you there as soon as
we can tomorrow, there is no point you being late for the ferry
waiting for us."* as much as I'd love to have stayed, Adam was
right. Danny agreed it was the best thing for us to do. We had
been back with our good friends DSMS and already it was
goodbye once again. Rumour had it that a ferry would be

leaving in a few days, if you were to miss it, you could be stuck for another week, the wrong side of the Caspian Sea. This is why we had to push on so much though Europe. The Caspian Sea ferry can make or break your Mongol Rally.

Baku was an 8 hour drive away, in the darkness It didn't seem appealing at all. DSMS were to follow us out of the small village and park up somewhere to sleep away from all the locals. Setting off into the darkness followed by Gnomes we watched as DSMS dropped back until their headlights became a distant light on the horizon. We both felt awful we had started the day with such high spirits, back in convoy having a blast with our new fond Georgian Driving techniques, but had wasted a day away waiting with no result. I asked Lee to put some uplifting tunes. Not a hard task as he had downloaded a 1000 song Spotify playlist for the rally. He pressed shuffle, but what song should appear as we saw DSMS disappear? *"The Boys are Back in Town".* We didn't know whether to laugh or cry.
It was nearly impossible to see the road ahead, a few times I nearly drove off it as the side of the road was all the same color as the road, a muddy dark brown. We had just started to make progress when I slowed due to two men in uniform stood in the middle.
"oh fuck, oh fuck, oh fuck." I said. *"This may not be official, be on your guard."* I added to Lee.
"Just pretend we don't understand them and they will get bored." Lee replied.
It was a good plan, Lee wound the window down, "Hello" they said. Without thinking Lee replied with "Good evening." I couldn't believe it, well done for playing the I don't understand them game mate!

I offered them a cigarette and in their disgust they declined. That was my plan out of the window. They took our passports, wrote in a large book our names and car registration and we were on our way. It must have been official and luckily, they asked for no money. Driving on and on for another hour into the early hours you could hear the Cleo being driven by Russell just screeching every now and again trying to avoid crashing or going off the road.

"THIS IS STUPID!" I shouted to myself and pulled over outside a shop at the first point of civilization I could see. Everyone got out of the cars and I said with all my honestly, *"This is just stupid, what an unnecessary risk we are taking here. This town is the last one for a long while, from there it's darkness until first light, you can probably see me wrestling the car off the side of the road every time I miss a turn, just as much as I can hear you slam on when you're about to either go into the back of me or head off the road yourselves. I think it's best we get some food and drink here, either find a cheap hotel or camp somewhere out of the way and put our head down till first light, then we can get up really early and do this whilst we can see, without taking a sill risk."* Everyone seemed to be persuaded, everyone except for Lee. He seemed off and began to argue back that we needed to push on. Holding my ground along with backup from Gnomes he eventually backed down but then went into a mood of not talking to me as we browsed the all-night shop.

The shop assistant was lovely, she spoke English very well and got on with Hattie and Jessie from an instant, giving us directions and introducing us all to her father, the owner of the shop. *"Can we help you with anything? maybe even help you find a hotel?"* Like music to my ears.

We awoke in a small budget hotel after following a lovely gentleman in his Lada here the night before, it was around ten dollars each, this was a bit pricey but it was better than a death drive to Baku in the dark. Lee woke up and instantly said *"I'm sorry about last night, this was a good idea, I just got annoyed as id downed energy drink and power chocolate. I was focused and got into the mindset of getting to Baku, not a roadside motel, I was ready to go the whole way."* What a guy. I was also wrong and rude to Lee at some points on the rally, just as he was to me occasionally, however you won't find any stories like that about me in this book, I don't want to look like a dick. (Sorry mate!)

Packing up the car in the 6am sun, we were joined by Gnomes. With no one else around we unloaded the worn tyres from the day before, and placed them next to some other rubbish on the roadside. Not a minute later, an elderly man stepped out of his house and dragged both tyres inside. Well we were glad someone had a use for them. It was already too hot but with no time to complain we hit the road on the last push to Baku, the gateway to Asia. We had stayed the night in a town called 'Soyuqbulaq' or *'The town named after a sneeze,'* as I called it. About an hour's drive east from the border of Georgia and where we had left DSMS to fend for themselves. From there it said on maps it would be a 7-hour drive to Baku, so with it being 6am, we should be there for this afternoon.

It felt fantastic to be up so early and on the road in the sun knowing that we could clock off at 3pm and hopefully book a ferry over the Caspian Sea. It was much safer being able to see the road ahead and within no time we were making progress. Gnomes were cruising behind until they pulled in at the side of the road and waved frantically from the passenger window for us to turn around.

"I bet they left something at the hotel" I joked to Lee. But I was far from being correct.

Their car had completely cut out and wouldn't start. I popped the bonnet and had a look around, nothing seemed out of place so jumping in the driver's seat I turned the engine over to the sound of spark but a lack of compression. The alternator belt felt as if it was jammed and would only turn an inch. It wasn't good at all.

"Were going to have to get it back into town to a garage, we passed one not too far back, but the problem is that there is a big hill and we can't tow you as the strain it will put on the rear of our car could completely destroy our axel So we're going to have to push." I said to the group. Lee drove off in the Fiesta to check whether it was a garage we had passed three or so miles back and returned swiftly to help. Jessie steered as myself, Russell and Hattie pushed their heavy little Cleo over a mile, Lee was driving behind us slowly with the hazards from the fiesta warning traffic that there was a hazard on the road, we would have used the lights from the Cleo however they didn't work at all.

Hattie swapped with Lee as we pushed and pushed the car for over an hour, over the big hill as Jessie steered it down. I saw a tractor coming in the opposite direction and flagged him down, showing him the tow rope he laughed and drove away. Thanks mate! Second a minibus, but I was greeted with the same reaction. Third a taxi with an Azerbaijan police officer in the passenger seat who spoke little english. *"This man will tow you far"* said the policeman signaling to the taxi driver.

Fantastic. He had seen the Clio break down a couple miles back and wanted to help. He called up a taxi and ordered the driver to help us. What luck!

He attached the tow rope to the car and we were on our way after about 10 minutes we pulled up to a house just off the main road. *"It's early so mechanic is not awake yet."* we completely understood, it was around 7.40am and we were expecting to have to wait until at least 9am. This was until the policeman entered the mechanics house and demanded him to wake up and fix the car for us. The mechanic woke up, the policeman went to work and the taxi driver stayed with us to help with translation.

The mechanic got to work and took a look all around engine bay, he started the engine and fiddled with a few things around the alternator, back to the ignition and back to the engine he spoke to the taxi driver who tried to translate. *"No car"* we were told, but we didn't understand.

"Can you fix it for us?" I asked but the look of confusion was clear they didn't know what I meant. Picking up tools I tried to use a global game of charades to act out the fixing of a car. still no luck.

Lee got out his translator app and translated a few sentences, but no luck again and again. *"you are asking too much in one go mate, try simple words."* Lee typed again and showed him the screen, nothing.

My turn, I borrowed Lee's phone and I typed 'Car health.' Into the translator app. He seemed to understand and crossed his arms to make a giant X, it wasn't good news but we were getting somewhere with information, then I typed the dreaded word. 'Dead.'

With a sad face he put his thumbs up, pointed at the engine and said *"dead".*

My heart sank, he pointed around the engine and a few dashboard lights and it clicked. He was better at charades than I will ever be. I turned to Hattie, Russell and Jessie who all looked miserable and broke the bad news to them. *"So by what I'm getting from him is that there was no oil in the engine, even though you were topped up there must have been a blockage and no oil was getting into your engine, your oil light had signaled it but with your dashboard lit up more than the Blackpool Illuminations it was probably just mistaken for an electrical fault. With no oil getting it at all over the past few days, your engine had run itself dry and seized."*

Another taxi driver had pulled over to see what all the fuss was, he had been sent by our good friend the policeman to try and translate. With his help I found out my diagnosis was correct and the engine was completely done for. However, this was then followed by good news. *"I will take the day off to help you."* he said. *"I will find you a replacement engine in Georgia as there are none of your car's in Azerbaijan". then we swap engine over."* This news was greeted with a smile, they knew the cost would be high but they had an option and a possibility to carry on with the rally. it was now 9am and our early start to get some miles under our belts had completely failed.

"You guys push on to Baku, it will be days before we find out what we can do and all of our car visas are only valid for 4 days. So, we may have to change our plans. There's no point you guys being stuck in Azerbaijan as well." Jessie said Lee and me.

Although losing a member of our convoy, leaving them at the side of the road when they drove miles and miles to help us with our rear axle problems was the last thing we wanted to do, she was right. Almost in tears, we said our goodbyes, after giving Russell, Jessie and Hattie a huge hug, we got into the fiesta and drove until they were mere dots in the rear-view mirror.

"Goodbye Team: Two fake Yanks and a Scott and good luck."

Complete silence for two hundred miles. Me and Lee didn't speak to each other because after all that had happened, we had nothing to say. We both felt terrible, sick and upset for Gnomes. There was nothing we could have done; I sent a WhatsApp message to them even though I knew it wouldn't send until the next time we had WIFI.

'Get yourselves back to Georgia and get that engine swapped, we will be waiting for you in Uzbekistan. This isn't you out of the rally, this is a bump in the road to Mongolia. We miss you already and can't wait to have Convoi Exceptionnel back together.'

We were so upset that whilst passing around the city of 'Ganja' not one joke was made about it. Azerbaijan was probing to be the worst place on the rally so far, this was proven when we stopped for lunch and WIFI gave us information on Adam, Danny and Oli (DSMS).

"We were almost killed." -
A short story by Adam Skerritt

We had wild camped about 2km away from the border next to the railway track, made a fire, grabbed some noodles and decided (luckily) not to set a tent up and just sleep in car. After pulled the mossie nets up over our broken driver side window we whacked a Harry Potter audiobook on the radio.

Not the most comfortable sleep next to the live track but at least we could get some shut eye. About 2:30/3am a car skidded up and 2 blokes got out talking in Russian, started shining flashlights on us and our belongings in the car. Completely unsure of what to say to a 3am Azerbaijan visitor and already being pretty done with the sodding country, I asked them what they were doing and told them to stop shining the torches. A bit of speaking in Russian made me come back with *"English, United Kingdom..."*.
It was at this point I knew I had messed up.
They jumped back in their car and drove off. I felt uneasy and had a strange feeling this was not the end of it all. Raising the seats back up, seatbelt on, key in the ignition I told Danny to get the border up on maps just in case, he also agreed it was weird and with both of us having some experience with iffy situations abroad, we got focused. I remember for a moment we thought It was all over until full beam headlights came from the small village towards the border as the sound of a speeding car filled our ears. The car pulled over next us and a guy popped up from lying down in the back. Without thinking I quickly turned over the engine but the car pulled in front of us to block us off within an instant they were out and surrounding the car.
Headlights on full beam, car revved to its highest point I turned the wheels in full lock right, dumped the clutch and did the tightest U-turn possible, only just missing one of the men and nearly sending him over the bonnet. They shouted and gestured at me and Danny whilst running back into their car, Quick thinking made me flick the headlights out and in complete darkness, made a break for the border.
In the rear-view mirror, we could see them trying to turn but thanks to a much larger turning circle it took them a little

longer. However, from that point, the chase was on. Danny was great and kept his composure well, giving me clear directions through the darkness, we were both running full on adrenaline at this point.

Entering the first village I needed the headlights due to large walls, ditches and lack of streetlights. We got some air over the railway tracks and sped off at 60 mph through the tiny roads. No matter how quickly we went, the chasing car gained on us. They knew the roads like the back of their hand and definitely had an advantage over a pair of tourist ralliers with an eagle on their roof. Just as the car had the opportunity to pull alongside with what I imagined to be a maneuver to take us off the road we reached the last bend to the border and the friendly sight of Army patrol. It's the first time I got the Micra going sideways and not the last on the rally!

Emergency breaking right at the gate and as the guards came out the chasing car skidded into a U turn and drove away just before it hit the lights of the border patrol.

The guards were confused, I had to spend almost half an hour trying to explain we didn't want to cross back into Georgia, we just needed their protection. Eventually understanding they let us park up next to their hut in a dark abandoned garage. With the windows open and the mozzie net up we fell asleep listening to the peaceful sound of cars sneaking through the backroads over the border and the odd screaming goat. Knowing that Oli was having a night by himself in no-man's land with only a tin of peaches and his sleeping bag in the rain, I suppose we really couldn't complain.

That was until Oli informed us about his night the next morning. The LUCKY BASTARD spent it in a lovely hotel a few miles away from the border, where a nice family had taken him and paid for a taxi to return him to the border the following morning.

That is why, you should always, triple check your visas. Not just for your own safety, but the rest of your team. Splitting up is never a good choice. - *Adam Skerritt*

In the roadside shop after filling our bellies and using the all we could eat Wi-Fi we sent one final message to our loved ones with an update of the past few days and our early morning farewell to Gnomes before rejoining the boring road all the way to Baku.

I mean honestly there was nothing, nothing the entire way. Just the same dirty landscape and shouting locals when you refuse to stop and buy their goods. The only good thing about it was the road was pretty much a straight line all the way across and that it was new, flat tarmac.

Imagine a long road with a dusty landscape around it, old buildings, shops and towns pop up every now and again and the odd interchange that sends another road in a straight line into the horizon in another direction, that is Azerbaijan. So why were we rushing to Baku?

We needed to get the Caspian Sea Ferry, this ferry leaves whenever it wants and costs whatever they want to charge. It has no set timetable or spend, its complete luck if it turns up at all and if there is enough space for you to squeeze on it. To get a ticket you have to return on the hour every hour to a small booth until he eventually gives you a little information and a riddle that sends you off around Baku before arriving back to his booth none the wiser. It's the most blind part of the trip and the biggest test of patience you could ever have. On top of all this, if you spend over

154

three days in Azerbaijan with your car you are instantly fined and made to pay tax on your car at an extortionate amount. Unless you are in a holding pen at the ferry port, that is your only way getting around the fine. That is the reason you should never do what we did, you should never, ever even consider taking the Caspian Sea ferry, always go through Iran.

With our plan to get to Baku, grab some information about the next ferry is and camp it out in the port until it arrived, we drove on and on into complete the complete nothingness of Azerbaijan. Until finally, we reached the coast of the Black sea and followed the coast into Baku. Me and Lee had completely forgotten to print off out Turkmenistan Letter of Invitation that we had received from 'The Visa Machine' just after we set off on the rally, The visa machine were fantastic and helped us with every single visa we needed, I couldn't recommend them more! The only thing we had to do was print one bit of paper, that we seemed to have forgotten.

Baku is the capital of Azerbaijan and you can easily tell once you are there as it's the only part of the entire country where there is actually something. It's all crammed together on the coast and you can see where all the money is spent, they built the flaming towers for the Olympics, Huge skyscrapers covered in LED screens to show some fantastic animations, but that's about all that's good really. Pulling over in the centre of this extremely busy capital we withdrew hundreds of dollars from a cash machine for the ferry and went off to find somewhere to print out LOI's (Letter of invitation).

With a complete stroke of luck, we happened to pull up outside the Academy of English language, we couldn't believe out luck. *"they will be able to help us, they may even print our LOI's for us"* Lee said. I couldn't have agreed more, what a stroke of luck.

"Excuse me, is there somewhere around here that we could print a document, a library or office we could borrow a computer for a few seconds?"

We paused, in our shock we got the reply.

"Me. No. English."

You have got to be kidding us.

If you happen to live in Azerbaijan and wish to learn english, do not go to the Academy of English language, they know fuck all.

Finding a library on the My Maps App, we headed deeper into the city, found the library and to our surprise it had no computers and one old woman behind the desk who just liked to start at us, thankfully across the road we saw a printing shop, almost as quickly as we entered we were out, LOI's in hand and ready for some well-earned dinner. A local pizzeria won the dinner choice award mainly due to the FREE WIFI sign in the window. As soon as Wi-Fi connected to our phones we were greeted with the most amazing messages.

"Cunning stunts are in Baku, were booked in a great hotel called 'East Legend Hotel' it has a pool, you should all join us" - Richie, Baz & James.

"Don't Smell My Shoes are about 2 hours out, we will book in the hotel when we have better Wi-Fi, see you in a few hours" - Oli, Danny & Adam.

"Were in Baku, the ferry is tomorrow, meet at the Ferry port for 10am" - James and Jade (Mini Adventures)

The Convoy was about to re-form, sadly without our Gnomes but there was nothing more we could do. After scoffing down pizza we were about to leave when a bunch of students invited us over to their table for a few drinks and a chat. It would have been silly to miss the opportunity so we stayed a while to talk about our lives back home and the trip ahead.

It was fantastic to jump into the cold water of the hotel swimming pool and share a beer with CS and DSMS. Having just some of the convoy back together, all under one roof was truly fantastic. Baku was swarming with ralliers, the Facebook page and WhatsApp groups were going wild about a possible meetup that evening at an Irish pub. But we were so focused in swapping stories, drinking cheap beer and smoking cheap cigarettes.

Before heading out into Baku we sent messages of hope and support to Gnomes who we still had no update from whatsoever, we really hoped that they had a solution but we had to take it in that may have been the last we ever saw of them.

Arriving at the pub we all ordered a large beer and toasted to our fallen compadres and our adventure into Asia. With what was left of Convoi Exceptionnel and a bunch of other ralliers all ready to face Asia I announced, *"Turkmenistan awaits! May the odds be ever in your favor, Cheers everyone!"*

Chapter 11 - Days 16 - 17 - I died choking on a dry biscuit and this was my hell on earth.

We all wanted to make sure we were all as prepared for what was about to unfold as we could possibly be, little did we know that there was absolutely no way we could possibly have prepared for anything that was going to happen over the next few days. I wish I could just write *"DO NOT TAKE THE CASPIAN SEA FERRY"* 300 times along with 15 Pages of screaming, however I best tell you all how it went down...

Arriving at the port an hour early we met up with about twenty other rally teams including Mini Adventures. With Gnomes back in Georgia looking for another engine and RallyMcRallyFace taking it slow and cruising through Turkey still, this was what was left of Convoi Exceptionnel. Mini Adventures, Cunning Stunts, Don't Smell My Shoes and me and Lee in Team Away from Keyboard. Seeing James and Jade again made us all extremely happy, it had been over a week since they split off from us and we had hardly any contact from them. Like a small family reunion, a group hug was in order.
We were all beckoned into the car park and headed over to passport control, with a quick check of our details, customs was the next stop. (A small building with no sign explaining it was customs at all) We handed them our Car V5 and the Azerbaijan Car Entry document. As did twenty other ralliers. He separated the documents, stamped them and turned to us all *"Wait."*
That was the only instruction we were given. In the baking hot sun of Baku this wasn't an easy task. Those who didn't

158

have ferry supplies and had turned up this morning, there just happened to be ferry for them had no idea what time anything would be happening, so the idea of leaving the ferry terminal and heading into the city for food and spares was close to impossible. If you miss this ferry it could be another week before another arrives, missing it is not an option.

a few hours passed, sun cream had been applied to everyone and we were starting to get a little bored of standing about doing nothing with no information at all.

12pm hit. Nothing.

1pm Hit, Nothing.

Likely then, Customs come running over, *"we need all drivers"*.

After three hours of absolutely nothing we were told that all of us hadn't paid tax on entry to Azerbaijan and that every driver needed their form back, the V5 back and needed to go to the 'Pochta Rossii' to pay $15 per car. Why we weren't told of this when we handed the forms in, we have no idea. but you just have to throw your hands into the sky and shout *"Mongol Rally"* with things like this or it will drive you insane.

With now close to thirty teams sorting out plans of what to do I couldn't take the noise and confusion anymore and along with Danny we shouted everyone to a silence. *"Right, there is no point us all going there, why doesn't everyone just give me their sheets and $15 dollars, I'll get you all a stamp and bring it back. Simple."* Within seconds I was bombarded with forms and dollar, feeling like an Azerbaijani stripper I got all my notes together. Danny volunteered to come with me and thankfully nice rallier who spoke Russian volunteered to come with us. He translated 'Pochta Rossii' to Post Office ordered an Uber and away we went.

The post office was a quick enough task, handing over the slips one by one along with $15 each, there was no problem until I have to pay a $3 fine for Mini Adventures who had been caught jumping a red light. (Which I never got back... James!) Even though the amount was so little, I only had the exact money with me, I ended up withdrawing money, this cost me £5 in exchange fee to pay a $3 fine that wasn't even mine.

No bother, 28 Stamps later, a final opportunity to stock up on cigarettes and a quick pint, before you knew it, we were back at the port handing in everyone's forms.

"Here we are Sir" I said with a smile but once again I was greeted with the same response, *"wait."*

It was 3pm, a waiting room had been opened to give everyone the well needed shade thankfully It also gave everyone the opportunity to use the toilet as most had been holding in a piss since the morning. By 5pm Lorries had started turning up, driving right past the car park and behind the huge wall of shipping containers and buildings, It was almost as if we had been completely forgotten about, this was until a port police man came over and gave the fantastic signal "Go, Go, Go" waving his arms drastically in the direction of the ferry. Lee jumped in the car, Ignition on, 1st gear selected and we were the first car racing down the road to the awaiting ferry. I pulled up to a policeman with a huge smile and awaited the next instruction. *"Hello"* he said, *"Hi, erm, lovely ferry you have here"* I replied not knowing what to say at all. *"You all need to go back and park."* Within seconds we had been turned around and were back where we started. The same policeman who signaled us to go, walked over, raised his head and said... "Wait."

It wasn't long till a bus turned up to take on the foot passengers, Lee, Danny, Oli and Jade all had to jump on whilst Myself, Adam and James were named on the V5 meaning we had the job of taking the cars though the borders. We watched as the bus set off, revving our engines impatiently as 8pm hit and sunset began, *"Ten Cars!"* was shouted from one guard to another as 10 rally cars were counted out, thankfully, me being number 9, I drove off in convoy with the other teams back down the road I had been down an hour earlier before arriving into another holding pen.

Another hour passed as one singular guard went though the other eight cars before me. He was looking for contraband, Drones (that are illegal in Azerbaijan and most of the Stan countries) and anything they can pocket once you turn your back. Once your car was searched you were allowed though the next gate into the next holding pen, I watched as the que grew shorted until it was finally my turn. Once each door, the boot and the bonnet were open he began looking though only the most expensive looking bags, clearly not bothered about anything, "Can I have this" he said as he pulled up our compass. Our compass was broken with a bubble due to the extreme heat of the car so it wasn't worth anything at all to us, however the last thing I wanted to do was give the guard the satisfaction of getting free stuff with the horrible day we had.

"WHAT IS THIS!" He shouted at me whilst smacking me over the head with our map off the dashboard. He was a complete arsehole and liked to show his power over those he could.
"It's a map of Georgia, Armenia and your 'wonderful' country of Azerbaijan." I replied as sarcastic as I could.

He opened it and started pointing around it *"This map is very bad, it shows Armenia, who are bad and this zone here is a conflict zone, you cannot have a map of this. So, I take this map from you."* I couldn't be arsed arguing, 12 hours I had been waiting and completing painfully annoying tasks for this terribly organized border. I wanted to just get on the boat and be on our way to Turkmenbashi.

"Fair enough." I slammed the car doors shut and drove into the next holding pen.

"You get out and go to Immigration" shouted another guard. Miserably I walked over to the shipping container that had been crudely converted into an office and handed over my documents. At this point Richie from Cunning Stunts came over, offered me a cigarette and said *"I will never return to Azerbaij-sham again."* I couldn't have agreed more. Since entering the country all we had was negativity. With border problems, car chases, rude locals, endless tax paying and no system of how to get on a boat, enough was finally enough.

We waited till past 11pm until each rally car had been processed The Lorries were loaded up and a huge ramp into the hold opened for us to drive down, it was extremely steep. We all made it down with ease, until we realised it would be a struggle to get back up in reverse as there was no chance of a turning circle. But that was a problem for Turkmenistan. Grabbing supplies from the car I picked up bread, cheese, sweets, sausage rolls that somehow once again Lee had managed to find and a large pack of biscuits for the convoy to share. We waited on the top of the deck outside as we watched all foot passengers get processed and make their way onto the boat, by the time everyone was ready it was

1am and everyone was tired, angry and in the need of a good night's sleep in a comfortable bed.

"There is not enough room for you to have beds and we need all of your passports."

Oh, for fuck sake!

Looks like we were making camp on the airplane style chairs, all us ralliers put our gear together and second off part of the boat, knowing that if anyone who looked suspicious went through our things, we could challenge them. It was warm, smelly and the toilets were already blocked. But this isn't a five-star luxury travel. This, is the Mongol Rally.

You make the bad times good and the good times brilliant, it's all about attitude, once again we had to change our attitude and embrace the problems, once you embrace what happens everything becomes a joke rather than a problem and you end up enjoying yourself more than ever.

We went onto the highest deck we could, sat in the light of the moon, smoking, playing dice and drinking some of the emergency beers we brought on board. Some ralliers had managed to some chicken and rice from an on-board canteen but when I asked for no meat and a bowl of rice was placed in front, I was completely put off.

BING BONG.

A huge tannoy system announcement kicked into action waking up most of the boat that still hadn't left port at 3am.

"Mumbles, mumbles, mumbles, Mongol Rally, mumbles, mumbles, passporta's" were the only words we could make out. Like a school of fish, we all grabbed our car V5's and headed to the desk. There was one woman who spoke English, she said she was an English teacher who would help

with translation. *"The price it $100 per person and $200 per car"* ... You what! we had already paid close to $200 just to get on the boat, with car tax, bridge tax and whatever taxes you could think of at the time. we began arguing with the woman and trying to haggle, *"If we all don't pay, they can't charge us that, I'm up for paying some more but nowhere near that amount."* James shouted to everyone. Luckily for me and Lee it would have been a maximum of $400 however for teams of five it was $700 just for a one-day trip on a boat that served one meal a day and had no fully working toilets. We all hatched a plan to haggle and think of an agreed price, just as we were about to put the plan into action the worst thing happened, some bloke from another team (a father and son team) had had enough, handed over his passport and paid. No matter what we said or did now changed nothing. We were beaten and it was all down to that knob giving in. Angry, tired and annoyed we paid the $400. We knew this woman wasn't an English teacher, as she counted out the dollars, occasionally putting some into a money box, the rest dropping into her handbag.

"Convoy meeting time." we all met outside on the top deck, I let everyone know that it was almost $200 for the visa for Turkmenistan along with $100 to get the car in then whatever they fancied to charge us on top of that, this meant a total spend of $900 to get into Turkmenistan from Baku just for me and Lee from Team AFK, it would be over $1000 for DSMS And CS. Determined not to get upset we decided sleep would be best and we could start tomorrow fresh. At 4am Lee, James and Jade headed inside to get some sleep whilst myself, Adam, Danny, Oli and another large bunch of ralliers lead out on the top deck of the ship, under the

beautiful stars above and fell to sleep with a lovely sea breeze.

I awoke in the morning sun of the Caspian Sea, wait.
no.
OH GOD NO.
NO, NO, NO, NO, NO.
THIS MUST BE A DREAM.
We hadn't moved.
It wasn't a dream, we were still exactly where we were the previous night, the port of Baku. Not knowing the time due to a dead phone (Fucking iPhone) I was about to wake the others and tell them the miserable news when all of a sudden, the engine started and we were on our way.
Finally, 24 hours after arriving at the port, we began our adventure across the Caspian Sea and into Asia.
We met up with all the other teams however one seemed to be missing, we looked around the ship and couldn't find them, their car was gone. They got off the ferry?
"Oh yes" James from Mini Adventures spoke up. *"I had to let them off last night, one of them fucked up by getting their Visa in Turkey and it didn't start for another two days, so he wasn't able to catch this ferry as he would arrive in Turkmenistan too early."* he explained.
"Oh, no poor guy" could be heard from the back of the crowd.
"Tell you who's a poor guy, My Mini." It turns out James had to reverse up the steepest ramp possible as his car was the only one blocking in the team who had to abandon ship. It got up the ramp well but supposedly the smell of clutch now lingered the hold.
We all spoke about security on the boat, always having someone with the bags and general ideas to make the time

on board best for all. I didn't car I just wanted to smoke. I had quit smoking before the rally, about 6 months before actually. I did it when my baby Sapphire was born, I didn't want her to grow up knowing the smell of smoke and relating it to me. It was hard for me to quit because I'd never had a cigarette I didn't enjoy and they truly did relax me and give me a moment to myself in a stressful situation. Luckily after quitting I've managed to have a good relationship with cigarettes, I would only smoke on holiday and special occasions. The crossing usually takes about twelve hours so I had stocked up for the ferry, finishing off the last in the pack I went to my bag to grab more. Finding the front pocket of my bag open and all my cigarettes gone made me wish I had paid more attention during the Mongol Rally official ferry briefing earlier.

Hours and hours passed as we wandered around the boat wasting time doing absolutely nothing. I managed to sit down and spend a few hours writing notes on what had happened so far on the rally just in case I thought about writing a book afterwards. What are the odds eh?

Lunch wad dry bread with an apple, yum!

Dinner was the same warmed up food as the night before, with an apple, yum!

Before we knew it, it was dark again, we ate all of our supplies except for the biscuits, warm, full and happy another game of liar's dice started on the top deck, calling out numbers slyly and using the term 'Snake eyes' every time we wanted to say 'one one's' made us all have the giggles. Finishing a gifted cigarette, I tried one of Lee's biscuits.

"Cough, cough, cough, FUCK ME" I was choking. Not because of a bit of biscuit was stuck in my throat, but because the

biscuit was the driest thing I had ever tasted in my entire life. With a touch to the lips the entire moisture of the top half of my body was soaked into its crumbly form, without thinking I put half of it into my mouth and within seconds I was dying of dehydration and wishing I could drink the entirety of the salty Caspian sea that surrounded me.

"Try one of these, they are good." I lied to Adam.

Grabbing a biscuit, I watched as he put it into his mouth and almost fell into a dehydrated coma, *"ITS SO DRY!"* he screamed spitting biscuit all over the dice. We all erupted into laughter and found the name 'Biscuits of DEATH' appropriate for the crumbly bastards. No one dared to try one after that so I had to get creative, I had to get rid of them one way or another. I hatched a plan and created a cunning game.

"So were going to play dice, whoever comes last has to eat the biscuit whole in one bite, whoever is second to last has to do it in two bites and so on and so on until whoever wins does not have to eat one." Everyone was happy to play. James and Ritchie from CS joined in from this point and the tense game was on.

Danny was first to be out, gambling on silly numbers. We all watched gob smacked as he accepted his fate and crammed a large biscuit of death into his mouth. Emergency beer had to brought over to save him from his fate. I know all readers must be thinking that we are over exaggerating however they really were that bad and were honestly the driest things we had all ever tasted, I was out second, having the biscuit in two bites was just as bas, then Richie, Adam and James leaving Oli the winner. Oli showed his good sportsmanship by sharing Adams however instant regret was shown over his face.

I asked those who tried one to describe them in no more than five words for this book and here is what some of them had to say:

Danny: Please can I die now.
Alastair: It tastes like sand.
Adam: I'm going in dry.
Jade: Turkmenistan in biscuit form.
Oli: Worse than the Azerbaijan border.
Lee: I don't remember buying them.
James: I've never tasted death before.

Close to 11pm we had made it to Turkmenbashi, we were officially in Asia. The unload process was similar to the loading process, lorries get to go first, anyone with a rally sticker has to wait for no reason whatsoever. Whilst waiting to get to the car the convoy got speaking too another team who were a newlywed couple, they were doing the rally as their honeymoon, this was so amazing and they seemed so badass until we saw a large 4x4 behind them, it was her father and he was their support vehicle. *"WHAT, you have a support vehicle and your dad is technically on your honeymoon?* we asked. *"My mother is with us as well"* was the blokes reply. I couldn't have thought of anything worse. The Mrs., the mother in law and the father in law! Lorry after lorry left the boat until the one parked over the hull door blocking our cars in had left. Like the scene out of The Lost World - Jurassic park when the T-rex is released from the boat a huge alarm went off, everyone stood clear and the hydraulic hinges started to open the huge steel door. Looking into the darkness we saw the rear of the Mini and then finally all of our cars parked up side by side ready to continue their journey.

I never thought we I'd have wished to have been back in the cars so soon, however with the absolute nightmare of a ferry, the cars were greeted by all as good friends, the mini drove up and out, the first onto Turkmenistan soil, followed by DSMS, CS and finally me in the AFK Ford. I handbrake turned in excitement as I picked up Lee before remembering about our broken axle and technically, we were still at a border crossing. Zooming off into the darkness heading towards a large building supporting the only light for a good few miles we were ready to get out Visas and see what Turkmenistan had to offer.

A lot of frustration and endless waiting hours. That's exactly what it had to offer.

After a quick wiz round the Turkmenbashi border/docks we parked up outside customs. Knowing that we had no visa for Turkmenistan only an LOI we knew this border would take a while. Please go to *"Chapter VII - Turkmenbashi Border"* for the exact order of how to complete entry into Turkmenistan. First at customs we handed over our LOI's in a huge pile and waited for over an hour only to then be told by a trucker they weren't processing us as they did not understand English. Luckily with Philo speaking Russian after some nods of the head and shouting from Philo, processing began. There were close to thirty ralliers and we all had to go through the same process so what do we do? The most English thing we can think of. We form a que.

After another hour (Two hours down) we get to the front, handover our passport for a small slip and are sent to the bank, this is luckily in the next office. Into queue two and another hour later (Thee hours down) we paid for our visa which is about $190 per person, got a stamp on the form and back into the que to get the visa printed and into your passport. after just over an hour (Four hours and 15 mins down) at the front of the que they then start processing ralliers again. They had stopped because of angry local lorry drivers who refused to que and just jumped in, this is the most frustrating thing and the only thing that you can do is voice your opinion (which they don't understand and then the customs guys start refusing to serve or avoid you) 45 minutes later we have a visa in the passport! I'm allowed into Turkmenistan! however my car isn't. (5 hours down) I hand my V5 over to the desk and another two hours of complete silence passes until Philo calls me over *"They need to know what route you wish to take, they then give you a slip to show your route to police along the way and if you are not on the route you said, you get arrested"*.

"Well that sounds reasonable, where do I sign?" I replied sarcastically.

I drew the route on the map, got it stamped, signed and sorted. *"Motor Customs"* I was then informed. (7 Hours down) I walked right to the end of the building and within 15 minutes I was in Car Immigration, another 15 minutes passed and I was sat with the Veterinarian next door, he asked if I had *"goat, pig or chicken?"* on board before stamping my form and sending me next door to 'Plant Immigration' finally after another half an hour of not understanding a word I was told I had the form all stamped and I was heading back to the bank to pay $60 for the *'I have absolutely no idea what this is for stamp'* (8 Hours down). Stamp in hand, Turkmenistan Customs form, V5 and passport returned we were finally ready to leave

Turkmenbashi, I returned to the car to find Lee fast asleep with his face pressed against the window and a lot of smashed glass on the floor next to our car. Whilst I was sorting the car out, Lee had the opportunity to catch up on a bit of sleep. Adam had planned to do the same however whilst he wound his driver's window up it had gotten caught and smashed all over the floor. *"I may have messed up here, anyone know where I can get a Nissan Micra driver's window in Turkmenistan"* he said with a smile. Adam knew he had messed up and would probably have to spend the next month of the trip with no driver's window though the sand and rain, thankfully his attitude towards the rally was truly inspirational and I knew he wouldn't let that phase him. I just hoped Danny and Oli thought the same.

With the engines roaring we drove to the gate with the plan on pushing on into the capital and getting well deserved rest there (and hopefully a pool) however we were greeted with an Inspection pit and guards that wanted to see the entirety of the cars insides and ask for free things along the way. 9 Hours it had been since we arrived in Turkmenbashi from the boat and my goodness did it feel good to be finally getting back onto the road.

"You need to park here and go pay taxes!"

Oh, for fucks sake.

I'd had enough, I just looked at the DSMS and CS lads and bust into a fit of laughter. Not being able to control themselves everyone joined in, Lee snorted some of his water and almost threw up, this made us giggle even more. We couldn't believe we were in such a stupid, annoying situation where the simplest of things take hours to complete. I left for the tax office as passengers stayed behind to watch the cars, protecting them from thieving guards. We had been warned they were possibly the most corrupt we would encounter. Well after forking out hundreds of dollars for tariffs we didn't understand, we didn't take any chances. Two soldiers approached the cars hands resting on their assault rifles. They began peering into the backs of the cars, despite being completely unloaded and checked at the previous checkpoint. One began pointing at our loudspeaker and wanted Lee to explain. This seemed like the opportune moment to showcase our sirens and loudhailer to the guards and chorus of the rally car gizmos filled the compound, much to the amusement of the soldiers. The screeching, wailing and light bars flashing drew some unwanted attention though as their superior officer came out of a hut sporting a magnificent large red cap. As he approached the soldiers stepped away rather sheepish, knowing they encouraged this racket that must have woke him. He walked up to Team: Breakneck Tweed's Red 4x4 Panda and to everyone's surprise, smiled. He shook their hands and proceeded to sit in the driver's seat, marveling at the wheel being on the wrong side. Next thing we knew he was racing around the car park as his soldiers cheered him on. It was a much-needed lift for everyone after the arduous border checks we all had to endure.

I ran to the tax man, sat in an office for a while in complete silence as he wrote a slip, then headed to another office where the woman gave us one stamp and sent half a mile back down to the bank to pay it.

Finally, after TWELVE HOURS of border, we had paid for everything needed, had all documents signed and the gates were opened.

We had entered Turkmenistan, our journey through Asia had begun.

Chapter 12 - Days 17 - 19 - The Country where nothing makes sense.

Turkmenistan is the strangest most messed up country I have ever had the fortune to enter, It's so wrong it's right, it's so good it's bad and all vice versa. I recommend it to everyone doing the rally, in one part you can be a millionaire and another part a God.

We were joined outside the gate of the port by DSMS and CS, Team Mini Adventures had gotten through first and set off south to the capital hoping to take it easy with more time to get there.

Benzin (petrol) was or next point of call, we were all low and before tackling our first boiling hot country we thought it would be wise to give our cars a drink and get ourselves enough food and water in case of an emergency. Using Maps.Me the mobile app we drove past two petrol stations that didn't exist before finding one to fill up, they had no water or food for sale but at least we now had the chance to push on and find somewhere.

The single attendant filled the tank to the top and I asked him how much with the international sign of rubbing your fingers against your thumb.

"One".

One what? I was highly confused.

"One dollar".

A WHOLE TANK OF PETROL FOR A DOLLAR.

I turned to the rest of the convoy and shouted *"Boys fill them up to the top, Uncle Alastair will pay for this, your first fuel stop in Asia. Don't say I never get you anything."*

We were joined by two other teams at this point, 'The Bongolians' and 'Around the world in 998cc', They were all great lads who we had gotten to know well over the 53 hours of Black Sea Ferry and Turkmenbashi border. They joined us in the charge all the way down to the capital, Ashgabat. Once we left the petrol station and the last few houses of Turkmenbashi, I completely fell in love with Turkmenistan. It looked like the surface of mars. Hill upon hill of sand surrounded us in its boiling hot landscape as you drive into the same scenery repeated again and again for miles. As soon as you see it you know you're not in Kansas anymore Toto.

Camels ran across the road and next to you as you drove by them, actually wild camels. I couldn't believe I had driven my crappy little car all the way to wild camels. It didn't seem like much to Lee, but for me that was a fantastic achievement.

After a few hours driving we found a house supporting the sign 'cafe' upon entering we found it was completely empty except for large rugs with the owners asleep and a woman stood at a table with a fridge hooked up to three car batteries. We bartered for some water and headed back to the cars, Baz from CS managed to exchange some dollars to the local currency 'manat'.

Baz bartered and managed to get 400 Manat for $30, we have no idea if this was a good deal at all but away we went. I drove into the horizon with the afternoon sun high in the sky, The Bongolians ahead and the others behind. I was taking in the scenery when.

SLAM.

I hit the brakes hard.

INDICATOR ON

I pulled over at the side of the road. Lee had no idea why I had pulled over so quickly and without warning. I looked at myself in the mirror, checked the car was okay and turned to Lee.
"You are going to have to drive mate.
I fell asleep."
I couldn't believe it, the endless boat, soul destroying border and countless hours of on and off naps had killed me, I didn't feel tired at all but the heat along with no sleep must have just finished me off. Thankfully as I drifted off my brain kicked into action saving a crash and probably our lives.
I tried to explain to Lee about what had happened, I started the sentence but after just a few words I was gone. My head resting on my watermelon shaped pillow. I had drifted to sleep through complete exhaustion.

I awoke a few hours later to the same landscape that I fell asleep too, the road itself here was rather flat and well looked after, every now and again you had to dodge a sand bank that had formed in the wind, but that was nothing. Out of nowhere, suddenly. Civilization.
We had arrived in the town of Serder, It was a little more glamorous than Turkmenbashi, In the middle there was a large, bronze statue of camels surrounded by water fountains on a beautifully green grass hill, however the buildings around it had all seen better days, It was almost as if they had 'tried to polish a turd'. This town had been run down a while and by adding a few good roads and fountains every couple of hundreds of yards did brighten up the road, but nothing else.
We were looking for a bank, the ones we passed on Maps.Me once again didn't exist and shouting ATM at passersby was

starting to get annoying. We had dollars and we knew that that was a stronger currency than any of those you could find in central Asia. We pulled up to the most stereotypical 'Hot country cafe' supporting Coca-Cola umbrellas, small huts to sit in and loud music. *"It seems like a tourist cafe however there were absolutely no tourists around, just us 13 blokes and our five smelly cars. Do you take dollar?"* They seemed to understand and shake their heads. I gave it another go, pulling out a dollar bill and saying *"We eat here and pay in dollar?"* Once again it was a no. I was hungry and there was no chance of seeing a bank anytime soon. I pulled out a $100 bill, *"They don't take dollar lads"*.

Money talks.

We were shown our seats and brought out a menu we couldn't read, Baz luckily had a point and say picture book, it was just a small book filled with pictures of anything and everything from cars to pigs and food to countries. It worked well, we asked for Fanta, meat, salad, chips and bread. They came out with huge dishes of all along with 1l bottles of Fanta. Eating like kings in the warm shade we had such a good laugh with our new convoy joiners and ate until we could eat no more.

"How much will that be?"

Lee managed to get a currency converter up on his phone, it turned out that it was 3.5 manat to the dollar or 4.5 manat to the pound. Working in dollars he had a look through the menu, *"For 13 people, all that food and drink looks about $52, not bad at all I'd say for what we ate! everyone put in $6 each and they have a nice tip."*

The waitress and the owner came over and shook our hands, I honestly think we were the only tourists who had stopped there in years, If not ever. Their son had spent the entire time whilst we were eating sat next to our cars and shouting at youths who came anywhere near them, for DSMS this came as a blessing as a lack of driver's window meant that they now lacked a main component for car security. I didn't tell them but their lack of window also relaxed me a little as the Ford Fiesta Mk3 is one of the easiest cars to break into, this took the attention off my car.

The calculator came out and they showed us the exchange rate, 17 manat to the dollar. This couldn't have been right. Checking it again their calculator came to the same amount. They were asking for a mere $12.

With us all eating like kings, car security and even some water for the road we doubled what they wanted and left once again heading to the capital.

Feeling 100% refreshed, full from a large lunch and the car stocked up with water. I took the wheel and pushed us onto the capital Ashgabat. After long drive in the sun with ever changing landscape we saw the toll of driving in a country with extreme heat, no driving test and cars that were falling apart. An old lorry had crashed into the central reservation of a downhill dual carriageway. Its load had gone over onto the other side causing a huge pileup. Blood, car parts and helpers littered the road, it most have only happen no more than 10 minutes before. Everything was under control, slowly passing the wreckage in the distance we could see Ashgabat on the horizon.

Entering the city, we saw the most amazing buildings, they were all pearl white with marble, bronze and golden arches. It looked like the Vegas of Asia. Clearly a lot of money had gone into re-building this city, it was re-built to a fantastic standard after a large earthquake in 1948 and anything built since then has a whole book of rules, they must follow to make the building as spectacular as the one next to it. Everything was extremely clean, the white buildings looked like they had all been freshly painted, no litter at all could be found on the streets and 80% of the cars were new and painted in a gloss white. We had found out before the rally that the governor of Turkmenistan decided that all cars in the capital MUST be white. He instructed local police and army to pull over and impound all cars that were not white, they were then kept until the owner either had the cars destroyed or made arrangements for a respray. We also heard a rumor of a place called Turkmen-world, a place that was built to rival Disneyland. Adam and myself had this crazy idea that it was a rundown fair in the middle of the desert operated solely by one man. He would change hats and put on fake mustaches to try and trick you to thinking he was someone else. We never found out if Turkmen-world existed or where it was, nevertheless we wouldn't have the time to go. If you want to do the central route and you wish to finish the rally in 6 weeks, you ain't got time to be going on rides.

We were looking for a hotel, knowing that the exchange rate was insanely good for us having dollars, we headed for the Ashgabat Sports 5 Star Olympic hotel. It was starting to get dark and the idea of a 5-star hotel with pool, sauna, gym, food and a 24/7 bar was just purely brilliant. We stopped to ask for directions, walking into what should have been a busy shopping mall, we entered to find it was completely empty. Nothing and no one could be seen, just a completely empty store.

Crossing the road, I headed to a supermarket, I found that it was closed, peering through the window I could see that it

178

was also empty, just signage on the window made it look like a regularly used store.

Eventually we found a different hotel, it was dark, we were all exhausted and we noticed other rally cars were outside. Wait, that's...

Mini Adventures were with us, James and Jade were heading over with huge smiles.

"We have had the strangest of days, woah we are happy to see you guys. We were going to book into here but it's the same price as the 5 Star Sports hotel down the road and they have a swimming pool".

This hotel was 5 stars as well but it lacked a swimming pool and was also the choice hotel of the Honeymooners and their parents, who were lovely but we were still extremely unsure what was going on there. They weren't sticking with the rally tradition at all, having a Land Cruiser backup vehicle carrying spares was a big 'no no' to The Adventurists, also we had heard a rumor that they were well in the money and were only staying in the best hotels drinking the finest wines. If this rumor was true or not, we were yet to find out.

The moonlight bounced off the white, bronze and gold buildings as we checked into the Sports Hotel, showered and headed to the bar. The hotel itself was extremely grand, right next to the Olympic Stadium it stood towering over its neighbors, inside it advertises its capacity of over five hundred rooms. However, the only ones who seemed to be staying there were our four teams from Convoi Exceptionnel and a convoy of three who had just made it up from Iran. Even the staff numbers were low, I only counted four the whole evening, two on the desk, one in the bar and one waitress. Then I realised the recurring theme of Ashgabat, the entire city seemed to look the part from the outside but from the inside it was completely empty. It was like a behind the scenes from an old movie where all the building fronts were in place but nothing else seemed to exist. The entire city is completely underpopulated but overcrowded with hotels, houses, shops, casino's and everything you could possibly need, just no one there to actually need it.

When we got to the bar, we ordered drinks and paid with our US dollar. Pint in hand the barman issued our change in Manat, *"35 Turkmenistan Manat change."*

Wait.

That can't be right.

"We got 17 manat to the dollar earlier today? also its 3.5 Manat to the dollar." I said.

The bar Manat replied with "10-dollar, one beer, 35 manat change."

Fair enough, so that means we're getting the official exchange rate in change, so technically.

"THE BEER IS FREE!!" well, it was with every exchange of dollar to manat.

"That and it cost us 30 manat to fill our tank earlier, so a beer and a full tank of petrol is less than 10 dollars" James informed us.

We then began asking the barman about how the exchange rate was worked out, we were getting 17 to the dollar at one point, 3.5 to the dollar now and it only cost us 1 dollar to fill up our benzin tank.

"Different part of Turkmenistan. In the city it is 3.5, outside of the city who knows? keep the money in the city."

After a small debate between the convoy and the barman it worked out that what he was saying is, the cities charge the standard 3.5 to the dollar but it seems outside the cities it isn't allowed to be so high, it keeps the rich, rich and the poor, poor. We didn't know how to feel, by drinking and staying here in such luxury we were paying towards someone's second Yacht whereas ten miles down the road we would have had everything for half the price but they wouldn't have made any money at all on them. It was a strange feeling but with my stomach screaming for food we all ordered pizza and drank until the crazy Turkmenistan Karaoke had finished. Well-deserved rest was in order and a bit of luxury in a cozy bed was greeted happily. Two days on a ferry, one sleep in the car and the plan of camping under the stars in the Kara-Kum desert next to the Darvaza gas crater meant we weren't getting quite the rest we needed.

I woke up before Lee, he was snoring extremely loudly and the air conditioning must have clicked off in the night. Sweaty, tired and feeling a little sick, I messaged Adam, we thought the best way to combat our lack of sleep was to try out the hotel facilities. An hour in the pool, fifteen minutes in the sauna and then a huge bucket filled with cold water thrown over your head was exactly what we needed.
The plan today was to head into the city to find a garage to fit a sump guard, the roads from now on we're going to be a lot tougher than what we were used too and even told rumors of ripping a sump clean off your car.
For those of you who don't know what a sump is, it's a hollow depressed oil pan underneath your engine that is used to store the engine oil that your engine pumps around to lubricate. In simple terms, it's what you want to protect most in your car, if you get a hole in it or rip it off, you have no oil, then if your engine runs, it seizes due to lack of

lubrication. (like Gnomes found out) Then it's game over for your car and your rally dreams of making it to Mongolia.

A sump guard is a thick bit of metal bolted under your engine that protect your sump from damage, we had been told by ralliers before that its necessary to have a sump guard and without one you are playing with fire.

Cunning Stunts already had one fitted, as did the mini, DSMS and us in the AFK car were the only ones lacking.

Once everyone had arisen, breakfast went down swimmingly before pushing on from our five-star accommodation to the messy garages on the outskirts of Ashgabat,

I won't bore you with what happened, all you need to know is that it was a complete waste of three hours, no one really understood what we wanted, CS tried to even get a set of knobbly tyres but when a garage pulled out a knife, they definitely got the wrong end of the stick.

Following one bloke, we finally felt like we had gotten somewhere, following him for twenty minutes we ended up at a huge Nissan dealership and were told *"Just buy a new one"*, He was referring to our cars. What a complete waste of time.

We spent the last part of the morning grabbing supplies, we needed, food to cook on our stoves, endless bottles of water in case of emergency, snacks, fruit and juices. You don't know how much you appreciate vitamins until you do the Mongol Rally. Once again, we were back in our convoy, Convoi Exceptionnel was back in business, I called a meeting before we set off. I told everyone about what I had heard about the road north from Ashgabat, Its bad, but manageable. Lee told us all about the Gas Crater being 5k's off road in deep sand and how we must stay together to help each other get there.

It was at that moment we made the decision.

We agreed that from now on we would stick together as long as we could. We all had the same route, the same timescale and the same 'go get it' attitude. With strength in numbers and our teamwork, as Convoi Exceptionnel we would make it to the end.

We went to the first petrol station we could find, filled up our cars, with a smile we took out our dollars, we would have had local manat but the bar bill the night before out of hand. Cunning Stunts went first, filled, paid and waited, then me and Lee in our AFK car, filled, pai...

wait.

How much?

"That's $100 for all four cars"

WHAT.

"That's $100 for all four cars" as he pointed at them all. We knew CS had just paid, turns out they were fleeced and without thinking, parted with $40 to fill their car and jerry cans. We had filled our car and cans and he wanted $100. 10 minutes later and a large argument with him I paid $20 for both mine and DSMS's Car to be filled.

James in the mini was next, he filled up.

"$6"

This attendant was an absolute joke.

He was obviously playing the game 'whoever has most sponsors on their car pays the most' game, little did he know, we had played that game many times before and never lost. Finally, 1pm hit and we were away, north from Ashgabat in a completely straight line all the way to Darvaza. George Ezra on full, underneath the hot sun. The car was running perfect, I was feeling good the road was smooth. for a while.

BAM, THUD, *"FUCK", "OH GOD"* THUD.

The road was still tarmac; however, it was completely full of holes, I'd never seen a road so bad, there seemed to be no one using the road but us, however it has had its fair share of beatings from lorries, cars and by the looks of things landmines. 275 km of this long, bumpy road completely surrounded by desert was only halfway out of Turkmenistan, it was another 300 km north from the Gas Crater to our point of exit into Uzbekistan at a place called Dashoguz. Our spirits were not to be broken just yet, as a team we pushed on at a good rate, I was nervous about our rear axle giving up on any of the potholes, but I remember thinking to myself, if it's going to go again, it's best to go now close to the city rather than in Mongolia in the middle of nowhere.

We pushed on and on swapping with each other to lead the charge, when it was Mini Adventures time to lead, we could all see the road taking its toll on their exhaust. Every bump or rock they hit, scraped the back of their exhaust causing sparks to fly. The roof rack wobbled and the knobbly tyres strapped on top were shacking themselves loose.

What should have taken three hours took seven. It was about to start going dark, the sun set in the distance and we were still 30k's from the turn off for the Darvaza Gas Crater (The Gate to Hell).

"We may not make it before sundown" I said to Lee.

"I know, then its 5k's off roading until we get to the crater, if it's too dark, we may have to camp next to the road and see it in the morning". he replied.

I thought to myself for a while about back in Blackpool when I was planning with Lee in my living room, I had this Idea

that we would arrive in the sun, pitch our tents and enjoy a cold beer when it got dark next to the scorching fire.
I replied.
"Nah mate, doesn't matter what happens, were getting there, we are getting there tonight, putting up our tents and enjoying a cold beer, just as we planned on doing." I announced.
No one could have expected what happened next.
"Okay mate, but we may need a miracle." Lee said with a sigh.
At that point, I overtook the miracle.
The miracle was in the form of a convoy of 6 other ralliers. The Bongolians, Around the world in 998cc's, The Honeymooners (along with mother and father), Team Over 9000, Breakneck Tweed (in a 4x4 Fiat Panda) and more. I knew that together, 10 Teams strong we could all make it to the crater. Pulling over at the turn off point, we got out of our cars to assess the situation of what we could see as the sun set.
Soft Sand.
Everywhere.
So much sand.
A rally car was stuck half way up a very steep hill and parked next to the roads were the locals waiting for us.
There are mixed reviews of the Gas Crater locals, some say that they purposely tell you the wrong routes so you end up getting stuck and then end up paying them to tow you out. Others say they are helpful, offer to take you there by motorbike and look after your car if you leave it on the road.
I would like to put this rumor to rest.
They MOST DEFINITELY point you in the wrong direction, when you go the right way, they push in front and slow

down to try and stop you, once you stop, you are stuck. They are complete and total dicks.

With 10 teams and a dream, the 4x4's went first to scout out what was to come as Mini Adventures floored it straight off the road and into the sand.

They were stuck instantly.

Every team helped to dig them out, we all pushed until eventually they were free. On the second attempt we watched as they set off, taking air over a small dune, crashing back down to earth before going over the main hill.

"If the mini can do it, we all can" said Ritchie from CS.

We all jumped into our cars and away we went, into the deep sand, 5k's to our destination.

Cunning Stunts floored it, up and over, taking no ease, POWER was their attitude. DSMS were next copying the same route as CS as their little Micra bounced over the sand, Then with Lee as my Co-driver, I floored it.

Though the first of the soft sand the mighty fiesta drifted through with the engine screaming and the front wheels struggling to keep any traction at all. Over the first little hump we bounced, I cringed at the thought of the rear axle snapping now, but with no time to even think about it, I pushed on keeping the accelerator flat onto the floor until I Reached the top of the hill, It was gravel and rocks, I stopped turned to Lee and celebrated.

"We did it mate, fuck yeah, well done mate, good callouts." I was so happy.

"Don't celebrate yet, another 4 km to go." said Lee.

I had completely forgotten there was more to go, I was taking it in small chunks. As I looked down the hill in the last of the sunlight all I could see was kicked up sand and brake lights.

Allowing the dust to clear, we could see the road to follow, keeping a good distance behind the car in front we followed them for another 3 km, soft sand made it extremely hard but with regular gravel stops we kept cool and coordinated as much as possible, taking it hill by hill, we limped over them, drifted around the corners and until we had only 1 km left to go. The road split three ways and we had no idea which way to go, we had been deciding amongst ourselves when a few teams turned and stopped behind us.

"It's this way, Up the hill and over, our guide though Turkmenistan says he has done it before and this is the way to go". Said a bloke from one of the cars.

Wait.

Remember that guy from the boat whop screwed us all over by paying what they asked? it was him.

I wasn't going to trust him on this one as well, was I?

"It's too steep" I announced as everyone looked over at me.

"It's too steep, you will get close to the top but you won't get to the top, that little dip ⅔ of the way up, that's what will get you, it goes very steep from there, It just looks like you can can make it from where were standing."

I could tell this guy wasn't happy I had just called him out, so he jumps in the car with his son and their guide and floors it. He did extremely well to get it up to about ⅔ of the way until their car crawled to a holt and the tyres dug further and further into the ground.

If you happen to be reading this book mate, Good effort! but Teamwork makes the dream work.

I looked ahead, one road had been blocked with stones and could only be accessed by going through a sand pit.

Lee took the words right out of my mouth.

"That's the way! It must be why the locals have dumped all those stones in such a huge plie! They don't want you to take that track! By taking that track, you get there without their help and they make no money."

Lee was 100% correct, all of us worked together to take some rocks from the pile and add them to the pit, giving the cars traction as they plowed through. Once it looked good, I got into the car,

clutch in,

first gear selected. Lee stood perilously close to the stone causeway we had just built, pushing part of it together with his foot. Pointing at the exact point in which to ride on top of the stones, I took a run up and sailed across the deep sand pit without issue.

I took a moment to look at the top of the hill to the left to see the bloke and his son waving their arms.

"Sorry mate, looks like you will have to pay you way out of this one too."

I floored it over the pit and onto the road and over the valley. In the distance we could see the glow from the crater, the gate to hell was so close and my spirits were instantly lifted. I was about to take the last turn town to it when I saw a Nissan Micra struggling to push themselves out the dirt further down the road, DSMS had missed the turn off and plowed straight into the soft sand.

I couldn't leave them behind and I couldn't tow them. Flagging down Team: Breakneck Tweed in the 4x4, I caught a lift over to them, hitched up a tow rope and pulled them out of the soft sand. Within a couple of minutes, I had returned to Lee and our trusty Fiesta before braving the last of the soft sand. He had started to get anxious as I had gone out of sight and the light was fading fast. We would have used our light bar but it had been shaken loose and only lit up our bonnet, blinding the driver. We still needed to watch for rocks and it was getting increasingly difficult as night set in. We had to make it. Onto the soft sand, over a few rocks and back onto the main track. Then, there it was, dead ahead. The Darvaza Gas Crater, also known as the door to Hell.

In celebration I pulled right up to the fires and cheered, along with DSMS and Cunning Stunts we took picture after picture, screaming *"WE DID IT"*, beeping, flashing the LED bar, we couldn't have been happier.
That was until we remembered, we were being so selfish and hadn't given a thought to Mini Adventures. It was pitch black and they were nowhere to be seen.
I found Breakneck Tweed again and explained we had to go back to help. They were more than happy to help, grabbing the tow rope and jumping in the car we saw the mini come over the last hill.
It looked and sounded bad.
One working headlight, the roof rack had been torn from the front of the bonnet, Dents had appeared all over and the ground clearance was none existent, the entire suspension had collapsed.
I didn't know what to say to James when I saw him.
"I fucking hate Turkmenistan, it's given me a stress nosebleed" were his words.
James had been a rally legend from the start, not only was he doing the rally in an old classic mini, he was driving solo the whole way with a passenger who lacked in DJ skills. I could understand why he was upset, unless he could fix it, his rally would be over. We didn't know what to say however the mood was broken quickly when we saw the father & son

189

team having to pay to be towed off the hill by locals. This wasn't rally spirit, but karma finally went full circle.

We took photos and videos for our sponsors of the car driven right up to the burning hole in all its glory, The Door to Hell is an unofficial rally checkpoint, it's one of the best places to go to in Turkmenistan. wait.
It's the ONLY place to go to in Turkmenistan and I wouldn't have wanted to miss it. We were only one step away from complete perfection.
"Cold beer here, $4 a beer" a man shouted from his 4x4. Pricey, but well worth it in the middle of a desert. Now that's a local that I will happily pay.
"And there we have it Lee," I said. *"Perfection."*

I awoke early once again because in the night I had been greeted by a true rally gift, some say that the Mongol Rally isn't complete without it, yes that's right I'm talking about the trots.
Brilliant, I was 279 km north of the closest toilet and 317 km south of the second closest toilet. Completely slap bang in the middle of a flat desert landscape. Luckily I could see a large rock about half a kilometer away, this was to be my salvation and my privacy, once I got there, toilet roll in hand I could smell that I wasn't the first person to think about this, I completely understand why you are told to dig a hole and bury it because the sight and smell that awaited me was one from a horror film. Nevertheless, when you've got to go, you've got to go. Back at our camp I noticed that our passenger side back tyre was flat and the roof rack had seen better days. It was sagging and rocking slightly so needed to be tightened. I quickly ratchet strapped it to the car as a

quick fix, feeding the strap through both rear windows, up and over the roof. Then out came the tyre pump we borrowed from DSMS. Somehow though all the checking and double checking during all the prep for the rally, my tyre inflator was sitting in a box at home in the shed. A quick blast and we were good to go. Well, that was until I looked at the Mini, in the daylight it looked a lot worse. We could see James trying to shift the roof rack back into place with no luck, we all knew what we had to do. Grabbing what we could we spent an hour hammering, bolting and raising the mini as a team, by the end it didn't look great but it worked and was ready for the journey back to the road.

After a quick breakfast of cereal bars purchased from Blackpool weeks back before we left, we jumped in the cars ready for the return journey back to the road, along with the rest of Convoi Exceptionnel. Due to me and Lee both having a great teamwork when driving off road we offered to lead the charge, we knew to leave space on the good gravel for those who need to stop behind us and also keep the power down on the soft sand. We took an alternative route back an off roading mini bus had just arrived and departed to from that direction and informed the ralliers it was shortest road back to the main road with little deep sand.

Off we went.

Lee was driving, he was excited to get behind the wheel and do some proper off-road driving. Powering through the soft sand he navigated the convoy through the winding sandy tracks, occasionally passing trucks who were collecting rocks from a local quarry. We were making good time and good distance.

"Crackle Crackle" the CB Radio had just kicked in, *"Erm, your exhaust is hanging off"* said James from Mini Adventures.

Getting out the car, taking a look, I could see he wasn't wrong, there it was dragging along the floor. It was no bother but had to be reattached. I dug a small put in the sand to get under the car easier before crabbing a 10mm ratchet, fixing the pipes back together and tightening it up.

By this point everyone else had caught up, all the other ralliers who camped with us the night before. This road was a lot easier than the road chosen the previous night so spirits high as we posed for photos filmed each other tackling the sand on a drone. Eventually we made it back to the road. Our exhaust was hanging off once again, the Mini's suspension needed a tweak and many other cars had war wounds needing attention.

"I think it's time for a montage" I announced to all.

On our car stereo I played 'The Darkness- I believe in a thing called love' on full blast as we all tinkered away on the cars. I re-attached the exhaust but also noticed it had nearly sheared where it connects to the baffle. Pumped up all tyres and strapped another ratchet strap on the roof rack. Well, I say I, I mean more both me and Lee. Lee had no knowledge of mechanics but was extremely eager to learn so anything I could talk him through and get him to do, I would. But most situations ended up with him being my tool boy and fetching the things I needed whilst I crawled underneath.

After half an hour on our car and some time spent on the mini, we were ready to tackle the 327 km to Dashoguz. Dashoguz is a city in northern Turkmenistan and the capital of Daşoguz Province. The Uzbekistan border is about 10 km away at a place called Yablykangly. Try saying that after a few beers!

That was our heading. With no sign of any petrol station for miles the jerry cans were emptied into the tank. The road condition was just as poor and pot holed as the previous day, but progress was to be made. It was definitely the hottest day of the trip so far; our water was warm and with no air conditioning we were sweating every second. The plan on the trip was to just drive with the windows down however in Turkmenistan this is close to impossible. As soon as the windows go down it's almost as if someone turns a huge hairdryer on in your car. The heat becomes instantly unbearable. Along with all of that, sand is blown into your car at a high speed destroying your skin, eyes and equipment. DSMS must have been having a shit time in their car with no drives window, luckily, I had passed on some dust masks just as we left Darvaza that I threw in the car just before we left, in case we lost our windscreen.

There I was moaning about the heat when we pulled over to help a man at the side of the road. He was a cyclist touring the world and completely out of water. He had all of the correct gear but with the heat of the day so unbearable his rationing had gotten out of control. Jumping out of the car I filled up his water bottles and swapped storied with him. His plan was to cycle another 100 km and wait till sunset where he would push on in the cold until darkness fell.

I thought we were badass traveling by shit car ⅓ of the way around the world, but there we were with engines and horsepower next to a true legend with manpower and a bicycle.

We drove all day, North in one straight line, it was a rather uninteresting day until,

"Clunk.

Clunk.

Screech.

Clunk.

Screech.
Clunk."
"ROARRRRR"
"What the bloody hell was that". Lee shouted.
Ah yes, I thought. I forgot to tell Lee about the baffle.
It had finally snapped and detached itself from the car, that
was the first clunk. It was then driven over by our back
wheel, the second clunk. Then DSMS swerved trying not to
hit it, the first screech. It then bounced off their car, the third
clunk. Into the path of Mini Adventures who swerved out of
the way causing screech two, which lead to a tyre dislodging
from their roof rack and bouncing off into the desert.
Causing the final clunk. The loud roar then came from our
car without a baffle and a disconnected backbox we sounded
like a true rally car. It was loud, it was annoying and it was
close to 300 km to the nearest welder. We were certainly in
for a loud ride though Turkmenistan.

Finally, after hours of driving and spot of tinnitus.
Civilization.
A petrol station and a roundabout. Now, there is nothing
strange about a roundabout, it was as normal as ever, but
when you have driven close to 500 km in a straight line, it
comes as a shock. I made Lee do three laps of the
roundabout before realizing it was also a Police checkpoint
so with our heads down, we pulled into the station for a well
needed rest, food and fuel. $2 for a full tank, so in celebration
kebabs were purchased by all except me and Jade. We had to
go for the vegetarian equivalent, Ice cream. For someone
with the trots this didn't feel good at all, Jade announced she
was feeling a stomach problem occurring too but with no
sign of non-meat based solid food around. We were screwed.

"If we push on to the border now, we could be in Uzbekistan by 6pm." Lee said.

It sounded like a good idea, Turkmenistan was the weirdest place I had visited so far but It didn't feel good to have driven through it all in three days hardly stopping. I was extremely excited to be going into the next country, I was excited to get the exhaust fixed to avoid destroying my hearing but everyone seemed to like the idea. *"Get me out of this shitty place"* James from MiniAd shouted.

His Mini was taking a beating and for the first time on the tip you could tell he was extremely unsure if he was going to make it all the way to Mongolia. With a new plan, back into the cars we went and for the first time since the ferry began our journey east. (After another three times around the roundabout that was).

We pushed on, exhaust roaring for two hours until we entered Dashoguz. Whizzing straight through to get to the border I revved the engine loud next to some cyclists causing them to crash into one another and fall hard onto the gravel road before arriving at the Uzbekistan border. A guard approached me with a huge smile.

He closed the gate in front of me and shouted *"Closed, Nine O'clock tomorrow please."*

Turns out the border closed at 6pm and 5:49pm was too late to process 4 foreign cars.

"Looks like we have Dashoguz to explore."

We were all completely covered in sand, at least two layers. Our hair had turned brown and I couldn't imagine the stench that would have been coming from not only ourselves but our car too.

"Cheap hotel, shower and drinks are in order I do believe" said Lee. *"You know what mate, I couldn't agree more."*

With the Convoy altogether we spotted a few hotels on the map, the closest one was just a few clicks back where we came from, 'Eric Hotel'. *"Let's go see if Eric is home"* said Adam. Our moods were fantastic, we had defeated Turkmenistan, we had the chance for a warm meal & a shower and in the morning we would cross into Uzbekistan. Pulling up at Eric's hotel the convoy laughed at how much noise our car was making, we were making heads turn at the sound of our tiny 1.1 roaring through the streets. *"Eric hotel?"* I shouted at a local with my foot down on the accelerator pretending I couldn't hear him over it. *"yes yes, here here."* Brilliant.

I knocked on the door, no answer.

The window, no answer.

the back door, no answer.

Ah,

The intercom, no answer.

Then just for a laugh I screamed at the top of my voice *"Eric!!!"* We all erupted into giggles, jumping out their cars the convoy began walking around just screaming *"Eric"* and looking confused. It was like the scene in Jurassic Park three when they lose their son and shout his name over and over again with no luck. Looking like complete idiots a crowd of locals looked on and started shouting back. they were probably shouting *"bloody foreigners, sod off somewhere else"* but we didn't care. The next hotel it was.

A Man approached me, *"Hello mate, are you Eric?"* ... He replied soon after but I couldn't make out a word. *"I don't think its him lads."*

Eventually we found a hotel, It was a little more than we wanted to pay so we thought with the last bit of daylight we would just search a little more. Then we saw it, a huge, grand hotel not only with Wi-Fi but a 24-hour bar. It was worth finding out the price. Adam ran in to find out the price and returned with the news. *"Good news or the bad news first?"* Oh god.

"The good news is that it's the same price as the hotel down the road. The bad news is that she doesn't know where Turkmen-world is either."

Laughs erupted as we unpacked our gear. Out of the two hotels we found at the same price, this was much grander. It was a no brainer. We entered the lobby and the haggling for a cheaper room began. I had been in charge of haggling throughout the trip, so it was Lee's turn to give his haggling a go. When we were at the launch party many weeks ago, we were given stickers for our car, it was a map of Turkmenistan that looked like an official stamp along with some writing we couldn't read. This logo was all around Turkmenistan and Lee used it to try and blag that we were special guests from the government of Turkmenistan, he showed her the sticker and she seemed a little shocked, after about 20 mins of conversation I returned to find that Lee had managed to get absolutely nothing from the bill.

Full price it was.

To be completely fair on Lee, not only was the last of the group to pay but the woman behind the desk had a price book in front of her that the manager refused to let her budge on. Turkmenistan hotels are mostly owned by the government and have VERY strict prices and taxes they have to pay.

A quick shower, fresh clothes on and our underwear soaking in the shower meant we could get to the bar quick, I arrived down first to give Caroline and the girls a call.

God, I missed them, I missed them so much.

At points I would tear up slightly when thinking about them, I knew how proud they would be of me for getting so far but even though I was on such an amazing adventure, I would be missing some extremely important moments of family life. I missed my little girls first steps and words, something a father should be around for, not on the opposite side of the world.

The phone call home lasted close to half an hour, we were catching up on anything and everything we could, constantly expressing our love for each other. As upsetting as it was to be traveling further away from them every day, it also meant that the time difference worked in my favor., It meant at 10pm Turkmenistan time my children were still awake just finishing their dinner at 5pm.

Looking around I spied Adam, Danny and Lee doing the same thing whilst Oli made love to his pint of lager. Adam and Danny had spoken so dearly about their partners and introduced us all too them from time to time, it was great being with other lads in happy, committed relationships just like myself and Lee were. It meant we weren't on the town every night trying to catch an STD, we focused completely on friendship, culture and good memories. Danny and Adams only quest that involved local women was the one that got Oli laid. A quest that both myself and Lee were happy to get behind.

We said our goodbyes on the phone, as much as no one wanted to put the phone down, hunger got the better of us. As much as we would have loved to talk for hours, we had lived off warm water and benzin station food for close to two days. We were drinking our beer when James and Jade joined us. For some reason James had changed into a full three-piece suit whilst Jade had changed into a stunning red dress.

"What's the occasion" I asked.

"It's a farewell party tonight, were saying goodbye to this shithole" he replied.

Turkmenistan had completely broken James however his mood at the border to Uzbekistan had finally changed. He could almost taste the freedom.

Hungry and happy we sat down in the huge dining room at a large 30-person table only to be joined by the Italian honeymooners and their parents. They turned out to be a good laugh, you could tell they had money and that they suited hotels as grand as this but under all that, they were just another rally team in search of Adventure. Even though I couldn't understand why you would convoy around the world with your parents, they were very friendly and I started to regret a few comments I had made earlier in the week.

"Hello my friends, are you here for food"

Finally, a waiter had appeared.

"You come with me to kitchen"

He had pointed at me for some strange reason, nevertheless I followed him to a large kitchen with its lights off and no one around.

"Kitchen closed."

Why he couldn't have said this at the table, I have no idea.

"Is there anywhere around here we can get some food? it's been a very long day and we could do with a good meal" I asked once we were back at the table.

The reply we then received shocked us all, still to this day I will never know what this man was trying to translate.

"I can get you chicken, nice chicken, boil in swimming pool. after soup has clucked and defrosted. We make rice and ask for no rice in case the rice need swimming pool. Maybe two hours near."

We all looked at each other in complete amazement, not knowing where to begin with a reply. *"yeah mate, sounds great"* Danny shouted before looking at us all, *"I have no fucking clue what I have just ordered".*

It looked like we were getting boiled rice and chicken from the local swimming pool sometime within the next three hours. Both myself and Jade being vegetarians we knew that it was going to be a night on the pot noodles.

Turkmenistan, your country is the wildest place I have ever had the fortune to visit, I loved parts and hated others. You make so many ralliers want to give in and so many others strive to beat you. Your currency doesn't make sense at all, your buildings are mostly empty and your hotels overpriced. On top of all this, no roads so far have been as bad as yours. They honestly suck.

With all this said, never change. You are truly fascinating and I wish for all ralliers from this day to experience exactly what we had. Now, onto Uzbekistan.

Chapter 13 - Days 20 - 23 - "Sir, your 'Crow' is broken."

We woke early, as did the rest of Dashoguz once we fired up our exhaustless car. I had already done all the morning checks and topped her up with oil. In the hotter countries our lovely fiesta had been drinking a little more than usual, but that's nothing to worry about if you keep an eye on it and top it up when needed.

I inched forward to allow DSMS access to their car, we had double parked them and blocked off access to opening their doors the night before as their lack of window made it very appetizing for thieves. After a short drive and a shout of "ERIC" out of the windows at every passerby, we arrived at the Turkmenistan to Uzbekistan border. This border had a lot of negative past on Caravanistan website and other rally forums due to the guards stealing rally gear, violence and even looking through your phones and computers for explicit images. Anything to get you fined. I was a little shaky as it would be up to me to get the car through safely as Lee walked with ease through the border. Not only would I be looking out for potential thefts but what would happen if I saw one? I couldn't go to the huge guard brandishing an AK47, *"hello mate, that's ours, give it back!"* Could I?

Upon entering the border, we parked up and headed to customs.

"Drivers with me, car passport and passports needed, also what's your favorite football team, mine is Chelsea"

What?

We seemed to have hit the jackpot with the nicest border guard yet. He was called Aysun and he loved speaking to tourists and practicing his english. If it got us safely though a

201

border, we were more than happy to oblige. *"What's your name? do you have a wife? what does UK stand for?"* the questions kept on coming but he seemed to be filling in all the paperwork for us. Myself, James and Adam were having a great time and within a few minutes we were done. heading back outside for the dreaded car search we were stopped by our good friend Aysun, *"My friends, if anyone from this point ask for money or things, you say that Aysun told you not too and they must come see me."* Brilliant, what a guy! My nerves dropped completely. Knowing the guard had our backs was a fantastic way to start our trip into Uzbekistan. Within no time we had said our goodbyes to the Turkmenistan side and crossed no man's land. This happened to be a huge fenced off area of broken road filled with large pot holes and concrete barriers, to the left and right were towers filled with guards. It was the one place we didn't want to break down, it was the one place we didn't want to...

oh no.

Sheep dip.

There, right in front of us all was the largest sheep dip we had ever seen. A huge, deep pool of water that must be driven though. Filled with chemicals and god knows what else it kills any bacteria or disease that may be attached to the bottom of your car. I wouldn't have minded doing this normally but with a very small exhaust just dropping from the bottom of our engines, if we stall and it sucks up any water. We were done for.

DSMS went first making it look easy, I roared the engine and just floored it. Without thinking I hadn't even looked at the guard who was meant to be giving me the signal to go, I just went for it, the sooner it was done the better. Making a huge wave we hit the water almost splashing the guard and roared out the other side. I was expecting some bollocking from the other side but I was greeted with laughs from the sound of our car. Passport stamped, Car passport stamped and away we were, straight into Uzbekistan. But first we needed local currency, usually just on the other side of the border is a local just waiting to swap money with you, they are usually hidden from the guards and in the most dodgiest places you could ever think to look, just as we started looked we weren't shocked at all to find a half-naked man in a basement of a nearby house wanting to swap money. Not knowing the best exchange rate, we swapped some smalls in the hope to get more in the next town.

Benzin (Petrol) would be needed soon. But without thinking of filling up in Turkmenistan we had entered a country where benzin was illegal. That's right, we had been told by many ralliers before that you have to buy petrol on the black market in Uzbekistan, not only that but you have to do it quite a few times to get from one end of the country to the other. With the plan to get our exhaust fixed and a sump guard fitted with very little money we were ready to see what this Uzbekistan had to offer.

We flew straight into the town of Shavat looking for water and daily supplies, the next big city was Urgench but the need for fizzy drinks, breakfast and cold water was too much. Pulling over I was escorted by a local man into his shop *"Welcome to Uzbekistan, we celebrate with feast"* he shouted whilst handing me some sort of solid leather fossil. He seemed very friendly but I had no idea what he wanted me to do. Impatiently he tore off a large chunk before popping it in his mouth and crunching away. *"What is it?"* I asked again and again but no replies were given. I grabbed the supplies we needed and haggled on the price but still this man was pushing me to eat some of this miscellaneous food. It was at this point I turned it over, what I had been looking at was the insides of a cut open fish, it wasn't until it was turned over could you see its face, eyes and mouth staring back at you. *"erm, vegitariana? erm, vegitarinski!"* he looked at me blankly. Luckily Oli and Danny popped into the shop at this point *"Hey guys, try this, I've just had some and its divine"* I lied. Then proceeded to watch them tear up the dried out Smokey fish and crunch away. Danny was disgusted but Oli crunched away merrily, disgusted and amazed, I watched as the mouthful of fish was swallowed, Oli gave a smile "Not bad" the bloke in the shop cheered before leading us back to our cars and asking hundreds of questions.

"I know exactly where this is going." Oli said as he grabbed the fish from Danny, push a carabiner through its eye and hooked it to the roof rack allowing it to swing around wafting its smell for all.

Lee found a garage on Maps.me, *"Here looks like a good place, it's in the next city, it has a review I can't read but a review nonetheless. It's an hour away and it means we can get our exhaust fixed, a sump put on both cars and Mini Adventures can maybe sort out their suspension."* Everyone agreed, back in the steeds we were and in the glorious sunshine we cruised down to Urgench. As I was driving over potholes n the car seemed to wiggle every now and again over the back wheels. Thinking it was just the road conditions I gave a few tests to figure out the problem. Breaks seemed fine, Steering is all good, I thought. Over a flat bit of ground, I turned left and right wiggling the wheel only to nearly lose control of the car at the back end. Something was wrong but I couldn't tell. *"This mechanic close mate?"* I asked. Lee looking confused directed me the last few miles over some terrible roads to the mechanic. Once arriving outside what just looked like a house, I just jumped out the car looked under the rear wheels at out axle to see everything was in order, the weld was holding strong. I followed the axel looking for problems until *"Ah there's the issue."*

"Hello my friends, what are you doing here" said a man with very good english as he approached our cars with a smile. *"We need a garage to fix our exhaust and replace a shock absorber"* I said. Lee looked at me in horror as I hadn't told him about the shock yet as I hadn't had time. *"We need a garage to fit a sump guard and raise our car"* said DSMS and James from Mini Adventures said "I need a garage to get my steel wheels bashed back in and tyres put on." We were all in need of something. *"You have come to the wrong place, we only do air conditioning mechanics."*

Bugger.

The man shrugged and returned to his house.

We stood outside planning what to do next, we were all low on Benzin and no other garages seemed to be within the area. All of a sudden, the man returns with another bloke beside him. *"We can fix all three cars today, park up here, sit on our outside bed and use our Wi-Fi while you wait."*

Dazed and confused we looked around at each other completely unsure of what just happened, but this is the Mongol Rally! Of course, I'm going to let two air conditioning fitters weld, repair and adjust my car.

I drove our tiny fiesta onto two wooden planks supported by rocks so they could see the extent of the damage, passed them the baffle and they were soon at work. Retreating to the shade we were treated to free grapes and water along with the unlimited Wi-Fi, It was a true god send, it was the first time in weeks that we had the chance to relax in the heat. Although our cars were a little broken, they were all still running fine, they were all pushing on. Our little fiesta felt like it was dragging its back legs with our rear axle, exhaust and shock problem but that didn't matter. The cars were all still cracking on with the main quest line and that was our journey to Mongolia.

Our exhaust was fixed, I drove a Lada for the first time ever with James as we went to get his wheels whacked back into shape. The Lada was well looked after, perfect bodywork topped off with Ferrari badge hubcaps. Our host had given us an address, upon arrival a man shouted his son to collect our wheels from us and start the work. Out came this child who looked no older than 8 years old.

I wish I was joking, he was definitely no older than 8. Grabbing both mini wheels he lugged them into the shop, pulled the tyres off with an iron, threw the steels onto a machine and it began pressing them back into shape. After a few minutes on each wheel they were onto the other machine, whacked a few times with a hammer and re-sealed with the tyres in place. Finally inflated to 30 psi before handing them back to me and James. Both of us hadn't noticed that as all this was going on, neither of us had said a word, we just stood their gob smacked that a child no older than EIGHT had just fixed our tyres and asking for the price of *one dollar, one tyre.* Still, completely gob smacked we gave him $5 before picking our chins up off the floor and returning to the Lada to head back to the others.

Back at the mechanics they had DSMS bonnet open, rear of the car jacked up and the springs from the rear suspension had been removed. For air conditioning fitters they really knew what they were doing, foam inserts were created to raise the springs before fitting them back onto the mighty Micra. One of the blokes takes a quick look under the bonnet wondering how to make and fit a sump guard, after a quick look around he signals DSMS over to show them a problem. One of their engine mounts had come undone, it had managed to detach itself due to a broken washer and was resting nicely on the thread of the bolt, one more turn and it would have been game over. They were extremely lucky. With ease the bolt slipped back through the frame and tightened to secure the engine. The reason why they were lucky was due to the man spotting it and the bolt still being there. If it remained it would have not only put strain on the other mount but one more jolt and they could have had their engine fall out. Whilst traveling at speed this would have been enough to completely flip the car and easily cause fatalities.

Just as we were about to get back on the road, who happens to join us other than our good friends Cunning Stunts along with rally veterans La La Lada, those bad boys had seen our pin dropped on WhatsApp and re-joined the convoy for the push though Uzbekistan. Upon realization of the suspension on the Micra, Ritchie instantly wanted in *"Can I book in for the morning to have my suspension jacked up?"*

Oh my, it looked like we were spending the night in Urgench. From the other side of the yard I suddenly heard what sounded like a scuffle and raised voices with Danny and one of the air conditioning blokes, thinking a fight was about to kick off I ran past their motorhome to see a man shouting at Danny.

"You must, you must visit Khiva. You come all this way and you don't visit Khiva, our beautiful Khiva"

The man seemed extremely passionate about Khiva but instead of giving us more information, he continued with his confusing words.

"Khiva is nice, you must visit Khiva, I SAY YOU MUST VISIT KHIVA!"

After calming him down we eventually found out about this Mythical place Khiva.

Khiva is one of the most noteworthy of the cities and towns of Central Asia, is situated on the left bank of the Amu Darya in the southern part of the modern region of Khorezm in Uzbekistan. It is a unique monument town, completely preserved in the cultural style of the region. In 1967 it was proclaimed a town-reserve and since 1990 one part of Khiva — the Itchan-Kala — was recognized by UNESCO as an historical monument of world significance. *(Thanks GOOGLE, I couldn't have said it better myself)*

Put simply, Khiva is one of the oldest Cities in Uzbekistan, its preserved from a time long ago and according to the locals, a truly unmissable sight. It looked like we were going to Khiva. Whilst waiting for the 'mechanic' to finish on the DSMS Micra, myself, Jade and James went for a wander. We were looking for a bank because with only dollars in hand locals either didn't accept them or made up an exchange rate that only worked in their favor, with no luck in two of three banks we headed to the final one. James and Jade stopping every now and again I managed to get ahead a little.

Opening the door, I spied a guard at the desk, I exchanged a smile and walked up to the counter. The mood instantly changed.

"Do you have an ATM?" I asked as friendly as I could.

The guard stood up, looked over at a second guard to my right. Everything seemed normal until he pulled out his handgun. The other pulled out a baton and began shouting *"No, No, No!"* He shouted as he violently swung the baton at me getting closer and closer. I stood there frozen still not knowing what to do until my brain kicked into gear and informed my legs to get the hell out of there.

I met James and Jade on the steps. *"Turn around, keep walking and don't look back. I'll explain everything"*

All packed up, we were Off to Khiva. The exhaust was still scraping every time we hit a tiny bump in the road. I began missing the deafening sound of no exhaust. At least then the sound was consistent, in a low D flat. The sound engineer in me was beginning to show as I cringed each and every time we scraped along the floor. Arriving in Khiva in the dark was extremely strange. Lack of street lamps and broken roads meant we were completely relying on our headlights to dodge car killer potholes as we drove through a giant doorway that seemed to be part of the world's biggest sandcastle. The entire old city seemed to be built inside an old sandstone fortress, it was completely mesmerizing. Our hotel was located within the centre of the city, surrounded by small market huts and bars. After a spot of dinner and a quick shower using our en-suite room hosepipe, all of the convoy completely crashed. Looks like Khiva would be waiting until tomorrow.

Imagine waking up to the loudest call to prayer you could ever hear in the hottest landscape you have ever entered. On top of that you leave the hotel into a sandstone fortress where different languages are spoken by all. Tiny market stalls have all been set up on the corner of every narrow street selling jewels, jewelry and prayer hats next to their family camel. That was Khiva. Right from the set of an

Indiana Jones movie. We could completely understand why it was on the much needed 'to do' list for Uzbekistan and also why the locals spoke so fondly of it. It really was a place of beauty.

After unsuccessfully finding an ATM we were eventually approached by a young lad on a bike with a carrier bag full of cash and I mean bags upon bags of currency. We checked with the hotel owner that it was genuine (as after all, we would be paying him with those bills) before exchanging US Dollar for Uzbekistan Som. It was at this point we realised why the kid had so much money. *"100 US Dollars' worth please!"* This worked out to 833994 Som. That's right, Eight hundred and thirty-three thousand, nine hundred and ninety-four Som. His quick counting though bundles and bundles of notes gave us the opportunity to pose next to the huge piles of cash for photos. After close to an hour of fanning our faces, giving away free money to each other and throwing money in the air to *'make it rain.'* It was time to head back to our Air Conditioning mechanics, get our exhaust raised a tiny bit more and have CS car raised.

We were back in convoy, me driving the AFK Ford, Adam driving the DSMS Micra, Ritchie driving the CS Ford and Jade driving the Mini Adventures mini. Pah! Just kidding, Jade was still yet to take the wheel of the Mini, even though we were 4933 miles into the journey, she still hadn't driven the car. Arriving at our mechanics, we were once again greeted with grapes, Wi-Fi and an outside bed in the shade. Our car was back in the air again. We showed the mechanic how he had welded it up at an angle and now it was scraping on every little bump. Not wanting to cut and reweld everything he had done the day before, it was suggested to brace the pipe to the underside of the car, holding it up. We got out some (metal tape) that had been hiding in our toolkit, and the mechanic got to work. Whilst waiting for Cunning Stunts car to be finished, I was so bored I must have smoked close to twenty cigarettes in three hours. For someone who had quit smoking before coming on the rally, this was extremely bad. I remember making myself promise that as soon as I was home, I wouldn't touch another. It was getting on into the afternoon where I was approached by DSMS. *"This is a bit silly, all of us waiting here for you guys to have your cars sorted when we could be pushing on and you can meet us tonight in the next city along Bukhara. If we set off now, we will find a hotel or camping spot and let you guys know where we are."*

To be completely honest I knew this was going to happen sooner or later. We had now spent close to two days waiting around for what should have been a quick garage stop. At that point, fuel started pissing out from underneath the car, he had split the fuel line whilst peeling back the heat shield less than a few inches from his lit cigarette. On top of all that we didn't have sump guards and our rear shock was knackered with no chance of a replacement from these guys. I guess they don't use Ford Fiesta parts in the Air Conditioning trade. After a quick discussion, we realised what was best, shook their hands and wished them farewell. *"We will see you tonight in Bukhara, mine's a pint of lager."* Two more hours passed and the mechanic had come up with a solution to our fuel leak while we continued to hang our heads, knowing we just had to let the air conditioning mechanic work away no matter how long it took. To our surprise he had cut another fuel line. This time on his own car. He found some excess pipe under his motor and began a little transplant surgery. He may have been a fool, but he was lovely remorseful guy and only wanted to help. The ford belonging to Cunning Stunts stood strong with new raised rear suspension. Eventually our exhaust was back in position. After paying less than $20 for two days work, there was only one thing missing now, good old benzin. We asked them if they knew of anywhere we could get some fuel for the cars, without it, there was no chance we could get to Bukhara.

Following the Lada, he took us down a few backroads, alleyways and dangerously pot holed roads. We were expecting at any point now to see a dodgy black-market fuel dealer syphoning petrol from a large barrel into empty water bottles. Pulling around the corner we couldn't believe our eyes as we were greeted with none other than, a petrol station.

"What?"

This didn't make any sense at all, we were told over and over *"Benzin is Illegal in Uzbekistan"* but there we were ,filling it up by the pump and paying a very good price for it, not only that but it's octane level was the best since turkey at 96. Finally, we were on our way to Bukhara to meet the rest of the convoy, at first, we were leaving the busy city, then onto the beautiful outskirts. Large wooden houses surrounded by beautiful green landscape surrounded us, horses and carts were being used by farmers and old Lada's beeped as the overtook. I was a beautiful road full of character. Every now and again we would pass a building or house that looked so interesting, I remember wishing I had the time to pull over and take a look. This opportunity came sooner than I thought.

Clunk.

The sound of scraping metal against the floor once again echoed around the car. I looked at Lee. He looked back with the same face, the sort of expression that reads 'oh for god sake.' I pulled over, there it was, once again completely disconnected, dragging its sorry self on the floor. *"Fuck this"* I got the hammer out, jacked up the car and began whacking it as hard as I possibly could until it was in three parts. It was a lot harder to be split apart as they had welded it at every possible place. Once it was off, I grabbed the entire exhaust and strapped it to the roof rack leaving only a tiny downpipe poking out from the engine underneath the car. *"Looks like those guys should stick to air conditioning."*

Both me and Lee were in the same mood. Annoyed that what we had just spent two days fixing had already broken after only traveling 11 miles. However, we both knew that no matter what we could always push on and get it fixed in the next town. With the agreement we weren't turning around, we pushed on into the sunset, exhaust roaring, chasing after Cunning Stunts and hoping to meet with the rest of the Convoy that evening. We raced on, the scenery had changed quite dramatically, from windy roads surrounded by farmland we now found ourselves on a completely empty road once again surrounded by sandy dunes. With that in mind, we floored it.

Hours passed, the same boring uninteresting road lay ahead, with no sign of Cunning Stunts they must have had the same idea, power. *"According to Caravanistan its 300 km of great road followed by 50km of terrible road into Bukhara"* Lee said. *"It can't be any worse than the road through Turkmenistan"* I replied, before being instantly proven wrong. Just as darkness fell, we hit the most terrible road so far, it was a lot worse than Turkmenistan because the pot holes were much wider and deeper. Along with that, every now and again it went into single track due to the road just disappearing into one giant hole. We were on our guard working together to dodge the biggest and deepest. Terrified that at any point our welded rear axle could snap again at any time. As if that happened not only would we have to get it fixed, we would be stranded in the middle of the most dangerous road of the trip with lorries speeding past. We pushed on as quick as we could as locals overtook us at speed. They really must mess up their cars over there, going through shocks and springs like crazy, not one of them slowed down to pass and after drove straight over large pot holes just to save waiting behind us. Then the worst thing happened. Well maybe not the worst, that would be the axel. A 'metal dragging' noise could be heard over the roar of the exhaust-less engine. There was nothing we could do. We had to get out on the most dangerous road of the tip so far, in complete darkness to find our problem.

Lee being the smartest grabbed some emergency lighting beacons that he had packed with him, putting three of them onto 'beacon' mode they emitted a very bright flashing red light which he placed in intervals behind the car making a clear signal to other cars of the obstruction. The Flashing beacons made our breakdown look like a major emergency and all traffic to our amazement actually slowed down and gave us a wide berth. With those on and our hazards I jacked up the car and began to take a look at our problem.

There it was, just a small issue. The last bit of exhaust under our car had come loose from its mount, they were held together with large rubber mounts that over time just degraded, they did well to last this far but Uzbekistan was too much for them. Luckily, I took one off the back of the exhaust and threw it in the boot when I hammered it apart, it just needed swapping and we would be on our way.

oh.

"Hello?"

A man had crawled under the car with me, I had no idea who he was but he joined me, grabbed the end of the exhaust and held it in place while I grabbed the spare rubber mount from the boot, within seconds it was swapped over, we jumped out from under the car, I was about to shake his hand when he started frantically looking around, down the road, in the ditches, everywhere.

"Have you lost something?" I asked, but with no reply a friend of his turned up, spoke to each other and began looking around.

"Thanks for your help, is everything okay?" Lee asked.

Nothing.

What on earth were they looking for? I felt stupid for not figuring it out any sooner. Tapping on his back for him to turn I smiled and pointed at the roof of my car. Laughter erupted from us all.

They had been looking for our exhaust thinking It had fallen off recently, they didn't realize it was strapped to the roof overhanging the front and rear of the roof rack in all of its glory.

These guys had pulled over in their huge truck seeing us in distressed and helped us putting themselves in danger. There was only one way to repay them. *"Do you smoke?"* I parted with a packet of cigarettes to each of them, fired up the engine and pushed into Bukhara. It was getting close to midnight when we entered the city centre with absolutely no idea where everyone else was. We needed Wi-Fi. Stopping outside what looked like a hotel, Lee walked in to ask about

Wi-Fi to find it was actually someone's house and most of the family were asleep on the floor. Moving on we eventually found a hotel, persuaded them for the Wi-Fi password and followed the dropped pin to the rest of the convoy. We followed what can only be described as a labyrinth of streets between houses and walls over, terrible road conditions made from gravel, sand a rubble it took over 45 minutes to travel less than a mile through these streets. Setting car alarms off through the city as our poorly car roared with high revs, and no exhaust, dragging itself over high manhole covers and deep sewage spillways, littering the streets. Until there parked in the middle of a sand pit was the Mini. We had found them and once again our convoy was complete. They could hear our car before they even saw us. Gob smacked that our exhaust was completely ripped off they showed us where to park, helped me back our fiesta through a narrow door and showed us to our room. *"I think, tomorrow we should all look for a garage! We only just got here too, the Mini's exhaust fell off twice as well so they need that fixing and we still don't have a sump guard. The hotel owner knows a place he can take us too, He's a nice guy."* Said Adam. It was extremely relaxing to hear that a garage was already lined up for us in the morning, this meant we could have the exhaust and shock absorber looked at and maybe even replaced. DSMS had gone out of their way to sort this out for us when their car had no problems at all they were great team players and an absolute dream to be traveling with. I couldn't believe that their only issue throughout Asia was a few dented rims.

Green fried eggs, jam, crusty bread and meat were all laid out on the table for us. Breakfast wasn't that appetizing at all, let alone for me who was still struggling with the trots. I just couldn't manage to shake them. I ate the most absorbing things I could find, Bread, rice and biscuits of death and still no change! Nevertheless, the rally must go on. We were all in a good mood knowing that finally, real mechanics would be looking at our cars. The hotel owner thanked us for staying with him and asked us to pass on his details to ralliers behind us before jumping in the DSMS mighty Micra to direct us all to the mechanics. With their only being three seats free in the car, this meant there was only one place left for Danny to sit. *"Looks like I'm on the roof then."* The winding labyrinth was just as confusing as the night before, the daylight didn't help at all, we had to keep right up the arse of DSMS as the streets were so short and narrow within seconds if we missed them take a turn, we would all be completely lost. Eventually we made it to the gates of a huge compound. It was around twenty garages all next door to one another with cars, parts, oil and modifications laid out everywhere. It looked like a scrapyard, this was exactly what our cars needed. *"Let's go shopping lads!"*

Mini Adventures were escorted into a small garage with an inspection pit ready to have their exhaust re welded and hooked back on. I drove the AFK ford onto a ramp and within seconds it was raised in the air. After showing our mechanic our exhaust, we then pointed out our rear shock. *"Can this be fixed or replaced?"* I asked, but I was only replied to with a smile. *"That must be a yes then."* We retreated into the shade to give the mechanics time with our car without us hovering around them asking questions. As a good deed we purchased a load of beers for our hotel owner and passed him some stickers for his daughter. We were very lucky to be in this compound. Almost everyone wanted to help, almost everyone was offering us cigarettes and next door was a brilliant shop that just so happened to be ran by a lovely woman who spoke English. I hadn't felt this relaxed in days. I took the chance to stock up on engine oil as we were still burning a little more than usual. James managed to find some engine oil for his classic mini too! I mean what are the odds? within an hour our exhaust was welded back together and back in place securely. It was a proper job and they even braced the pipe to try prevent it happening again. Without having to ask they began to remove our rear wheel and take a look at our rear shock absorber. I took the time to visit the garage working on the Mini.

"Stop"

It was Adam shouting. Just as James was about to reverse his Mini from the inspection pit Adam realised a huge problem. The mechanics has welded his exhaust on but not high enough to clear the inspection pit. Put simply, if he reversed out the garage, he would have ripped it off completely once again. Tools came back out and work continued. I took a moment to have a cigarette with Adam and just talk general rubbish. All of our conversations we had made no sense and usually involved stupid voices that were not our own. Filled with Alan Partridge, Monty Python or deranged Harry Potter quotes. With playtime over he managed to speak to a garage about getting a sump fitted. Finding some very thick sheet metal he managed to get the translation though and for a small $18 dollars a sump fitted to the front of the mica. What a bargain! This really was the place to be. Everyone within this compound were kings of 'The Bodge Job' creating and fabricating anything and everything to get the job done. This was proven even more when It came to our shock absorber. With no luck of finding a replacement he managed to find the closest size and then began dismantling our old shock. With a hammer and a welder, he managed to create what only can be described as 'Frankenstein' an abomination creation of a shock absorber using parts from our old and miscellaneous metal he found scattered around his workshop. Once completed he passed it over to me and Lee to make sure we were happy with the strength. *"It's perfect"* I said. Lee had a look at it unsure what to think however once it was in place on the car, it looked like it had always been there. "Well what do you know, a perfect fit." The job he did was truly magnificent. He asked for $120 in return for his work. He had worked nonstop for three hours, broken a few of his tools and even used quite a lot of resources from his workshop. The amount seemed fair but we still haggled him down to $105. $100 went to the mechanic and $5 to the hotel owner for bringing us to him. Mini Adventures bill came to $60 which was way too steep. I just wished I was around when they were making the deal, my haggle skills were on point and I loved giving it a go. However, Adam did brilliantly and worked them down to $30, any less and we would have had some trouble on our hands. With a tyre shop being so close I even managed to get two valves changed and all of our tyres pumped up for a fantastic price of $2. I said goodbye to the mechanics using google translate on Lee's phone. Unexpectedly they took the phone from me and began typing with their large oil covered hands, after a short while he handed it back to me. Once again, we were greeted with the same message as the Turkish mechanics back in Istanbul.

"Your 'Crow' is broken."

Two languages both 4,000 miles apart had somehow informed us that our 'crow' was broken using Google translate. Once again not knowing what they meant at all, we tried to figure out the correct translation but sadly with no luck we needed to push on. *"If it's as bad as it sounds, I'm sure our crow would make an appearance soon"*

As I started the engine of our trusty Ford it felt new again. It felt like we were setting off from Blackpool all over again with a completely faultless car. Both myself and Lee were feeling positive and with it being only 2,15pm it made our idea of getting to Samarkand a reality with just over 6 hours until sunset. All of our cars were side by side, all fixed up, I dropped my shades onto my nose, revved the engine, released the handbrake and released the clutch before releasing.

"Shit, I forgot to get a sump guard!"

I wasn't going back now. The open road was ahead where we could make brilliant progress, instantly we found another station selling benzin on the pump at a quality of 86 octane. This 'illegal' benzin was so easy to come by and at such a brilliant price. We filled up before flooring it all the way to Samarkand.

Once we arrived at the city outskirts it was around 8pm, A cheap hotel was found on Maps.Me and the idea of just relaxing, getting some good food and an early nights sleep was on everyone's mind. We were about half a day behind schedule but that didn't matter, we had gotten use to using the most of the sunlight during the day and being at our destination early to enjoy what sights they had to offer, whereas lately we had been setting off just after lunchtime and rushing all the way without seeing any of the sights. This had to change not only did it affect our distance; it also took a kicking at our morale.

Finding a fantastic, cheap hotel in the city centre was fantastic, it was just down a few backstreets and oh wait dead end.

It was just down the road, turn left, no wait, dead end.

It was just. We eventually gave up, Dan went to find the hotel owner, made him jump in the DSMS car to take us all the way round to the hotel. Once unloaded, everyone jumped in the shower almost instantly, the muggy hot weather had given us all a layer or two of sweat. I showered with all of my washing ensuring that they were completely soaked in washing powder whilst I stamped on them. Clean clothes are a complete luxury on the rally, you don't realize how much you miss them until you put on a fresh t shirt. Eventually we all made it out into the city, after an hour of searching for somewhere for food that accepted dollars and did anything other than meat, we eventually settled down to ice cold beer and one of the largest food platters we had ever seen. It was at this point we realised we would be saying goodbye to our good friends Cunning Stunts. Tomorrow they planned on heading east through Tajikistan to tackle the famous Pamir Highway, whereas we were heading north, still over some huge mountains but nothing as challenging as the Pamirs. *"I wish you all the luck on the Pamirs and wish we were able to do them with you."* Lee said as we all raised our glasses and gulped our beer empty. Tomorrow we entered our next country. Tomorrow we tackle the mountains of Tajikistan.

Chapter 14 - Days 24 - 25 - ISIS, The tunnel of Death & Free Apples.

Once again, the car was reloaded in a strange Jenga like style, the engine was topped up with 5w/30 oil and the windscreen was sprayed with rainex as we pulled out our best Consuela impression from Family Guy. The bonnets were slammed shut and we were on our way.

For about 5 seconds.

As soon as we left the hotel grounds we were pulled over by the police outside a beautiful Mosque. *"Shit, maybe we shouldn't have come... oh no wait, they just want photo's"* Fantastic! Jumping out of our cars they posed with us gathering crowd of tourists and locals. Cunning Stunts had raced off east however both DSMS and AFK stayed and posed to the camera. Just as we were about to get back in the cars and move a little more down the road, James and Jade turned up, the crowd went wild at seeing a classic Mini Cooper so far away from home.

Back out the cars we were when the policeman came back over.

"Look everyone it's Machina Mr. Beana."

Laughter erupted. Of course, Mr. Bean is a well known lovable character. He is known all around the world due to his ability to generate humor without speaking a word. He is practically a mute. Just his awkward presence and hand gestures make him the character he is and he wouldn't be Mr. Bean without his Mini Cooper.

Everyone wanted photos with Mr. Bean, sorry, James and Jade. We took the opportunity to get ourselves some snaps as well of them standing awkwardly with complete strangers. Then finally after almost an hour we were on our way out of the city. Just as we began to see the city outskirts, we noticed that Mini Adventures had pulled over. Thinking there was an issue we span round in the crazy traffic to join them. Approaching the mini, I opened the door to ask what the problem was.

"Erm, I don't have any money" said James. *"Well, I do, In the bank. But I don't think I have enough USD to get through this border"*

Shit.

I hadn't even thought about it. Put together both myself and Lee probably only had around $150 left. DSMS were in a similar situation. Being in a large city it was decided that our best bet was to turn around in search of a bank. After three complete wild goose chases, I ended up asking a chap on the street where to find the closest bank. He randomly grabbed Oli's arm and pulled him into his car saying *"Yes, Bank, I'll take you there."* Looking like Oli had just been abducted, the convoy followed close behind the car whilst Oli and his new friend listened to what sounded like Uzbekistan's equivalent to ABBA. Arriving at the bank, we said our fond farewells and like everywhere we stopped, drew in a crowd.

We took it in shifts to enter the bank, those with Mastercard were fine, withdrawing money quickly but for those like me and James with only VISA, no one would take our cards.

"Were going to just have to chance it and hope we have enough. I'm sure that Tajikistan will have somewhere to withdraw." Our only hope was that the Insurance, tax and bribes would cost less than we had.

Driving once again out of the City we had just passed the point where we turned around. Just as I was about to make a sarcastic comment such as *"You know, I think I've been here before."* I stopped myself only to see the sign VISA, MASTERCARD, DEBIT, WITHDRAW.

"Well.

That's convenient."

Finally. Loaded with dollars, smiles and full tanks of benzin we pushed on to the Tajikistan border.

I was so excited to be heading to Tajikistan, it was one of the countries I did a lot of research about before setting off. 93% of the entire country is mountains, it's part of the world-famous silk road and green tea just happened to be the national drink of choice. Although we could easily drive though in a day, I knew that the mountain roads would still be a tough climb for our tiny, overloaded cars. Following the twisted and winding roads out of Uzbekistan we were met with many dead ends, the road almost followed the border line perfectly until the road just ended, no more tarmac, just a dirt road lay ahead. Lee confirmed this was the way so we pushed on, the road got thinner and thinner as we bounced over dirt, gravel and potholes. We were all being so careful about what was ahead, not one team noticed the perfect, new, tarmac road that lead stretched out too our left. For about 10 miles we had slowed down to a crawl to master this road and get to the border safely, when the whole time just behind a row of trees was a brand new, fresh tarmac road. Soldiers could be seen ahead, all carrying AK47's and other automatic machine guns as they patrolled their area. Ahead was a huge iron gate that's stretched across the road, patrolled by many guards and surrounded by taxi's trying to grab all the foot passengers entering into Uzbekistan. We drove slowly up to the gate. Caravanistan had informed us that this border had only just re-opened for tourists, it was usually locals only and had a strict limit of the number of cars it let through.

Fingers crossed,

breaths held.

We approached the gate and gave a quick beep. Slowly the gates were pulled open and we were signaled to enter the border. Everything seemed a little tense, more strict than usual. We had heard on the news that a few days before there had been an ISIS attack on two American cyclists on the east road towards the Pamir Highway, they had been rammed off the road before stabbed and left for dead. If any border had the reasoning to decline us, take our gear or even question us, it was Tajikistan.

I drove to the first window, handed over our passports and waited in complete silence. I then drove to the next window, got out, singed a few forms and returned to the car.

"Something doesn't seem right about this place mate" I said to Lee. He nodded. Looking around we could see the rest of the convoy repeating the same processes we had. Ahead a guard was walking towards us, sniffer dog on one side, Machine gun in the other. He slowly checked around our car and indicated for us to open our bags.

Then he saw it.

The briefcase.

We had brought with us the briefcase gifted to us by the Adventurists. He wasn't happy at all. A locked briefcase at a border most definitely isn't a good idea. He demanded me to open it. I began to open by putting in the extremely hard code of 0000, clicked the left side, clicked the right and raised it open. He had expected to find something of value. Money? Drugs? Nope. Inside were 5 perfectly rolled cigars. Lee had packed them, from his last cruise at work, he had managed to get some time off in Puerto Rico and picked up two Cuban cigars and a few cheap local ones for the finish line celebration (if we were to make it).

I couldn't tell if the guard was happy or annoyed, He ended up whacking me on the back of the head with what felt like the back of his handgun, but anyway, it was nothing a free Cuban cigar couldn't solve.

With his new souvenir in hand he allowed me to move on whilst he searched the rest of the convoy.

Within no time we had everything back in our hands and we were through the huge gate on the other side. Greeted with the most mesmerizing views. Mountains and hills stretched for miles on either side, the hot sun beamed down onto the crystal-clear rivers in the canyon. I had expected to see some beautiful sights, but I wasn't expecting anything as stunning as this. The convoy had joined us on the other side, after taking some time for photographs we were once again in search of local currency. We didn't have to look long, Adam quickly found a shirtless man sat in the sun on an outside bed with a black duffel bag absolutely full of notes who he named 'Jabba the Hutt' and with a fair exchange deal he managed to get some Tajikistan Somoni, once again we were in a country as rich as kings with 1 USD equal to 12 somoni. With it being early afternoon, we pushed on through the valleys of Tajikistan completely in love with the stunning landscape. With an empty road we took the downhill stretches at full speed occasionally hitting our top speed (downhill) of 88mph. The Micra kept up well but Mini Adventures engine screamed and overheated at anything over 67 mph. We slowed as we passed through our first village. At times it looked like we were in the south of France with beautiful hillside houses and then at other times poverty brought us back to realization as children chased goats through the streets. Passing through the first town DSMS raced on as we passed a policeman at the side of the road, he smiles at DSMS. I was about to wave and smile when his baton and whistle came out. With one furious blow and a wave of the baton, I realized.

Oh.

Wait.

I'm being pulled over.

"Shit, Looks like its haggle time."

Mini Adventures had been pulled over too. They asked for my passport which stupidly I handed over without question. Moving onto James in the Mini, he did the same. *"Come to my car."* he said.

Following him, I turned to James and quickly whispered *"Whatever he says, play dumb as long as we can and then if he asks for money, say you will take the fine and go to the police station to pay it."* That was a trick I learnt from Charlie Boorman when I watched him in Long Way Round. Eventually people get bored and let you go. The policeman handed our passports to the policeman waiting in the car, pointed at his headlights and said *"On."*

It turns out, no matter what time of day it is, you need your headlights on at all times in Tajikistan. This we already knew, I had been told hundreds of times by Lee, So many countries enforce the rule so Lee had them on 99% of the time whilst he was driving. However, every time I drove, I just forgot.

He points his finger and within the dirt he draws '$100' and points at me. He then draws '$100'and points at James. *"What? I have no idea what you are saying."*

227

Of course, I did, but I didn't want him knowing that. No way was this legal. I wasn't paying $100 on the roadside to two policemen.

"I don't understand."

"I don't understand."

Me and James repeated over and over again whilst over exaggerating the odd shoulder shrug. By this point the Policemen could see we understood completely. A change of tactic was in order. *"Give me a ticket, I have no money, I'll pay at the police station."*

angry they shouted back "No, you pay now or go no further." I could see Lee in the car hiding the few notes we had left into the folds of the seats. Good thinking! The argument continue, James was as silent as ever as me and the police began raising our voices. After twenty minutes of no budging from either side, out of the blue, completely randomly, they gave us back our passports, made us put our headlights on and sent us on our way.

Suckers.

After meeting up with DSMS at the top of a beautiful hill, we let them know about what had just happened. How we stuck to our guns and paid nothing. "Corrupt Po-Po got No-no." They then informed us that they were also caught a little further down the road for speeding. Oli had been driving at 70 kmph in a 60 zone and was just given a quick slap on the wrist and sent on his way. I couldn't believe it, it's an on the spot fine of $100 for no lights but a slap on the wrist for speeding! ... MAD!

We continued on through the valley until we reached a petrol station situated at a crossroad. To the North lay a large mountain pass full of twists, turns and lorries heading at close to 3mph, it looked like a real struggle. To the east was a flat road with one sign, it read 'Pamir Highway.'

Fuck that,

Mountain road it is.

With our engines filled up to the top we began the ultimate climb, at first our cars we hot off the mark, changing gears at perfect times, keeping the revs high we began the climb. As we got higher the incline began to get severe, our cars began struggling. Locals overtook us dangerously on corners before break checking us, Lorries stopped in the middle of the road with no indication causing you to either slam on or go on the opposite side of the road. At times we would have to pull off the road, letting the speeding behemoth trucks pass us both from behind and oncoming in a racing line. They had momentum and if we were to slow them down, they would get stuck. We had to give way or be hit.

Everyone's cars seemed to be struggling. Our Fiesta was doing brilliantly, the fan span around and the water filled the radiator cooling the engine meaning that our engine stayed the same temperature as usual. Just the struggle of the overloaded car slowed us down. The Mini however was a different story, it couldn't do over 30 mph uphill. With 4 gears and an overloaded roof rack it dragged itself up the steep hill and around the sweeping bends. At close to 7pm we made it to the top of the hill in time for some low sun photographs and a cool breeze for the engines needing their well-deserved oxygen. The best part about it all was, what goes up must come down.

Below we could see a perfect road sweeping into the valley below. We had planned to push on North as late as we could until dark hopefully reaching a huge lake 200km away however with the danger of mountain roads and the heat of the day exhausting us, we decided it would be a good idea to camp somewhere soon. Not only would we be in the beautiful landscape of Tajikistan, we would have the opportunity to pitch our tents in daylight, get the hobs on the go, cook some good food and be sociable.

'The Mongol Rally' Spotify playlist was put on full blast, shades covered our eyes and we began the extremely quick journey down the mountain. No speed limits mattered as we hit a new record of 90 mph downhill. Even James in the Mini decided to open it up and hit a fantastic 70, we completely lost DSMS who sped off, winding around corners opening up their car as much as they possibly could before finding a safe place to pull over at the bottom of the valley.

"This random road going off to the right here near a huge wolf statue looks like a good shot" said Danny sarcastically.

Following them we slowly made our way down a small single-track road until we reached another T junction, to the right was a very normal looking single lane tarmac road. To the left was a dirt track though a gap in the trees.

"This looks like the best way, follow us" said Danny as he pulled the car down the dirt track, over a huge pothole, a small stream and through a bush. We followed slowly until the gap in the tree's opened up to a huge field full of apple trees.

It was perfect.

Away from road, light pollution and noise, this random road had taken us to one of the most stunning places I have ever been. The local farmer approached with his adorable children, not knowing a word of English, we shook his hand, offered him a cigarette and a sweet before pointing at our tents. He couldn't have been happier to have us, pointing where we could park and where to pitch our tents, we were soon out of the cars, tents up and pasta on the boil. Darkness crept in quickly but with smooth music on the Bluetooth speaker we were all sat back in our chairs relaxing and giggling until Adam looked up.

"Holy shit" he said blankly.

Looking up, I was greeted with the most beautiful view of the stars I had ever seen, they looked huge, burning bright, glistening as shooting stars could be seen sweeping by. It was truly beautiful. I then felt so upset. I was so happy to be there but I wished Caroline was with me. I wished that she could have been there to see the beauty of the sky with me. Although it cost me £8, I sent her a text.

"I'm looking up at the stars, I hope you look up at them too tonight. It doesn't matter how far away we are from each other, if we both look up, we have exactly the same view. I wish you were here with me to see them in a perfect, beautiful, cloudless sky. Pass my love onto the girls, I love you all so much xxx"

We spent close to an hour looking at the sky and taking about time and space, interspersed with the little children laughing and screaming, sneaking up on us and trying to get into the cars. Lee while grabbing a beer gave them the fright of their lives. He had placed his head torch over one eye and changed it to red approaching us spouting a terrible Arnold Schwarzenegger accent. Hilarious to us, but in hindsight, those children have probably never seen anything like that before. Unsurprisingly, they stayed quiet the rest of the night. Adam seemed to be extremely interested in space time continuum, the theory of relativity and his prediction of the big bang. Conversation had really hit its peak. Usually we would be talking about potholes and gear changes, but not tonight. Tonight, we relaxed under the stars listening to Marvin Gaye.

We woke up early, part of it was due to the early morning heat however the other reason was due to a really fucking annoying donkey that had been pretty much tied to our fiesta during the night. It wasn't much the donkey that woke us up however, it was more how every time the donkey made a noise, Danny decided to shout back.
"HEE-HAW"
"SHUT UP!!!"
"HEE-"
"FUCK OFF MATE"
I moved around, grabbed some clean pants and changed, I needed to stand up and stretch. As I pulled down the zipper of the tent I realised a child was stood directly outside the tent staring right at me.
"Well, thank fuck I put my pants on. Erm Hello?"
The child ran off giggling back to the farm. Danny looked right at me as if to ask *"did that just happen"* but no comment was needed. Slowly the rest of the convoy awoke, the child and his dad returned with a huge bucket of apples for our breakfast, they were extremely hospitable. Once everyone had gotten up, packed the tents away and loaded the cars, we couldn't believe it. It was only 7am. So, If you do the rally and find yourself in need of a place to camp with free breakfast and an early wakeup call the coordinates are **39.714782 LONG, 68.770151 LAT**. *(Please pass Danny's love onto the Donkey.)*
Looking at the map we could see the huge lake we were aiming for the day before, past that was the Kyrgyzstan

232

border and into Kyrgyzstan another huge mountain range. Strangely the roads looked like they went in and out of Uzbekistan, Kyrgyzstan and Tajikistan on the map, but we were too late to turn back now, we would just have to see how it all planned out. Osh is a town resting on the border southeast of Kyrgyzstan and our heading for the day. We said goodbye to our hosts and followed the dirt track until we were back at the main road. Just before we set off however I had to use the bathroom. I still had the trots and by this point it had spread. Lee, Jade and Me were all trying our best to hold it in at all times. It wasn't a good feeling at all but with determination to push on and not slow anyone down, we pushed on With it being so early we made brilliant progress, by 9am we were close to 100 km down of our 500km, 8 hour drive with a border in the middle. Bypassing the city of Khujand we finally got to the huge lake, this turned out to be a reservoir. Its blue water glistened, we just had to stop for a swim, it looked truly beautiful. After finding a place to pull over we all stripped and changed at our cars, we followed the locals carrying Lilo's and blankets ready for a day in the water. We then had to cross a live railway track without being ran over by a high-speed train. Once across the tracks we pretty much ran to the water, the sun was unbearable. Then, there we were, stood by the water's edge.

"It's brown"

"It smells of shit"

were just two of the comments I could pick out. This complete illusion of the blue sky had shone down onto the water that was actually a vile shade of muddy brown. It was complete disappointment.

"Sod it" I shouted.

I threw my clothes onto an old truck tyre lying in the muck and ran into the water along with Danny and Adam, shortly followed by the rest.

We were there, In the moment and I'll probably never be there again. I'd love to point at a map and go *"See that shithole, yeah? I swam in it"*

I lasted about 10 minutes before getting out and retreating to the car, closely followed by the rest of the convoy.

"So, Kyrgyzstan anyone?"

Due to the layout of Uzbekistan, Tajikistan and Kyrgyzstan boundaries we had to head to the border slightly south east from our location as if we carried on east, we would have hit another border for Uzbekistan. With only a single-entry visa we had already used, they most definitely would not have let us in. Nevertheless, the Isfara border into Kyrgyzstan was close by. Not only that but it was down as a quiet and quick border.

By 10am we were on the main road to the border, We passed through the town's traffic and around a small roundabout that for some reason held a giant peach or apricot, We had no idea why it was there, it wasn't till later on I was told it brings good fortune to the fruit farmers in the area. The border was mainly used by locals, upon arrival we were instantly escorted inside the Tajikistan side, passports were stamped quickly and we were on our way though no man's land. It was named perfectly as the road was almost impassable with sand, sharp rocks and potholes everywhere. I couldn't believe how quickly we were through; I was hoping that the Kyrgyzstan side would be just as quick, we could really make our destination of Osh If so.

Oh, my lord was I wrong.

No one seemed to be around.

Eventually we were told to leave our cars and head to passport control where we paid $10 each for 'something'. I then had a quick meeting with the general who also asked for $25 towards car tax and $10 for tax tax. With absolutely no idea what I was paying for, I had to hand over the money. It was just easier and quicker. I mean, what else can you do? Say *"Hello Mr. guard, please don't take all my money"* as he leaves his fully loaded pistol on the table next to you. After another hour of waiting and a quick car search Adam and the rest of DMSM were allowed to go. With their foot to the floor, they left the border and were first to have their tyres on Kyrgyzstan soil.

I followed about thirty minutes later with Lee. We stood on the other side pondering about what we had paid for but glad we were finally out of the border.

Just as we were waiting for James to appear a guard runs over to me and Adam, "CAR DRIVER COME BACK".

We had no idea what we had done, but we ended up having to walk back into the border V5 in hand. With the guard checking our V5 he slammed them back into our hands and pointed at a hut on the opposite side of the border compound. We made our way across to meet James. He was stood in there with the most miserable scared look upon his face. Before we had the chance to ask what was wrong the guard behind the desk just began shouting at us at the top of his voice before snatching our V5 documents.

"I think he fancies you" said Adam looking at James.

There is a time to make jokes and a time to not say a word whilst at a border. However, to Adam, these rules didn't apply. Whilst trying not to burst out laughing the man continued to shout and stamp documents before demanding another $20 and sending us on our way.

What should have been a quick border turned out to be three hours of waiting with no other's passing through but us, either we were the first to pass through this border on the rally or these guards just really couldn't be arsed doing their job. After what had felt a lifetime, we had finally made it all onto Kyrgyzstan soil and It hadn't even hit 2pm. We pushed on following the two border lines to our west. As we winded in out of three different countries we were unsure if we were to accidentally end up at another border patrol as the road just occasionally went in and out of its neighboring countries, we were making great progress upon the flat ground, then through the mist and clouds ahead, we saw it. A huge mountain road.

twice the size of the one from yesterday with much harder inclines.

We pulled over to discuss a plan. *"Just go at your own speed, watch out for locals,"* and *"Don't do anything stupid"* were passed around, but we ended up on agreeing with "Drive it like you stole it and floor it."

We went first in our fiesta, somehow could go the fastest uphill, both myself and Lee knew the car inside and out, knowing the biting point, engine sound and clutch really help with inclines as if you know all those things you are in complete control and can match the rev's at the necessary points to exclude any power loss or loss of speed. Behind us was Mini Adventures, with the slowest car and the most likely to overheat, being in the middle allowed us all to pull over safely as a group if needed. Then DSMS taking up the rear ready for any issues. We were like a pack of wolves with the pace keepers at the front, the weakest in the middle and the muscle at the back.

With our convoy in position we began the climb, it wasn't as bad as we expected but it certainly was a struggle, just as we thought we were close to the top we saw the hill extend again and again as we ever so slowly increased our altitude. We were really pushing our cars. Not only did they have to put up with the battling heat and overweight luggage but they were trying to breath in the lower altitude whilst climbing up very steep inclines. Pushing on we were overtaken by angry locals but we learnt not to care. The higher we got the more amazing the view until finally the top could be seen, I took over a lorry who smiled and waved at us as we passed, a very friendly chap indeed, before putting my foot to the floor and making it to the top of the hill. The sign at the top read '10,000ft'. I couldn't believe it. It was quite a bit off the Pamirs but it was still an excellent accomplishment.

Wait.

Something didn't seem right.

We were at the top quite a while with no sign of the convoy. Just as we were about to turn around the lorry driver from before beeped us and waved his arms frantically. Pointing back and mimicking smoke with both hands of the wheel, it didn't seem like a good sign. Doubling back, I cringed as I went back down the hill that we had just struggled for two hours to get to the top. I didn't have to travel far when I saw the white smoke billowing out from under the bonnet of the mini. Luckily James had managed to coast it into a safe place to stop before getting out. He seemed surprisingly cheerful in light of what had happened. Smoking and sat on a rock he smiled. *"Yeah, I knew I was pushing it when I overtook that lorry, it will be fine, it's completely overheated and spat its water out. Just got to wait for it to cool, fill it with water and hope it starts again."* We did exactly that. We lit a few cigarettes and waved at locals as they passed. At some points other ralliers passed, pulled over and had a smoke with us until it was time to test the mini. James topped up the radiator with his emergency drinking water before firing up the engine. It roared into gear and headed up to the top of the pass. Myself and Lee jumped into our fiesta followed by DSMS in their Micra until eventually we made it to the top for a few snaps at the sign.

It felt good to be at the top with the mountain pass over, we celebrated quickly as the need to push on took over. Engine on we took one last glance over the hillside before we-

Wait.

The Micra was not happy.

It really didn't want to start; the altitude had beaten it. Opening the hood, we all had a good look to see what the problem was. James and Adam took the air filter off, cleaned it out and even sprayed some WD40 into the filter whilst turning the engine (This is a good way to give your car that extra boost to start it) but no luck.

"Well at least it's all downhill from here" said Lee.

He was right, all we had to do was give them a push onto the road then gravity would take over. They would be able to coast it down the hill trying the engine and dumping the clutch as they moved. With every foot traveled the air would be thicker and thicker until the engine was happy.

With Oli, Adam and Danny in the car, we pushed them off the gravel and onto the road watching them cruise down the side of the hill.

"We best catch up" I said.

Eventually we caught up, they were moving at 60mph on a flat road, so either they had got the car going or somehow fitted a sail. What took us close to two hours to climb took around 15 minutes to get back down. The valley was stunning, one straight road with yurts scattered around. *"Yurts, already?!!"* I screamed at Lee. He was instantly startled at my outburst and confused for why I had done it. *"I can't believe I'm seeing yurts now. I was expecting them in Mongolia but not before"* I had no idea why, but I was furious. I explained to Lee that I expected to see my first yurt close to the end of the rally not at the start.

"Mate, its day 25, we have 15 days left."

Realization dawned on me, the rally was happening so quickly but at the same time so slowly. We were covering hundreds of miles a day and concentrating on one day at a time that I had completely forgotten that within another fifteen days we would be flying home. I felt sad.

'The last fuel stop for 200km' could be read in the distance and with half a tank of petrol burned away on the last mountain pass we were grateful. A quick stretch of legs, fill of the tank and a chat with the locals made me feel a lot better. I showed them the map on the back of our car and they congratulated us on the journey so far whilst toasting vodka and offering us a sip for good fortune ahead. *"be careful on big hill"* said one of the gentlemen who had taken a shine to me due to me wearing a Muslim prayer hat I had purchased from Khiva Uzbekistan. *"No, we are going north, we just went over it don't worry."* I assured him whilst he stroked my fluffy chin beard. *"No no, big hill and darkness"* he said whilst pointing in the direction we were going.

It didn't feel good to hear that at all, with the mini still recovering and the afternoon creeping away.

We said goodbye to our new friends, re-formed the convoy and started to cover some ground again. The Mini was at the front followed by DSMS and us in our AFK Fiesta when the CB radio cracked, it was James.

"Look at the size of that, I hope that's not the hill he was talking about."

Fuck.

Imagine being in the middle of a hot country, in an overheating tiny car only to see a huge hill covered in snow and windy roads ahead. I didn't know what to reply with. In the moment I decided the best thing to do was lighten the mood, so I replied with. *"Were not scared. We can't go round it, we can't go through it, we'll have to go over it"* in the tune to 'Were going on a bear hunt.' No reply was heard from James as we began the steep incline up the next mountain. Our fingers crossed, our engines roaring. after 30 minutes of none stop climbing, we somehow hit traffic. Being nowhere near the top this was a big worry. Thinking someone had broken down or crashed we made slow progress trying not to burn our clutches out on every stop and start. We were stuck behind two lorries with no view of what was ahead for quite a while until finally a clearing. We could see the reason why there was such a hold up. Traffic lights and some huge signs with strange drawings.

The signs signaled:

A TUNNEL

A GAS MASK NEXT TO A CROSSED-OUT FAN

BLACK SMOKE

WINDOWS AND AN UP ARROW

3 CARS

30KM/6KM

Which we translated into, 'Warning, tunnel ahead, No ventilation, Lots of fumes. Put your windows up, only three cars at a time through the lights and you must not travel over 30 kmph for the length of the tunnel.

Woah,

This was dangerous. A tunnel so long with no ventilation that was completely filled with CO_2 from all the cars passing through. Without time to think the lights changed. It was at this point I realised that our tiny ford was in convoy with the two large trucks in front billowing black smoke. Breaths held we entered, traveling at a steady 30 kmph in complete darkness, all we could see was the truck headlights ahead and the occasional few cars coming the other way. It was terrifying, for what was probably a few minutes felt like an eternity as we breathed as little as we could and kept focus on the rear lights in front, I remember worrying about DSMS who had managed to sneak in front of us when we were about to enter the tunnel, unknown to them what fate was to bring, especially without a driver's side window.

I started to panic a little, I'm unsure if it was the CO_2 inhalation or just pure anxiety but I was close to blacking out. I felt my eyelids slowly close as my eyes began to roll back slowly until...

AIR!

Thick air!

Pure oxygen tasting like dull soup.

We had made it out the other side. We welcomed the fresh air along with another truly stunning view. I completely understood why the man from earlier warned us about 'dangerous roads and darkness.' That was easily the most dangerous tunnel I have and will probably ever enter.

241

There is a tunnel in Tajikistan named 'The Tunnel of Death' that we avoided due to it being in the wrong direction. However, since then we hear that they have now added ventilation to it making the one we went through the 'New Tunnel of Death' and the old one 'The Tunnel of Slight Inconvenience'.

Having pulled over to wait for our convoy we were eventually joined by them, Adam, Danny and Oli all coughing trying to take in the fresh air whilst James merely replied with *"That's what my mini smells like every day."*

After retrieving our breath, we made quick progress on the downhill straights, hours and hours passed of long, un interesting roads only housing a few petrol stations. Until finally an hour outside of Osh, our luck had completely ran out. The road conditions went terrible, from tarmac to gravel, gravel to sand and sand to potholes. They had completely dug up the road and covered it in roadworks. Everyone paid no attention to any sort of signs, locals raced on both sides of the road bouncing over holes, mounds and ditches. We had slowed down to 20 mph in fear we would once again snap our rear axle. Mini adventures followed behind but with the beast of a Micra, DSMS pushed on. They bounced over everything blending in with the locals well until they were completely out of sight. Slow and steady progress took us into the city and at midnight we turned onto the road Maps.Me had taken us too. We had agreed to meet at a hostel called Apple Hostel however once we arrived at the point on the map, we were greeted with a large muddy slope and no sign of DSMS.

We had no way of contacting them, we didn't know if they had tried the next place or stumbled on the hostel. After close to another hour of looking, I headed down some dodgy back alleys only to find the Hostel, Micra parked inside the compound and three loud lads drunk on lager smoking cigarettes.

"Evening lads!" I announced as I entered the compound, *"Room for five more?"* They had already booked us in and secured us beds for the night, what beautiful blokes. I rallied the troops, drove our fiesta down the muddy bank and into the compound. The hostel owner was fantastic, she instantly showed me to my bed whilst Lee grabbed the Wi-Fi code to ring Mica. She then grabbed all my washing off me, Lee and James only to load up the washer then and there. *"It will be dry by the morning."* she said.

Fantastic! I was tired but in the mood to socialize, grabbing a few beers and cigarettes from the car I sat on an outside bench with Oli, Danny, Adam and two large men who were chatting away about Mongolia. *"It's a lot of fun, there are some water crossings but people will be there to help you through. We even ended up pulling a campervan through a few."* one of them said. By the sounds of things, they were traveling the world but in the opposite direction as us. *"What are you driving?"* I asked. The smirk appeared on their face as one of them pointed next to James's mini. "How the fuck did I miss that?" Parked next to the Mini was a huge, new Land Rover with roof tent, sump, bull bars, LED Bars, everything! It was completely kitted out to the max, a real adventure machine!

You could tell both the guys were ex-military, one had scars upon his face and the other walked with a limp he tried to disguise. *"We didn't feel like we belonged anywhere when we got home, did we? so we decided to belong everywhere."* Home from where? I don't know, I'm presuming Afghanistan or Iraq. They told us about where they had been and the bodge

243

jobs they had to do on their car and how amazing their adventure had been so far. It was fantastic and inspirational to hear about all the places they had been.

Lee joined us. Jumping in a hammock close by he caught up on Facebook, posted a few photos and re-assured his family all was well and our safety was still our main concern. I took the opportunity to call Caroline whilst finishing off a few cigarettes and beers. We spoke about what had happened the past few days, where we were and that in three days we planned to be in Kazakhstan! *"We only have three countries left!"* I said to her. They just happen to be the biggest. She missed me more than I ever expected. Here I was on the adventure of a lifetime taking it day by day, whereas she was at home or at our caravan in the lake district running the whole family without me or any support. As much as I was loving the rally, at that point I wanted to be home. *"It's day 25. The plan was to finish in less than 40, so I'm over halfway. I'll call, text, message and do everything I can speak to you every day. Keep an eye on our tracker! I'm off to bed now sweetheart, I love you".*

Chapter 15 - Days 26 - 27 - Shits, Drugs & Sausage Rolls.

I awoke from the hostel bunk bed before anyone else, jumped into the shower, changed and went outside to relax in the morning sun. On my way out, I bumped into Lee, he looked completely exhausted. I was about to asking what the matter was but before I had the chance to say anything he shouted. *"Someone took my bed, I had to sleep in the hammock outside!"* he was furious.

He needed a good night's sleep just as much as the rest of us so I felt extremely sorry for him. *"I went in the room and you were all asleep with all beds taken"* he snapped. He stood there waiting for a reply that I didn't have to give. Until it clicked. *"Mate, you weren't in that room, you were in the other across the hall!"* I said back to him sharply. I could see on his face that he didn't even think to check another room. I walked upstairs and into the other room to see two empty beds. I tried pointing them out but Lee seemed to embarrassed now to see anything. *"Go and chill in my bed, it will be a while before everyone is awake"* I ordered. Tired & defeated, he did exactly that. Ever since that day he has tried to make out that the hostel was double booked, however, I will never let it drop.

But sorry mate, you slept outside for no reason!

I took the time to relax on the outside bed, text Caroline and the girls, smoke a few cigarettes in peace. I even offered my help the hostel owner hanging up all of the washing. As Afterall, most of it was mine. Then I lead there, in the warm shade listening to the birds in absolute bliss. You don't get many moments to yourself on the rally, most of your time is spent in the car with your team or socializing with other teams as soon as you park up. I had completely forgotten about the enjoyment of personal space and time to yourself. I had relaxed for a whole fifty seconds before having to head to the toilets. The trots were still going strong with no sign of leaving. After a while I returned to the hammock to find Adam, Oli and Danny outside on the lounger. *"Ali, you need to sit down."* Adam said extremely seriously. *"Ali, you need to sit down and just listen for a second."* Danny quickly snapped. My heart sank as I slowly lowered myself into a chair wondering what the problem was only to find out from Oli, *"I don't want you to be too upset but..."* I interrupted, "WHAT, what on earth had happened and why are you dragging it out so long!!" I snapped.

"We didn't want you to find out this way, but Barry Chuckle is dead."

"YOU BASTARDS!" I shouted before entering a fit of giggles. I mean, oh, that's terrible, what a TV Icon the Chuckle Brothers were. I had worked with them closely before on their Qdos tour of 'The Chuckles of Oz' at my local theatre. I knew them very personally. Although DSMS didn't know he was actually a good friend. The way they tricked me was rather funny.

James and Jade had awoken, grabbed some coffee and joined us. We broke the news to them about Barry as we reminisced about The Chuckle Brothers appearances in old 90's television. After a while, the conversation turned back to the rally and the usual morning question of *"What's the goal for today?"* We were all exhausted and in need of time out of the car to drink beer and be merry. So, with Lee upstairs and asleep we hatched a plan. *"So, it's decided, we set off at mid-day from here once Lee is refreshed and James's washing has dried, then we get on the road, stop for some late lunch around two and hopefully around 5pm we'll find somewhere to camp on the River."* I couldn't have agreed more. As much as I love driving, covering distance and every day getting closer to that Finish line. We were all in need of a little chill out day where nothing needed doing to the cars, just 100% looking after our bodies and mentality.

After grabbing some supplies, relaxation in the sun and probably going through a full packet of cigarettes. We woke Lee, informed him of our plans and loaded up the cars. Lee woke in the same mood he fell asleep and just agreed to our plans to save any argument. We said goodbye to the hostel owner who signed our cars, took photos for the wall and told us of another hostel twinned with this one in Bishkek, two days drive away. *"I have called ahead and reserved you some beds for tomorrow night."*

Fantastic!

We assured her that this was the Mongol Rally and that anything and everything could happen to stop us from getting there, however she was quite happy to help us out anyway. Then finally we left for our wild camping spot by the lake. Osh was a beautiful place, being the second largest city in Kyrgyzstan I expected it to be like every other city, busy traffic, vendors stood in the middle of the road and litter scattered everywhere. I was completely mistaken. Osh is rather small, surrounded by beautiful hills, not too many cars and winding, clean streets. Nevertheless, it was time to say goodbye.

We joined the main road north, towards the Naryn River, the road conditions weren't too bad at all and the long straight, empty roads gave us plenty of time to mess around. I took over mini adventures at one point only to throw a banana right at Jade through the passenger window. They returned the banana allowing it to smash all over our windscreen. With Mario Kart now in play DSMS joined in weaving around us both. I got Lee to put his foot on the accelerator whilst I climbed half way out of the window still steering until I saw James casually driving the mini ahead with his steering wheel in his hand hanging out the window. He had a quick release and whilst traveling at top speed, he had detached it using only the steering column to now keep the mini in a straight line.

It was hilarious to watch however James had made on fatal mistake. When reattaching a steering wheel, you have to click it into place by steering it left and right. After a small panic we watched as the mini swerved onto the other side of the road and back into the correct lane as he managed to re-install the steering wheel. After a few hours of driving and messing around we pulled over for lunch just on the outskirts of Jalal-Abad. We had managed to find a cool looking cafe at the side of the road. The owners spoke no english and handed over menus in another language. We tried everything to ask what they had with no luck. We then tried explaining there were two vegetarians by holding up meat in one hand and a cauliflower in the other. Still nothing clicked as they began hilariously laughing at our attempts to make sense. Eventually we took to the translation apps. Pointing the camera at the menu they have a fantastic way of translating printed words into English.

With this said, there was no way we were to expect the translations to read this...

1) Manta Rays
2) MarMash
3) /-\ene

4) Steak
5) Chops
6) Garnish
7) Scrambled Eggs
8) Awe
9) Boop Kypasty
10) Awww Pilaf
11) Testicles and on the Sausage.

*"I'm sorry, I didn't quite get that last one, could you read it
again?"* I asked sarcastically. *"Brilliant boys, testicles! I know
what I'm having"* said Danny. After another discussion with
the waitress everyone settles on testicles, except for me and
Jade that is, we both decided that scrambled eggs would be
our best bet. The waitress kept coming over, saying words
we had no clue how to understand before almost wetting
herself laughing. Our food arrived quickly, the meat eaters
got what looked like a lamb kebab whilst me and Jade were
left with a fried egg each. I was hoping for something a little
more filling but the endless cola, Fanta and bread on the
table did the trick.
Then it was time to ask for the bill.
They had absolutely no idea what we were asking for, we got
money out in local currency, dollars and other currencies
along the way with still no luck, she just erupted into
laughter. At one point she got most of the staff outside to
laugh with her. *"I've had enough of this"* said Adam. At this
point he got up, walked over to the waitress and with the
most serious voice said. *"I know it may be funny but, this
morning we found out some news, it probably hasn't traveled
to Kyrgyzstan yet but I think you should know."* We all knew
what he was about to say. With our eyes wide, smirked faces

we watched as he informed her. *"Barry Chuckle is dead."* We erupted into laughter, she had no idea what we were saying and the tables had completely turned. The staff all looked serious as we giggled and cried as he continued to tell her. *"Chucklevision is no more, Paul's got no one to help him with his ladders now."* At this point I was wiping tears from my eyes from laughing to hard as Adam tried his best to keep his face straight. It was just as we had all calmed down the waitress came out with the bill, handed it over and in broken English she said *"Chuckle Chucklevision."*

This was the closest I have ever been to 'dying from laughter.'

It was at this restaurant we constantly had to tell unwelcome onlookers to stop rocking the cars. Looking simply isn't enough and it seems the standard of instead of kicking tyres, in Kyrgyzstan you rock the car with all your might side to side. It didn't that all our roof racks were mostly held on with ratchet straps ever since the Darvaza Gas Crater

Powered by Fanta, one fried egg and a full loaf of bread I was hoping that the bread would soak up my stomach ridding me of day 9 of the trots. Filled with hope we pushed on. The road we were following was to take us all the way to the capital Bishkek and then into Kazakhstan however due to its layout winding around the borders of Uzbekistan we found ourselves going west for quite a while. An odd feeling when you have been heading north or east for 26 days in a row. Eventually the road turned north as we made steady progress into beautiful valleys, instead of revving over large hills, strategically placed tunnels allowed us to keep our speed up through the hills. The river to our west was a beautiful shade of blue. I kept wondering if it was another

Illusion. A reflection from the sky like the last place we swam or if I was being double bluffed by nature and this one would be actually stunning. By 5pm I didn't have to question myself anymore when Adam pulls his Micra over to the side of the road next to some huge pile of rubble. *"I think we should drive down this lane here to our left and see if there is somewhere close to the water to wild camp"* he said. It was a fantastic idea; however, Lee had a much better one, *"Or we could go down this road to our right that definitely takes us down to the river and even has a campsite at the end."*
We couldn't believe it.
It did.
A strange easily missable dirt track off the main road winded down the hill to the river and at the end was hosting tents, camper vans and cars filled with families having a swim. Somehow, completely accidently Adam had managed to pull over at the exact turn off to a campsite whilst looking for somewhere to camp.
I mean, what are the odds of that?
Heading down the dirt track we were greeted to a flat field of grass, trees to hang our hammocks, Wooden bed frames to relax on in the sun and a beautiful view over the river. It was perfect. We instantly found somewhere to park and Danny made friends with some locals cooking on an open fire whilst the rest of us hung our hammocks, opened beers and got some pasta on the go. The locals took the opportunity to come over, introduce themselves and offer us some very strong vodka that we happily accepted. I was just about to get changed into my swim shorts when Jade came over.
"Heads up, don't use the toilets, I honestly will never be able to get that image out of my head" as she began to gag.
Oh god.

I had the trots, so did a few others, a nice toilet would have helped so much, but then I remembered this isn't a Luxury Villa Holiday, it's the Mongol Rally.

After a holding it in for quite a while, I had to visit the little boy's room. Halfway up the hill sat a small shack made from concrete blocks with M and # spray painted on the side. I presumed M was for male and slowly entered. As I opened the door, I was instantly wafting my face from every spooked fly fleeing the hut, just as I came back to my senses I was hit with the horrid stench, it made my eyes water at an instant forcing them to close tightly. I tried to take a deep breath but as I did, I could taste the vile air. Then, slowly, opening my eyes, I was greeted with a large hole in the floor.

From Turkey onwards, I had gotten used to there being no toilet seats and the occasional squat would be in order, but standing over a fecal mound on two rickety floorboards was not something I would sign off on. Not only that but a lot of those who had gone before me had somehow missed the hole and covered the foot placements in feces.

It was at this point I understood the term 'Shithole'.

"No thank you" I announced to myself, before turning and leaving the toilets in search of a spot away from the campsite and out of anyone's view.

I rejoined the group, shoved my shorts on and within a matter of seconds we were all splashing around in the calm blue river having a much-needed wash. Adam and Oli grabbed their crayfish pot, tied a rope around it and used a bottle as a float. They were hoping by the morning to have caught something to cook the next day. Danny could be seen with his new local friends drinking excess vodka and eating miscellaneous things they gave him which included melon and homemade lamb kebabs and very strong tobacco you put under your lips, he was ever so slowly getting drunk. Something seemed off, he didn't seem drunk, he seemed completely off his head. *"They are taking me on an adventure"* he screamed whilst swimming across a small inlet in the river, went around the corner and ran up the side of the hill going out of sight. A little worried we all left the water in search of him, but he had already gone. All the food we cooked were dished up and offered around the group along with a lot of beer, vodka and apple sours Jade and James had been hiding for a special occasion. As we pass around the booze, I see Lee munching away on something. *"Is that a bloody sausage roll?"* I didn't know where on this earth he was finding them but every country so far, he had somehow managed to locate and eat a sausage roll.

"Did someone say sausage roll? I'm starving man!" Danny had returned. *"They are off now, such nice guys, I got vodka off them and it tasted pretty damn good! Then we went for a walk and they kept hand feeding me things from a bush, I was so scared they were like drugs or something but before I could say no, they were in my mouth."* We couldn't stop laughing as we each made boyfriend jokes about his new friend. Even more when he realised that the things he had been eating from a bush were just peanuts.

Finally, all re-united, sprawled out on a large bed frame, we sat drinking beer and chatting about how far we had traveled and how far we had left to go. It was only a few weeks back we snapped our rear axle in Turkey, thinking it was game over I had pins saved on my phone about how to scrap a car in Turkey. But here we were, watching the moonlight appear over the calm river with some brilliant friends by our sides.

I woke, swinging slowly in my hammock to the sound of a screaming frog, As I looked towards the river, I laughed as It looked like Oli was stood in the water wearing only a Scottish Kilt whilst fishing.

Wait.

That exactly what he was doing. He hadn't caught anything sadly and with a quick retrieve of the crab pot we found that that was unsuccessful also.

It was 7:00am and the morning sun along with a cup of coffee we received free from Turkey meant we were back on the road quickly. The mood was excellent, everyone felt happy and refreshed, ready to tackle a long day's drive up to Bishkek. Driving up the steep bank back onto the main road we filmed our front wheel drive cars struggle for traction and bounce their way up to the top.

Myself and Lee took a GoPro and a Panasonic Handycam with us, Our idea was to film the entire rally and release a documentary about our trip however it wasn't until we had set off I realised how much of a painstaking task that would be, when we broke down it didn't feel great to start filming, when we finished a day's driving a long blog about the day just started to become a chore over anything so I had decided to just film what we wanted to film and enjoy the rally though my eyes rather hidden behind a screen.

We followed the narrow road through the mountains until we reached the Toktogul Reservoir, It was an extremely beautiful sight, the only thing that let it down was its 50 mile road all the way around the east side, if you were to head the west way around it, it would only have taken about twenty minutes but with no road to the west, the only road headed

254

east around it through the town of Torkent causing a whole hours detour.

Just as we headed through the town of Torkent we were flagged down by the police very quickly, all three of us pulled over to the side of the road as he came marching over to our fiesta. *"Its 50, its 50, you know the limit, its 50!"* A little shocked I replied quickly with *"I was only going 40."* His anger calmed in an instant as he replied with *"Very good"* before shaking my hand. *"You have nice car, where are you going?"* He had just pulled us over to see who we were and what we were doing, he had just tried to make it out we were speeding to make some money but could see from an instant we were having none of it. *"Gift erm, souvenir from England?"* This happens a lot on the rally, everyone asks for a coin, or flag, just something from England they can be proud of. I knew the exact thing. *"souvenir back there"* I said as I pointed at the back of the convoy. He knew instantly what I was talking about, a smirk grew upon his face as he pointed and shouted to his friends *"MACHINA MR BEANA!"*

We pushed on, eventually caught up by James and Jade he let us know over CB radio that our little prank cost him £3 and a few cigarettes before they could move on. Finally passing the lake we headed further north over more large hills, sweeping valley bends and the occasional tunnel. More trucks were on the roads today meaning that dangerous overtakes were used again and again just to keep us on schedule. We drove all day though the hot sun only stopping for benzin and food until finally at about 5pm we made it to Bishkek, our stomachs were rumbling in need for a good meal, thankfully we headed straight to Apple Hostel Bishkek where our host from two nights ago had booked us in advance.

Parking outside, myself and Adam walked in to a full hostel filled with teenagers all on their gap year trip, most of them like to label themselves as 'travelers' however the majority of them flew to Kyrgyzstan and couldn't believe we had driven all the way there in such tiny cars. I felt almost like a celebrity when I got to the desk and asked about our reservation.

Only to find out that there wasn't one. The hostel was full. Never mind however as the hostel owner had a hotel down the road, she was willing to give us rooms in for the same price. I headed outside to the carpark to inform the convoy of a change of plan, when I got to the cars, I could hardly see them due to the crowd around them. Some Network scouts had come out to ask about our cars and our journey. It was fantastic to see other scouts from around the world have an interest in our adventure as I'm an explorer scout leader myself back home. I showed them around the car along with the additional modifications including the 50 Inch LED Bar, CB Radio and 12v charging system before moving onto the loudspeaker and its selection of deafening sirens. The scouts then showed us a dashcam video of their car that they had flipped (lots of French swearing was heard as the car skidded and lost traction on the dirt and then flipped).

With play time over, DSMS lead the charge all the way to the Kazakhstan Hotel, specifically called that due to it being the final hotel before the Kazakhstan border. It was on the main road out of Bishkek with taxis and crowds all gathered outside. It wasn't somewhere that would have chosen to stay personally but their locked compound and door guard made our cars a little safer. We were booked into our rooms quickly, they were basic but rather large with big lounge area, bedroom and bathroom. We gave ourselves 20 minutes to shower, check social media and meet back up in the lobby before heading out for food. Giving ourselves time limits was a great Idea. If we logged onto the Wi-Fi and started checking up on lives back home, other ralliers and general news, we would often be sat there for over an hour before realizing how late it had gotten. So, time limit set and suck too we found ourselves outside the lobby enjoying a cigarette watching more locals shake our cars furiously via the roof rack before heading out for food. We must have walked around asking locals for over half an hour about places to eat and local interests however no one gave us anything as a suggestion. We were so sick of service station food, crisps and chocolate that we wanted a good meal to end a good day. Myself and Jade were feeling it the most as the only cooked food we had in days was one fried egg and a handful of pasta. I'd have done anything at that point for some cooked vegetables. Then we found somewhere, It looked really cool. An outside restaurant filled with loungers, curtains and cushions. We found a seat and watched the waitress come over.

"Do you have a menu?" Oli asked.

"No." she replied.

"Oh, okay, what do you have?"

"No" once again.

"People are eating, what can we eat?"

She seemed to understand us as her facial expressions were moving in relation to the way we spoke, she was just playing dumb for some strange reason.

"Erm can we get 7 beers please? Brewski?" Adam asked.

"No beer"

"Okay, cokes?" he compromised.

"No cola, just tea" she demanded.

"But they have cola, they have beer" Adam said as he pointed around.

"No no, you don't understand, they are friends"

This was getting annoying, she wasn't for giving us anything we wanted. It was almost as if she didn't like us and was trying to make us leave. With this being the only place open for food we could find, we had no choice. Getting nowhere fast with our stomachs rumbling we settled on 7 green tea's just so we could begin the food order.

"Food? what can we eat" Adam asked slowly.

"Soup"

Anything else?

"No"

"Right, looks like we're having soup, now to explain about these fucking awkward vegetarians" he said with a smile.

"5 Meat Soups, 2 Vegetarian soups" was slowly spoken.

She wrote '5 soup' down on her list and looked back at Adam blankly. Danny then took charge.

"No meat soup" he said.

Nothing.

"Vegetarian."

Nothing.

We didn't know how to explain what a Vegetarian was, completely defeated he shrugged and completely made up a word.

"Vegetariansky"

"Ahhh, Vegetariansky" she replied.

What? She actually understood what we were saying.

Shocked and amazing we really couldn't believe it as she walked back to the counter with her face pulled.

"What is her problem?" Lee asked rhetorically.

We waited for a while chatting, smoking and watching other waiters bring out kebabs, cola and beer for everyone but us, we asked them about other food but all they did was stare back at us blankly.

"Oh, look lads, here comes our food" said James sarcastically 7 Large bowls of chunky soup were laid out in front of us, It didn't look too bad at all. Lee went first, with his spoon he pulled out the largest chunk of boney meat before returning it back into the broth, it was almost as if he thought he was dreaming and had to re-dip his spoon to find out. Adam and Oli just went for it, one quick spoonful into to mouth.

"It's actually not that bad" said Oli.

I had the same Idea, I threw my spoon into the soup, put my mouth close to the bowl and...

"ALI WAIT!!"

James shouted at me. Jade was holding her spoon up with a giant ball of meat resting on top. I dipped my spoon deep into the bowl, only to pull out an identical ball of meat.

I was one inch away from eating meat, something I had managed to avoid for over 10 years.

I was starving, if it had been anything else in front of me at that time, I could have been persuaded to east my first bit of meat, but not today soup!

Both me and Jade waited whilst the others ate as much as they could. Once everyone had finished the waitress understood the word 'bill' instantly bringing over the final invoice, we informed her about the meat, which she agreed to take off the bill.

"How much?" Oli announced to the group.

2,422 Som. That's 35 dollars. No way at all were we paying that for 5 soups and some tea. Then we saw at the bottom of the bill 40% service charge.

You are joking me, she was rude, did not give us anything we wanted and fed the vegetarians meat.

Adam and Danny decided to confront her with 1,000 som in hand. We weren't paying any more. She called a man over who spoke better English then in front of us all pretended to cry. The man was furious and shouted *"You come here with all of your money and you refuse to pay thinking you are better than us all, we need money to live, you have so much money."* Tired and starving I couldn't be bothered listening. We left a generous 1500 som and headed back to the hotel. What a fucking joke that was.

Back at the hotel we all took turns to play a plug in TV pac-man game I purchased and brought with us on the trip. It was at that point I couldn't wait any longer, I had to call Caroline. I was waiting for close to midnight, this would be about 6pm back home so It would have given her the time to get the girls fed and ready to bed, but with the long day we had, I couldn't wait any longer.

Within seconds, I was on the phone listening to the world's most comforting voice. *"Babe, you won't believe what we've been up too..."*

Chapter 16 - Days 28 - 30 – "Why are you here?"

Kazakhstan lay directly ahead of us. Pulling up to the border que I waited in the hot sun whilst beggar after beggar asked for money. Lee had just run into a shop for supplies before joining the que of non-drivers. Once again, I was left to tackle the border alone with the car whilst Lee ever so casually strolled through.

Adam in the DSMS Micra was ahead, James in the mini was behind then way behind that was another team in their car completely covered in fake grass, I desperately wanted to go and say hello, but with all of our gear as my responsibility, I couldn't leave it.

After a short while Adam went through the gates with a few cars in front as the gates slammed shut on me. This was one of the busiest borders we had been too far, except maybe the Turkey-Georgia border, however this one seemed better manned and quicker processing. In no time at all, all the convoy were through the gates and at the first desk. For some reason, every border we had been at with James, he had been last through, we would usually be waiting for him on the other side whilst he stood there alone waiting to finish off. With that In mind, I gave him my place in the que, I could see some locals already getting rowdy, knowing James would have to put up with their pushing and shoving, I took one for the team. Adam in the DSMS Micra had passed the first checkpoint and moved on followed quickly be James until it remained only me and one man in a suit who did not push once, he just waited in line next to me. *"Sir, I am government official for Kazakhstan and I'm late, could I go before?"* As he flashed a badge in my face. Not wanting an argument, I agreed. *"Certainly!"* I said with much sarcasm. Approaching the desk, he had his papers stamped, looked at me and snatched my documents. Before I could say anything, he passed them through to the guard he stamped all of me documents without even looking.

"Is everything okay?" I asked the official. But no answer was given.

In complete silence he handed back my papers. Read out my name and said *"No bother for you on my side, straight though please"*

I didn't really know what he meant, but with stamped papers in my hand, visa's all sorted and my customs declaration I got back in the car and headed through the border. Along with the official I was waved passed two important checks before overtaking James in the Mini and catching up with Adam in a large barn. He had emptied some of the contents of the car as the guards asked the usual. *"Drones? drugs?"* before asking for *"England souvenirs."* Parting with a couple of pounds he repacked his car and set off to the final gate into Kazakhstan. I jumped out of the fiesta ready to open doors only for him to close them and ask "Big english coin" ...Luckily, I had a 50p coin in my wallet. grabbing it out and passing it over, he waved me off as he made James drag his belongings from the mini.

"How the fuck did you manage that?" James asked when he eventually caught up to us outside the border crossing. *"Government official business mate!"* I replied jokingly. He couldn't believe that yet again, he was last, yet again he was searched the most and yet again It had taken him the longest.

But there we all were, in Kazakhstan!

Our plan was to head to Almaty, the old capital. There we would find a hostel and enjoy the rest of the afternoon being tourists. We planned to go to a place called 'Car City' the place that supposedly had every part for every car ever, the complete mecca of car parts and accessories. Also, there was supposedly a giant wooden squirrel in the capital that the president of Kazakhstan spent the entire arts budget on. Something I personally didn't want to miss. However, with all this planned, we still had an early morning 210 km drive ahead of us.

The scenery had completely changed, from sandy flats and Rocky Mountains we were now faced with flat stretches, wind turbines and the occasional inspection ramp at the side of the road. Handy if we were to have a problem! We drove a quick 50 km north to Kenen before a large junction took us east on the main road (The A-2) to Almaty. The road was close to empty, fresh watermelon and other fruits were once again sold at the side of the road.

It was early afternoon when we made it to Almaty, our first stop was for Car City, James needed to see if they had any suspension cones as his had collapsed in Turkmenistan whereas me and Lee just wanted to have a good look around. It was huge, a giant indoor market for anything you could possibly need. Sirens, lights, shocks, wheels, mods anything you wanted all under one roof. It was great to look around however with no sign of Mini parts and everything being an accessory we would eventually have to leave in Russia, unless you actually need any parts, it's just a trip to browse. I ended up leaving with a bottle of DOT4 as the Fiesta's handbrake light was occasionally flashing around corners and whenever we slammed on our breaks. On the way out I

263

also spotted some large metal cable ties that I purchased on the thought that *"they might come in handy."*

We were soon out of there; James was no better off from when he went in with no one understanding what an Austin Mini was only 'Machina Mr. Beana.' We headed to a nonexistent hostel before pulling up at a place called Sky hostel. There were no signs about so Lee, Adam and Danny went for a wander whilst I stayed at the car for a few cigarettes with the rest. We were chatting away about the drive into Almaty, making jokes about dangerous driving when all I could hear was *"ALI WE FOUND THE HOSTEL"* I looked around to see no one about, *"IT'S HERE"* still nothing. Where was this coming from? *"UP HERE, I'M ON THE 13TH FLOOR"* I looked up to the building closest to see Adam on the roof terrace, half his body hanging over. *"It's got an amazing roof terrace and right now there is a wedding on, it's great, the groom is completely rat-arsed."* Fantastic! with our bags in hand along with passports and official documents we headed up to our rooms. each room was filled completely with bunk beds and a few camping beds laid out on the floor. It wasn't much, but free Wi-Fi and a roof bar definitely made it all better.

After catching up on social media and sharing a drink with a complete stranger at his wedding, I realised that I was starving. My stomach made a growl that I have never heard before. In the hot sun all day you just feel a tremendous thirst with not much of an appetite, however once the sun starts to head down and it becomes cooler, you realize how hungry you can be.

We instantly found a restaurant that looked the part, We entered and were instantly shown seats on an outside balcony away from other eaters. (I believe that this could have been down to our smell) Not knowing what food was on order we went with the usual drinks order of 7 beers. Within a matter of moments, three huge 3L taps filled with Carlsberg were brought out and planted on the table. Perfection.

We were then handed menus written in english.

Pizza, Pasta, Steak, anything you could want.

For three days, all I had eaten was one fried egg, bread, a handful of pasta and crisps. *"Your biggest cheese pizza please".*

Not long after our food arrived. I'd gone a little overboard being able to pour my own drink at the table so It was at that point I stood up and announced to all,

"Everyone of Convoi Exceptionnel, those still with us, and those far. Gnomes, Cunning Stunts and RallyMcRallyFace, I wish you all the luck in the world. I would like to raise a toast for someone who is still with us, although never speaking on CB radio and I've never seen them under the car trying to fix a problem. Celebrations are in order. I would like you all to raise your glass for Jade on her Graduation Day!"

Like stereotypical English tourists we cheered, clinked glasses and stuffed our faces with good food until we couldn't move.

After paying the bill we headed back to the hostel for more beer on the roof. It was at this point we found out that our cars were parked in a no parking zone. Luckily for us our hostel owner had a space of us at the rear of the building. The only problem about this was, it meant driving.

Adam took the Mini's keys for some reason, Oli drove the Micra and I took the AFK fiesta. We drove like maniacs around the corner. I forgot to put my lights on, Oli realised halfway around the corner that the handbrake was still on and Adam in the Mini 'drove it like he stole it'. Luckily, we all got to the parking space in one piece with no accidents before heading to the roof bar. An outside cinema had been setup. It was paying the film Inception in another language with both Russian and English subtitles. I was definitely too drunk to concentrate and with my phone running low on battery, I retreated to the room for my charger. Usually heading back to a hostel room was uneventful however just as I was looking around the room for a plug socket, I moved the wardrobe next to my bed slightly to see behind it was something I didn't expect at all. Shocked and confused I headed back to the balcony to speak to the guys.

"Erm, does anyone else know why there is a bolt action sniper rifle in the room next to my bed?"

Everyone laughed as if I was making a joke.

"No. Seriously"

Everyone marched to the room thinking I was making it up, but there it was in perfect sight, a bolt action sniper rifle. Kazakhstan you really have intrigued me.

Waking up with quite the hangover the desire for water and tobacco was strong. I found Adam on the balcony checking his phone in a better state than I was. *"There is no way I'm driving first mate"* I said. *"Feeling rough, are we?"* he asked, then I realised. I wasn't awoken with the need to go to the toilet, I woke due to another reason, maybe this was it, the trots had finally gone! after 11 days of pure annoyance, I was cured.

The plan for the morning was to find some car Insurance. Not knowing where to look, we resorted to finding a few companies online within the local area. Once we were all up, showered and re-packed we hit the road as early as we

266

could. After walking down a few roads and circling the same spot for almost an hour the first Insurance place did not exist. But no bother there was another one on the way out of town. We eventually found it and insured all three cars before midday. It cost about $19 each, fantastic for two weeks' worth of insurance (even though we would only be there for a maximum of 5 days) The best thing about international insurance specific to a country is that it insures the car, not the driver. This means that anyone, with permission from the owner is able to drive the car. This was perfect, James had driven the entire way completely by himself so far, I was so eager to drive his Mini and he was looking forward to a day's rest.

Returning the cars, DSMS had been gifted a Kazakhstan flag from businessman who seemed to be passing. It was the sort of flag you would stick at the front of your car if you were a town governor or mayor, clearly not for a Mongol Rally car. Once out of the city we pulled over to decide on which direction to go, of course the plan was to head north to the border of Russia at a town called Semey. *(Many jokes were made about the name of this place, we also found out that the english translation for this was Cemen, which is also hilarious.)* Semi was at least three days drive away, if not more however there were many roads to choose from. Eventually after a bit of research from locals and truck drivers we were told to head the west road around Lake Balkhash as the east road was described as a car killer, with that decided, once we got to Karagandy we could choose to head to the capital Astana or head east over to Semi.

The wait was finally over, I would be able to drive the mini, sliding into mini and fitting myself snug into the bucket seat,

I turned the key, roared the engine and apologized to Jade. She had to spend the day in my car with Lee. Not only can Lee's stories get a little long and boring but the smell coming from inside the car from both of us over the past twenty-eight days must not have been pleasant. But why should I care, I was in a classic Mini and the roads of Kazakhstan lay stretched out ahead.

Kazakhstan is rather flat, its brothers surrounding it take up all the scenery, for over one hundred miles it was just one, long, boring road up to Lake Balkhash. I expected to see a beautiful blue lake surrounded by greenery but instead we were welcomed to marshland and a dull, oil filled water. Without stopping to take any photos we pushed on for as long as we could until a re-fuel was in order. I loved driving the mini, even though it only had four gears it screamed through each gear and drove like a tractor. We pulled in for fuel South-west of the lake, I was watching Lee fill up the fiesta when I noticed a small ball of fluff sticking out of the bonnet.
"What's that mate?" I asked,
Confused, Lee walked around to the font of the car.
"Ah, yes, I thought we hit something earlier"
Jade started to laugh.
"YOU ARE SUPPOSED TO BE A VEGETARIAN"
I jumped out of the mini, headed over to the car and knelt. By this point everyone had come over to see the carcass of this tiny bird.
"Tweet Tweet."
Oh, you are joking me.
"The bastard is still alive!"

268

Slowly but carefully we all took it in turns to free the tiny bird without harm. Eventually he was free and rather happy but sadly lacked the ability to fly. We said our apologies before placing it in the shade with some water.

"We will call him Eric" I said, *"Whilst we were looking for him, he found us."*

With no time to lose I jumped back into the Mini, fired up the engine and...

'PSSSSSSTTT'

Water strayed into the air and steam rose from the bonnet. I looked at James as if to say "What did I do?" but he just calmly turned to me and said "Well, the radiator was bound to go at some point."

I couldn't believe how calm he was, He simply jumped out the car, grabbed a bottle of radweld and poured it into the radiator once it had calmed. Then he waited a little while, topped it up with water and there it was. Fixed.

I like to think I'm very relaxed in bad situations, but James takes the word relaxed to a whole new level.

We jumped back onto the road and continued once more in the blistering heat. Eventually we hit our mileage for the day. 500 km seemed to be a good target through Kazakhstan. With their shitty potholed roads, it felt good to still be able to get so many miles under our wheels. As quick as the day arrived darkness began to fall and our Idea of somewhere to camp was looking like a good choice. We just needed somewhere off the road with no civilization.

With that in mind DSMS took the lead down a dirt track, we followed it past quite a few houses, loud dogs and twisting mounds however no luck. Street lamps and scattered houses and flat desolate land meant we were in plain sight of the entire town. We pushed on down the main road a little further only to go down the next path and be greeted with the same problem.

I know what you are probably thinking *'Just wild camp anywhere'.* That was our plan but with our cars attracting so much attention, security wise for ourselves and our belongings was a bit of a risk. We would need to hide them from the main road.

With no sign of a spot to pitch tent, I chickened out a little. *"Look there is a town on the map 14 miles ahead, there will be cheap hotels and warm food, If not I'm sure we can persuade someone to show us a good pitching ground."* With no better plan everyone agreed. Everyone except Lee that was. Not out of spite or to cause any drama, Lee just dreamed of a rally where wild camping would be daily and hotels would be a treat, not the other way around!

The town ahead was called Priozersk, a small lake town part of the Karaganda region. On maps it appeared on a small dot and on all of our travel maps only a little information was given. 'Priozersk Site' read Maps.Me. I mean, that sounds safe, right?

Heading down the M-36 we took the right turn down to Priozersk, I was leading the charge in the Mini followed by my AFK Fiesta and DSMS. I drove into the darkness, around a roundabout and through an open barrier until in the distance I saw a large glowing sign 'Hotel'. What a spot of luck.

Just as I was about to turn into the hotel, Lights and sirens came on behind, it was the police. For some reason they were not happy.

"Where are you going!" they demanded.

"To this hotel" I said quickly.

"Why!? Why do you come to this town!!" he shouted back.

Trying to calm him, I paused for a moment before replying with *"Were traveling through Kazakhstan and need somewhere to sleep for tonight."*

I've never seen such a confused look on someone's face before. His English was rather good so I tried to get a little more information.

"Is there a Problem?"

"No problem" he replied. *"Stay here, but tomorrow you go, you get out of here".*

Deal.

With the confrontation over, we took a moment to catch up before shrieking at the prices of the hotel. We were about to pitch up on his back lawn when a local informed of us of 'budget hotel' just down the road.

Budget Hotel turned out to be fantastic. Pulling outside we were quickly greeted by two good looking ladies and their friends.

"Hello, what are you doing here in these cars?" said the first lady in complete awe.

Starting the story again I began to inform the group about the trip whilst the other went inside to hotel to check out the prices. *"Were thinking of sleeping here, do you know anywhere we can get some food tonight or is it too late?"*

"This way" she said. Both of them grabbed my hands and walked me down a pitch-black street asking me all sorts of questions. *"Do you live in England?" "What's it like in London?" "Can we meet up for breakfast in the morning?"* I thought at first something was odd. I felt like I was being lured into an alleyway where I would be beaten up until we entered a quiet restaurant.

They spoke to the restaurant owners who let out a huge scream. Upon heading this his entire staff force and family

ran to the foyer where I was standing in pure amazement.
"There are seven of them, they have USD and they are very hungry" said one of the ladies.
Within seconds the man smiled and nodded. *"He said he will cook until you are full, if you go get your friends."*
Perfect.
 On the way back to the hotel I hadn't realised how long I had been, I didn't even know if there was any room in this hotel all I knew was where I could get us all a hot meal.
"Also, if you want, across the street, that door with the light. That's where you go if you want a woman for the evening."
Scratch that. All I knew was where I could get a hot meal and a shag.
"You are okay thanks, I have children and a fiancé, but I'll be sure to pass on your offers to Oli."

I eventually arrived back at the budget hotel to find out there was plenty of room at a total cost of $9 each. A brilliant deal. Before leading everyone through the labyrinth of dark streets to our restaurant. Upon opening the door, we were once again greeted with the whole family. *"Please follow"* said the only man who spoke english. We followed him through the bar, through the kitchen and out the back to the traditional plastic chairs and Coca-Cola umbrellas. *"Do you have a menu?"*
No.
Brilliant.
After drawing, pointing and impersonating chickens, we somehow ended up with fries, eggs, salads and for the meat eaters a traditional Kazakhstan dish which I believe was a broth of lamb and goat. We were full to bursting and full of beer all for the total of $21.

A woman who spoke rather well English approached our table with slight caution. *"Why are you here? what brings you to our town?"*

Why does everyone keep asking this?

Once again, we informed her we were just travelers/tourists who happened to be passing and needed a place to sleep for the night.

"But, why of all places did you choose here, we don't get tourists here"

I didn't know what to say. Luckily the silence was broken by loud thumping music coming from inside near the bar. "We will stay open so we can dance with you." She grabbed Oli's arm, pulled him to his feet, held him close and seductively said *"Dance with me!"*

Oli was more than happy to oblige. Filled with beer, food and happiness we danced into the evening with our new friends.

Waking up early I grabbed a quick shower using the hose pipe in the bathroom, the only other person who was awake was James from Mini Adventures and we both had one goal in mind, breakfast. Stepping outside the hotel we looked around to see what we could find in a completely run down town. A bank was also needed so checking Maps.me we found the only one in the town and set off walking. Everywhere we went, locals couldn't keep their eyes off us. Occasional shouting in Kazakh was hurled in our direction as we traveled through the apocalyptic town. Many houses were completely destroyed, the ones still standing were covered in overgrown plants and looked completely deserted. As we crossed a main road straight ahead, we could hear military chanting. Looking around we saw soldier after soldier forming ranks and marching through a huge courtyard. The guards at the gate were staring directly at us with guns drawn.

"Is the bank close mate?" I nervously said to James.

"According to Maps.Me this is it." He pointed at a building that had been completely bombed. *"Looks closed to me"* he said. Heading back to the hotel we found a small market shop where we grabbed supplies for breakfast and the day ahead, I even managed to pick up a sausage roll for Lee.

The time finally came when we were ready to continue our journey through Kazakhstan, with everyone awake and full of food we said goodbye to the hotel owner, fired up our cars and began our journey out of town.

A police car followed us the entire way out, as we were leaving, I looked left and in complete shock saw an entire compound filled with military vehicles. Tanks, Anti-Aircraft Guns, Trucks and bikes. To the right was a huge monument created completely out of missiles.

"Where the bloody hell did, we just stay" I asked Lee who was just as shocked as I. Then we saw the large open gates we passed through the night before, only this time they were closed. A soldier completely confused ran to the gates and began to open them. Over the CB radio I had to ask James if he had any clue about what was going on but he was just as confused. I drove through the gates first, followed by the DSMS Micra and the Mini. It wasn't until we were clear of the gates, I pulled over only to see a huge sign we must have missed the night before in the dark.

'PRIOZERSK - Sary Shagan anti-ballistic missile testing site.'

Chapter 17 - Days 30 - 31 - Whoop Whoop, it's the sound of the Police.

Our plan today was to reach Karaganda, A long drive north on the same bad roads of the day before. Over the CB radio James had informed me that his mini was having a bad day. *"Could nobody late break today as my brakes don't seem to be working"* I'm sorry, what? *"Typical, I let Alastair drive for a day and I get a bust radiator and my brakes stop working."* Me being me, I presumed James was over exaggerating a little and his brakes would either need topping up or in need of a bleed. *"No seriously, watch."* James the proceeded to speed up and take over us both. *"Ready and BREAK!"* He slammed on his breaks as quick as he could.
Nothing.
Yeah, that's your problem right their mate! *"Just slow down using your gears and at the next town we will pull over to take a look"* I said over CB. *"looks like today may not run as smooth as planned."* I took the opportunity to give our car a once over. I looked to the left to see our left-wing mirror almost hanging off from when I snapped it trying to push it in when parking. I checked the temperature using the gauge and let go of the steering wheel for a moment. Our car drifted to the right slightly. *"Yep, the tracking is still out."* I tapped the break.
Nothing.
I tapped it again.
Nothing.
I pushed down completely.
There we go, now there is something! That wasn't a good feeling. Our breaks had air in them and we were leaking

275

Dot4 oil somewhere. I couldn't believe it. On the same day both of our car's breaks had decided to give up. At least ours were working a little, unlike James who had to floor it past lorries to avoid ramming into the back of them.

By early morning we past the city of Balkhash on the northern shore of Lake Balkhash until the road straightened out north heading directly to Karagandy, Looking around the flat landscape occasionally at the side of the road we would see a large graveyard in the middle of nowhere, huge plinths, headstones and memorials in bright colors. I have no idea why they bury their dead in the middle of nowhere, but the beauty of them are just incredible.

We pulled over in a small town for lunch, I slowed down quickly and pulled into a spot on the side of the road, DSMS followed suit and the Mini drove past with is engine roaring. *"Ah yes, the break issue."*

We jumped out quickly to see James wrestle with the car before using the handbrake to get him to a standstill. This was a huge problem that needed to be sorted quick.

We began walking around the town asking if there was a local mechanic, however we had no luck. Checking Maps.me we could see in the next town close to 100km away in Aksu-Ayuly there was a mechanic, however nothing could guarantee he would be open or have the parts to help us. James jacked up his Mini and saw the problem instantly. He has a split in the break line, thinking fast he grabbed a clamp and further down the line he clamped it on before using a cable tie to tie it out of the way. After a quick snack and cigarette break, we continued further north to the next town with our fingers crossed that we would find a mechanic. Just outside of the town we were greeted to a police car blocking the road due to a terrible accident involving a lorry and a car. I have no idea how the two managed to crash as the road was almost empty, nevertheless, both were looking terrible and blood splatters could be seen.

Being diverted down a dirt track the tarmac had completely disappeared. I had to floor it in second gear to avoid getting stuck and only change gear once our car hit the tough floor, the lorry in front suddenly stopped.

I slammed on.

I had missed him by an Inch, DSMS had no way of breaking in time so along with Mini Adventures they flew past us both bouncing over the sandy mounds. I only just managed to get the car moving again in the soft sand.

Eventually we made it back onto the main road to see DSMS and the Mini pulled up on the side of the road.

"That's it, they have completely gone"

His breaks had finally given up. James didn't dare move any further. He simply couldn't stop the car.

I don't know how, but after a short while I managed to persuade him to continue to the next town where we would find either a mechanic or at least a way to get the car too one. I would ride in the Mini with James driving, whenever we needed to slow down, I would pull the handbrake up high and he would slow down using the gears. I couldn't believe it, we pushed on and It actually worked. I mean, if we needed to do an emergency stop or slow down for a tight bend, we would have died 100%, but to keep us moving at a steady pace It worked all the way to the next town.

We turned up to the mechanics only to find a small compound, across the road in what looked like the town hall a wedding was going on with guests drinking and celebrating outside.

It was time to crash the wedding.

I got speaking to a young lad who introduced me to his father. No one spoke a word of english, however with a wrench in one hand and pointing at our cars, we eventually found the mechanics workshop. News must have traveled fast that we were around because an english speaking blocked turned up, told us to wait and headed inside. Whilst we waited, DSMS realised their roof rack had broken at one end and borrowed a Jubilee clip to fix it. I couldn't believe their mighty Micra, they had one slight problem in Europe due to their belt slipping and since then, had no problems other than smashing a window. That Micra was built brilliantly. The man returned.

"Problem Sir's, the mechanic is in Karagandy, he will be back in two days"

Bollocks. We were stuck. James didn't want to move any further as he was just tempting death. Maps.me showed one more mechanic just 3km up the road. *"This is it, this is the final time im driving this with no breaks"* said James. I couldn't have agreed more.

We drove the 3km up the main road before pulling down a narrow road. We were greeted with nothing. Just an inspection ramp. James without hesitation drove straight up and parked on top. *"At least now I can get a good look at the problem."*

He had a good look around and the problem was obvious, he had breaks full of air and it was leaking on the copper line right next to the brake drum.

Just as all hope was about to fade, a large truck pulled up with two men inside, they instantly jumped out and looked at our three cars. After a short time, he took a look at the mini and picked up his phone. He quickly dialed a number, spoke for a moment and forced the phone to my ear.

"Hello, Welcome to our beautiful country of Kazakhstan" said a softly spoken women's voice on the other end of the phone. *"Hello, erm, thank you?"* I replied not knowing what else to say. *"Now, my husband has taken a look under your car, he can see you have a problem with a Mini cooper? the Mr. Bean Car"* I laughed. *"He can get you a truck to take your car to Karagandy but it will cost you close to $100."* Woah, this was fantastic, we had been blessed with a solution. I spoke to James and informed him of this option but I could tell by the look on his face that the price was a little too much. *"We can't afford that, we need to get this fixed somewhere here, can you help?"* I passed the phone back to her husband and they continued to talk in Kazakh. The phone was then handed back to me. "Okay, if you do not want that then we have called the police."

Wait.

What?

"I'm sorry what was that you said?"

"My husband is chief of police, he will call a car to escort you the 100km to Karagandy, you will not need to stop as he will have lights and sound to move the cars out of the way. You will convoy with the police."

I smiled and turned to the group.

"Lads, you are never going to believe this."

Twenty minutes later we were driving north 100km with the police in front, everyone moved out of the way, parting like Moses at the red sea causing no need to loose speed or break, resting at a good 60 mph the entire way. We felt like celebrities as the sun started to set over the beautiful Kazakh landscape.

'SCREECH'.

A completely random local had decided to pull in front of DSMS and then completely floor it past the police. Within second the police waved us on as they floored it after them. Once again we were on our own, that was until we had caught up with them, they had pulled the local over at the side of the road, we could see bundles of cash were exchanging hands, we pushed on not knowing if they would ever return but within the next few minutes they were back with us and once again leading the charge.

Eventually, we made it to Karagandy in the darkness and the hotel that Maps.Me had taken us too. When we entered the city we made sure to not go fast at all. We were reminded of the dangers and horrors of an accident as we crawled past a huge head on collision on a busy junction. I was readied up with both hands clasped upon the handbrake. Whilst on the rally at times you feel immortal, you forget the dangers surrounding you and always and have the 'It will never happen to me' feeling. Luckily each time we had to stop we managed to get the car to halt or the traffic lights changed just as we were about to crash. It was way too close to comfort. Danny and Oli went inside the hotel only to find out that there was no room at the inn but luckily whilst leaving they had bumped into a cool guy called Esen who spoke brilliant English. Over the next 24 hours he completely changed our views on Kazakhstan.

A few calls later he had booked us into a very cheap apartment a short walk away. Then he led us around the corner to a huge compound with tall gates and an armed

guard. *"You need to park in here, it costs one dollar a day".* Not knowing how far away this apartment was were a little unsure. After a few questions he simply came out with. "You are in a very bad area, I will help you get some food, a good night's sleep and anything you need, but your cars must say here or they will be gone by the morning." He then proceeded to pull out a small knife from his pocket. *"I carry this so you don't have too."* it was at this point we realised he was scared for our safety. Our cars attracted so much attention. This was something he was hoping to hide.
"I once met another team who did the same rally, a few years ago, my friend said we should rob them and take their money but I believe in Karma, I believe that is the wrong thing to do, so I will help you and good karma will come my way." It was brilliant to hear him say this, especially because he was the one carrying the knife. With this said, the entire time we spent with him, not once did I feel uncomfortable or threatened. He was a genuine, good person. Adam, Oli and Danny were a little unsure about leaving their car with no driver's window so far away so once again parked so close to our car that no one could squeeze in. They then threw the tarp over the open window and slammed the door shut, trapping it between the door and the frame to avoid the rain, we each grabbed our bags and off we went following our new guide. During the dark walk he told us a little more about his life and his hatred towards the Kazakhstan government. He owned a small tyre shop with his friend and close too it he lived with his wife and child in a one room apartment. His pride and joy was his 1999 Lada and he was saving up for his daughter to go to college to get a good education. You could tell he was a complete family man who would do anything for them. He also told us that Kazakhstan

isn't the place for his daughter, she deserved the world. Therefore, he wasn't teaching her Kazakh or Russian, she would only learn and speak in English.

Eventually we turned down the final street, it was pitch black except for one light coming from a dark doorway. I knew instantly that this would be our accommodation for the night. The door was made from solid steel, a real heavy-duty door with a keypad on the front. It almost looked air tight, Stepping through, we then entered the downstairs apartment.

"What do you think my friends?"

It was quite obviously a brothel.

With it being so late and our host so kind, we all generously complemented the one stained bed. *"At least there is is a kitchen"* I laughed. I asked Esen for the code for the door but he seemed confused. *"Why would you want to leave?"* he asked. I think he knew the dangers of a nighttime stroll more than we did.

With our stomachs rumbling I explained to him we needed to swap some USD to Kazakhstani Tenge and get some food. His reply was straight. *"You will get hurt or robbed. If some stay here and some come with me, I will take you to get change and food"* Our guide looked after us brilliantly, he did exactly that. Myself and Adam walked to his Lada and he took us to get change before taking us to Burger King. We purchased about seven meals and a kid's meal for his daughter for when he got home as a thank you. I looked around to see everyone else in Burger king was suited and booted with smart clothes and expensive jewelry. This wasn't like the Burger King back in Blackpool, over 8000 miles away. Our guide could see my confusion and informed us that in Kazakhstan the only people who have enough money fast food or Burger King are those who own a business, it's too expensive for everyone else. If you eat at Burger Kings, you are somebody.

I couldn't believe it. What is seen as a cheap, quick and unhealthy meal choice back home was close to 'fine dining' in Kazakhstan.

With our large order in our arms, we headed back to the apartment in the Lada like hunter gatherers bringing back a deer to the tribe.

After feasting on a vegetarian burger and a mountain of fries, Danny tells me to *"look for the treat in the bathroom."* When I eventually went, I expected to find a hole in the floor and the usual disgusting smell. Instead I was greeted with a normal bathroom with nothing out of place. *"CHECK IN THE BIN"*

"Oh.

Right.

Nice one."

Inside the bin was two used condoms and a used cock ring. *"So, are we tossing a coin for the bed?"*

We awoke at 9am to our lovely host banging on our door. It wasn't his fault, we all agreed to be up and ready to go for then but all of us had managed to sleep in. I chose the floor the night before as the rickety bed with the stained sheets didn't quite take my fancy.

"I have mechanics at my tyre shop ready to fix your cars" With that said, we all jumped up. *"But first, coffee."* Even better! We said goodbye to our beautiful brothel before walking back to the cars with Esen, He told us his daughter almost cried when she received the kids meal from burger king the night before and he had taken the day off work

today to help us with whatever we needed. What a truly fantastic guy.

The cars were collected and in exactly the same state as we left them and driven round to Esen's tyres shop, well, we say tyre shop. It seemed to be just a few steps down to a door located outside a garden centre. But nevertheless, he ensured us that his friends and workers knew what they were doing.

They quickly jacked up the Mini and our Fiesta and began looking for the problem. James showed them the issue with his break line and it instantly meant a trip to the Karagandy car market on the other side of town. Checking our car, once the drum brakes were apart, we could easily see that our cylinders were leaking on both sides and that new seals were in order. I volunteered to go with Esen to the car market, it was a huge outdoor compound filled with shipping containers. I stood out like a sore thumb in a sea of local Kazakhstanis, All Esen had to do was walk with me into the middle and hold up the break line we had taken off the mini before local merchants ran up to us with their wares and offers. Within seconds we had a brand-new line for the Mini, but our seals were harder to come by. We entered a more modern looking building only to go to a store that completely specialized in brake cylinder seals. Within no time we were back at the cars with the mechanics working away. All for a total cost of £3.

With the mechanics working away on the cars myself, Oli and Danny decided to head out to grab some supplies, by the looks of things we would all be back on the road again by lunchtime. We quickly found a local supermarket and topped up on all supplies. Cigarettes, crisps, bread, cheese, sweets, chocolate and I even tried to buy some vodka to toast with, however I didn't know in Kazakhstan you cannot purchase alcohol before 12pm. I was heading to the till, when I saw a toy I just had to purchase. It was a scale model of a Kazakhstan police car. So, James could always remember his Police convoy. Once we were back to the cars, I presented him his gift, for it to be quickly cable tied onto his roof rack. Adam wandered into the garden centre and purchased a model of a worm which they called 'Professor Slughorn' and proceeded to tie it to their roof rack next to Edgar the eagle and the rotting smoked fish.

The Mini was first to be fixed, It was dropped from its axle stands and the breaks pumped and blead by myself, Adam and James, I pumped them from the driver's seat as James bled out all the air on one side, Adam on the other almost blinding him with DOT 4 as he tried to dodge the spurting oil. Once again, the mighty mini hard-working breaks. Once my little fiesta was dropped the DOT4 made an appearance and I topped up the lines. Our breaks didn't feel any different, they were still a bit spongier than usual. However, they weren't going to get any worse. They were once again safe. The only annoying thing was the CD player had stopped working due to taking in too much sand. No more music for us this trip.

"How much for all of your hard work?" We asked.

"I'm fine for money, but a donation to my friends would be lovely." He replied.

We couldn't have been happier to donate as much as we could spare, I think we ended up paying them around £25 for half a day's work, just think how much Burger King you can get for that! We were once again ready to continue our adventure.

"Ali, my friend can I speak to you?" Esen asked.

"I told you last night that my friend wished to steal from the rally teams many years ago. Well, I didn't tell you the whole truth. We did take their things. I am a different man now and as a Muslim man I believe in karma. So, I hope my help today has made up for my mistake. If you know the people who had a gold Fiat Punto in 2016, please tell them Esen is sorry."
I will mate, I will.

Astana is the capital city of Kazakhstan, straddling the Ishim River in the north of the country. Astana is Kazakh for 'Capital' so the capital of Kazakhstan is called Capital. The capital used to be Almaty however the president of Kazakhstan changed it 'just because he could.' It was also our next destination. The plan is to cross the border into Russia at Semi to the east of Kazakhstan near the Mongolian border, however it wouldn't be right to go this far through Kazakhstan and not visit its beautiful capital.
So here we were, driving NORTH WEST to the capital. The mood was brilliant, everyone was on fire. We were once again messing around doing silly driving and throwing things at each other's cars.
It was only 200 km to Astana so within a few hours we were there. We drove around for about an hour looking for a hostel until finally Maps.me gave us one that actually existed. Parking was an issue but a kind gentleman showed us to another Kazakhstani compound with huge dogs and even paid for us to leave them there! With the cars parked up safely, we wandered over to our hostel and jumped onto the FREE WIFI. It was a blessing.
I know many people would do the rally to escape from western civilization and social media, but with a family back

home I couldn't wait to give them another update oh where we were and how close we were to the finish line.

"13 days and I should be home my queen"
I told Caroline who I could tell now she just wanted me home. I'd had the most amazing adventure so far, but with two countries to go, I had to finish. There was no way I wasn't going to complete the Mongol Rally.
After a quick update and all the sweetheart talk, I passed my love onto the kids before it was time for food. We spent the entire night in a local restaurant drinking lager and eating good pizza. It was close to midnight when James and Jade lifted their head from their phones and said *"Our Visas for Russia don't start for another four days, were going to have to leave you guys tomorrow"*
My heart sank, Convoi Exceptionnel was about to lose another car.

Chapter 18 - Days 32 - 33 - I can't reach a Semey

"So, the problem is that we originally planned to take longer to do the rally. However, we then joined Convoi Exceptionnel and didn't want to leave. So technically we are ten days ahead of schedule and can't enter Russia for another five days. With that said, with no suspension and my gearbox playing up, I don't think I can do Mongolia." James announced.

My heart was still recovering from the news the night before. James and Jade met us in Frankfurt Germany and no matter what we always ended up back with them. Convoi Exceptionnel was about to go from three cars too two. It was heartbreaking enough when Cunning Stunts left to do the Pamirs. But now this!

I think I was upset a little more than the others. From the moment I met James, I felt like I had known him my entire life. Although I'd only known him a few weeks, we felt like we had been friends for years! He's a cracking guy who would do anything for anyone. Back home he is an Emergency Care Assistant and classic car enthusiast. But the best part was he shared love for adventures, motorcycles and stupidity.

I could tell that everyone else was upset too, we all had plans that we would arrive at the finish line in convoy to cheer the others on.

Wait. I have an idea...

"If we carry on as planned, we will be in Ulaanbaatar in seven days, if you guys wait your four days, then drive through Russia, by the end of the seventh day, you can be in Ulaanbaatar too! You will just have to enter Mongolia from Ulan Ude. We can meet in Ulaanbaatar and then do the final

leg of the journey together. We may even meet up with Cunning Stunts."

The plan seemed like a brilliant Idea, well, it was the only idea. *"But let's make this last day, the best day"* Lee announced.

Lee told us to pack our bags quick and head to the cars, before speeding to Semey on the east border we were too visit the giant, tent like Khan Shatyr Entertainment Center as it's supposed to be a 'can't be missed' attraction is Kazakhstan. He certainly wasn't wrong. This huge, tent like building could be seen for miles. We parked up in our ratty, mucky cars next to beautiful, expensive sports cars and SUVs. *"Bollocks to paying for parking!"* I said before heading inside.

Lee had taken us to a magical place, a huge westernized shopping centre that featured a theme park & aquapark on the top floor. *"I am paying, we are all going on the monorail."* We shopped around for a short while, I purchased a traditional Kazakhstan hat to add to my ever-increasing hat collection, Lee somehow managed to bag himself another sausage roll and finally a Sony Bluetooth speaker to play music on within the car. It had only been half a day without music, in fact, it had been less than that because we borrowed a speaker from James. However, at one-point Lee told me the most boring story about a birthday cake, I couldn't to listen to again. (Sorry mate, I've never known anyone who could make a story about someone's birthday, so boring.) So, it was definitely time to invest in another speaker.

"Seven tickets for the monorail please."

We were on, split into two carts we slowly made our way around the roof of the shopping mall on 'The tour of the world monorail.' It was almost like the rally in reverse. We passed through Almaty, Istanbul, Berlin and finally London, the whole experience didn't last long, but with good friendships surrounding us all, it was a fantastic memory to say goodbye to James and Jade on.

In the car park outside, it was time to say goodbye. Our plan was in action and if nothing was to go wrong, we would be seeing them in Ulaanbaatar in seven days' time.

However, we forgot one thing. This is the Mongol Rally, where nothing goes to plan.

 DSMS lead the charge out of Kazakhstan. It was market day to the outskirts were completely full of people walking in the roads, walking their donkeys and carrying fifty members of their family on a moped. This made a quick, easy exit from the capital into a three-hour labyrinth of trying not to kill anyone.

"Bloody hell mate, I almost hit that donkey then, watch out for it" I said down the CB radio.

Lee looked at me awkwardly.

Oh.

Yeah.

James isn't with us.

Eventually we were on the long stretch of main road west. It was smooth tarmac all the way, you could see that they were doing road improvements at this time, a darn good job of it too. Completely flat, two lane tarmac lay stretched out ahead of us. The weather changed drastically this day. No more were we in the hot climate of southern Kazakhstan, now we were in the northern wetter climate similar to England. Rain began to pour into the Micra through the windowless door meaning we had to pull over to set up a tarpaulin.

For some reason it was at that point on a completely empty road, we blasted out the song 'Gay Bar' and danced in the middle of the road.

We were all feeling low about leaving James and Jade but for some reason, a completely spontaneous dance in the middle of an empty Kazakhstan road managed to lift spirits. DSMS were also feeling particularly low due to the rain and temperature in their car. Throughout the Stans, they would have appreciated the lack of window however now in northern Kazakh, it's a whole different story. Luckily, they were making their way through the Harry Potter audio books on the long dull days and it seemed to keep their morale up high. We continued east as the brand-new road turned into long stretches of roadworks. Not like roadworks in the UK they are more of a complete road block with huge mounds of dirt causing you to go on a wet, muddy and sand filled dirt track around, most of them lasted a few miles however occasionally we would be stuck on them for much longer. They were completely uneven. a mixture of rubble and soft sand mostly. They were thin two-way roads but due to their poor, temporary condition you were forced to drive on the opposite side of the road quite often whilst praying a speeding local wasn't coming the other way. Occasionally the road crossed the brand-new tarmacked road we were unable to drive on to the other side where the dirt track would continue.

We were just about to cross until we spied a local squeeze his car through the dirt mounds and rocks causing the blockage only to start driving down the perfectly laid, new tarmac.

"This guy must have done this before, I'm following him" I said to Lee before racing past DSMS and following the while Lada. I could see that Lee was a little unsure about this as who knew what would be waiting for us at the other side of this? a sheer drop? the police? or angry workers? Nevertheless, I could see that Lee wanted an end to the bumpy almost impassable temporary roads.

DSMS followed as we raced at great speed down the fresh tarmac, after a couple of miles we eventually reached another blockade that we just squeezed through once again. We raced past car after car, truck after truck as we floored it at top speed down the empty straights, we watched as they all tried to maneuver around the dirt tracks situated on both sides of the road. Making excellent time we reached Pavlodar just as the day had finally gone and only the moonlight and headlights from the 1990's shone down of the road. We were distracted by blue flashing lights behind us. Oh bugger. *"It's the Po Po"*

We were being pulled over.

They sped ahead of DSMS and indicated for us to pull over. We did just that. Two policemen came out of the car with a radar gun in hand, tapping away it they went straight up to Adam.

"Speed"

"Yes, I was moving at some speed" Adam replied sarcastically.

"Where are you going?" they asked.

"Semey, can you reach a Semi?"

I burst out laughing in the car behind. The police instantly realised Adam was messing around so beckoned him into their car. He wasn't in there long when he was literally thrown out of the police car in haste as they sped off quickly.

"What the bloody hell happened then mate?" I asked.

"They said I was speeding, but their gun was turned off, then they started to copy out a ticket, Identical to one they created earlier with someone else's name and car. So, I just told them I wasn't paying anything unless at a station. Then they got angry and left."

The advice we were given from other ralliers in the past had really paid off, we had made it close to 8000 miles and still not paid a single fine or bribe.

With darkness upon us, the idea of warm food and a place to sleep was our first point of call. Option A: was to either find a cheap hotel then head out for food or Option B: get food and enough beer down us that we get drunk enough to want to camp in the terrible weather. Luckily however Option A was soon upon us, parking outside a Kazakh Ambulance station we found that situated above was the Hotel Anatay - Pavlodar. It was cheap enough with another woman who deserves the nickname Consuela (The maid from family guy) She moved slowly, never really told us anything about what was going on and the only English she knew was *"no, no, no."* The hotel and ambulance station both had CCTV so we were feeling safe enough about leaving the cars outside. Whilst grabbing gear from the cars, two men came out to say hello. They worked cleaning ambulances inside and out overnight, they were working all night and out of kindness offered to look after our cars. They seemed friendly enough as they answered questions we had about their town, their lives and where the closest place to get some food was.

After failing to understand directions the two men, who at this point had introduced themselves as Vladimir and Vladimir ended up walking us round to an amazing restaurant, it was Oktoberfest themed and served pretty much anything you could ask. The waitresses were in traditional attire and all looked very beautiful. The usual of beers all round were ordered along with Vladimir ordering something called 'Чечил' (Chechil).

"It's something we have with beer in Kazakhstan."

This strange stringy yellow bowl of what looked like noodles was placed in front as everyone began to dig in. It was the most amazing tasting smoked cheese we had ever had. It complemented the beer well and was easily the nicest thing I had eaten so far on the rally. My main was a pasta dish however I filled up so much on cheese that I filled up on Chechil, beer and cigarettes. Before we knew it, another day of the rally had ended, our stomachs were full and we were all fast asleep in the hotel.

As soon as I awoke, I grabbed a quick shower. It was quick because it was directly across from the reception desk and I still remain positive to this day Consuela was watching me the whole time.

Our bags were once again packed, I loaded the car with my large rucksack and began the daily checks. Oil level, DOT4 level, tyres, roof rack. I began ticking everything off the imaginary list in my head.

"Ali, were missing a wing mirror! someone has snapped it off!" Lee noticed.

"Actually, I was a bit drunk last night and when returning to the car.... yeah. I'll fix it eventually."

I could see that the mood around the convoy was low. Well, I say convoy, at this point we were now just two cars, a duo heading into the unknowns of Kazakhstan, Russia and Mongolia. Mini Adventures had sent us a message letting us know that they had started a slow drive to the border as the capital was a little too expensive to stay at for more than a day. It was good to hear that Cunning Stunts were also ahead of us by a day, they were crossing the Semey border into Russia that morning and hoped to meet us at the Mongolia border in a few days.

With the cars loaded and the wing mirror gaff taped in place temporarily and a quick stop for benzin, we were soon on the road heading slightly south east to Semey. 400 km lay ahead of us in the wind and rain, DSMS had their tarp up in the window leaving enough room to check their blind spot as they lead us into the foggy day that lay ahead.

Once again, we were greeted with a morning driving on good roads before the afternoon struck. Temporary roads next to the main road were once again tackled as the gaps between the barricades were too small for our cars to squeeze through. We took the roads as slow as we could manage. Slow enough to not completely destroy the car, but fast enough to make it feel like we were covering some ground. We started passing the odd Nodding Donkey by the side of the road pumping oil to the surface. I was finally greeted with the scene I was expecting before the rally, my own vision of Kazakhstan, a sort of cross between poverty along with new technology. You would see families at the side of the road selling fruit in hand-built huts, however at the same time they would have their car park next to them and a mobile in hand.

It was around 1pm when the roads got quiet, no one really has the need to come this way. the only thing in the direction we were traveling was the town of Semey. Over the next hour we had no one pass us in either direction. A completely desolate landscape. It was at this point we were greeted with 'The Mound' This giant mountain of dirt was placed in the centre of the road. There was absolutely no getting past it to drive on the fresh new tarmac that lay ahead, the only option was to take the dirt road south through forests, fields and washboard gravel not knowing where it would take us. Our GPS was already flashing to let us know it was clueless to where we were. We turned down the steep banking and began our journey south down the dirt track. We were taking it steady, bouncing along for around three miles when the gravel turned wet sand. Skidding and sliding I kept the revs high and the gears low to avoid getting stuck, since the Gate to Hell in Turkmenistan, my off-road driving had gotten a lot better. Eventually we were back on the hard stuff but with the car bouncing and crunching so much, I had to slow down. DSMS sped off, their mighty Micra sailing over each bump smoothly without making even a noise. *"Were going to get a flat tyre any minute now"* I shouted to Lee over the loud rumbling of our car.

Crack

The smell of burning rubber filled the car instantly as I slammed on the breaks. With my worst fears floating around my head, I jumped out of the car, with my eyes closed tight not wanting to look I navigated myself to the back of the car, it was at this point I took a breath and opened them wide. *"bollocks!"*
Our rear axle had once again snapped. Something a lot worse than a flat tyre. Something I had been fearing since Turkey. I jacked the car up at the rear instantly to try take the weight off the rear however it was too late, the damage was already done. DSMS had turned around to see why we had stopped, once they saw the axle their hearts sank too. *"So, the*

*situation is, we are on a dirt track that haven't seen anyone on
for hours, our car is stuck in the middle with absolutely no way
to move it. Yeah? I need a cigarette."*

I sat at on the soft sand at the side of the road chain smoking,
Adam came over with 'Lime Thins' a new Kazakhstan style of
cigarette with twice the nicotine and a hint of lime. *"You are
going to need these more than us."* I'm very good at dealing
with problems quickly but I couldn't think straight with a
sickly feeling in my stomach. Lee had been silent the entire
time, I could tell he was feeling just as bad as me, but with no
mechanical knowledge, he didn't really have a solution. I
jumped under the car and began hatching a plan. My idea
was to get a block of wood or pole from the boot, and ratchet
strap the entire axle at the wheel end up, onto the frame,
pretty much making our car a one-sided hardtail. Then using
a block of wood wedged between the axel and the drum
break, it would be enough to keep the wheel straighten the
axel in position to coast it slowly to the main road.

"It might just work mate!" I said to Lee who seemed
optimistic. My plan most definitely wasn't a permanent fix,
just a temporary measure to get us back to civilization. Just
as I was about to begin my almighty bodge job, a car came
speeding down the dirt track, I managed to get his attention
until he slowed to a crawl and eventually decided to stop.
"Hello, were in a spot of bother" I said. His reply was short
and straight "No English. Roushki?" sadly, no Russian from
our end. Lee was now sat on the side of the road where I had
been earlier, he looked lost and agitated as if he was about to
take up smoking. I grabbed his phone off him for the
translation app and typed away.

"Our car is broken, we need a flatbed truck to move it, we need to go to Semey. Our axel has snapped. Our car cannot be moved"

He typed away for a moment on the phone and his reply was short. *"You are out, the car is eliminated."* The sick feeling in my stomach started to return. I was seconds away from giving up and returning to my bodge job that Adam and Danny were currently starting to crack on with in my absence when I sent one final plea. "Can you help?" This time he typed away for much longer, after ten minutes of silence, I offered him a cigarette. He sparked up and left it in his mouth as he typed away. After another ten minutes he looked underneath the car, smiled and handed the phone back to me. I read the message and almost cried in shock. I had to read it again and again and again just to be sure it wasn't translated wrong. It read...

"My name is Ramil, I am a mechanic and I have a truck but I am on my way home, my wife is waiting. I can phone my friends with truck, they will take you to Semey where my friend can fix your car quickly. If my friends cannot get you now, I will come back and get you with my truck."

"Lee mate, you are never going to believe this." Lee was just as amazed as I, that one car, that one man to pass us within the last few hours just so happened to be our savior. One quick call later he returned to us and typed out *"They will be here in three hours, it is 100km to Semey with bad roads, you wait here for $100."* Truthfully, I wouldn't have cared if it cost double £81 for a 100km flatbed truck to take us to Semey. Sold. I packed away my bodge job gear and our friend left to

go home to his wife. The long wait began, I didn't want to sit in our car and put strain on the rear axle It wasn't till then, taking a look under the car did I see our friend Ramil's toolkit, when he was looking under the car he grabbed his tools out first to see if he could help and left them there. Luckily Lee had his WhatsApp number. Both me and Lee then vowed to get these tools back to our friend no matter what. He had done for us one of the most amazing favors, the least we could do was return his tools.

After an hour I had nearly gone through half a packet of cigarettes. Although we had a plan lined up, the wait was still a little stressful. *"I'm going to run out of tobacco soon"* I said to Adam scarily admitting I'd almost smoked the entire packet of lime thins he gave me earlier, but Adam being Adam just replied with *"Then just move onto the stuff behind you."* Turning around, my memory jogged back to some of the facts I remembered about Kazakhstan before the trip. a certain plant grows wild at the side of the road in Kazakhstan. That certain plant was Marijuana.

The entire fields surrounding us were filled with Marijuana, no one really smokes it due to their religion so there is hardly any market for it, it's never looked after and grows in acres. A new game was then thought of *'Let's try hid Marijuana on DSMS Micra to see if they notice.'* Eventually after three long hours our flatbed truck was here. It was old and blasting out black smoke, but It would be our savior.

Two men jumped out, they spoke no English but though hand signals and smiles they prepped up their truck and started to pull our little fiesta onto the back, I heard the creaking of the axel as the wheel slowly turned. The axel was twisting and contorting with the weight bearing it down as it

299

pushed slowly through the soft sand and gravel. The winch was stopped and started over and over again as our truck driver forced the wheel straight. It took close to an hour, but eventually our car was ratcheted on to the back and ready for its piggyback to Semey. Strangely I didn't feel upset or stressed anymore, I was happy. We didn't just lose a few hours driving, we gained another memory, another story another tale for around the fire when I'm back home talking to my kids about the rally. I had seen in Uzbekistan how something can be fixed or turned into the most incredible bodge job, our Frankenstein shock absorber was living proof. Adam, Oli and Danny followed behind in their mighty Micra with still absolutely no problems. The dirt tracks eventually turned into a concrete road filled with giant holes easily big enough to swallow a Micra. Occasionally we would bounce through one in the truck causing the worst grinding sound to bellow out from our car. It was at this point, I knew our rally dream would be over.

With our fingers crossed we were driven 100km to Semey, upon entering the town, we must have passed mechanic after mechanic, I was hoping every now and again we would be taken to one of the large upmarket garages until eventually we arrived at what looked like a shed.

The doors swung open to reveal an inspection pit, tools, piles of scrap metal and a welder. Frantically I reached for Lee's phone and typed into it. *"Is he a mechanic?"* I was ignored as they began to reverse the flat bed and line it up with the doors. *"Is he a mechanic?!"* I asked again flashing the phone. Nothing. I was getting a little annoyed and worried at this point that I was dropping my last hopes to get to Mongolia off with someone who didn't know what they were doing. Finally, a young lad jumped up and opened our door.

"Welcome" I snapped instantly *"IS HE A MECHANIC?"* He stepped back, looked at the car and replied calmly. *"No, he isn't, but you don't need a mechanic, you need an engineer."* This kid was correct, I needed an engineer, someone with the brains and the knowledge to fix the unfixable. I turned to look at the car when my heart sank that little bit more.

"Oh, that's nasty!" Lee said under his breath.

The rear axle had completely snapped.

Our rear wheel was being held on with a half-broken shock absorber and a break line, the tyre was completely flat where it had been pushed back underneath the frame and jammed itself in place. I looked at Lee, as our eyes met neither of us said anything. We knew this could be the end of the trip, our hopes were resting on this backstreet welder. It was impossible to remove the car from the back of the truck. The wheel was completely jammed, luckily with so many large blokes to hand they each got a hand hold under the car and began to lift. I couldn't believe it. At this point a jack was thrown under the axle, a new wheel was placed onto the car and slowly they reversed it off the ramp.

I don't care how glamorous he other garages looked when we came in, I want these guys working on my car! No one understood any of the questions we asked just as much as we did not understand when they tried to get information from us. Luckily the lad from earlier suck by us to try and translate the best he could.

"They say to come back at first light tomorrow, they will help then." said the lad. With it being 7pm, we took that as a 'we don't want to work now, we will do it tomorrow.' It felt good to have our car in good hands, but the next part I wasn't ready for, with no chance of a quick fix, this meant Oli, Adam and Danny from Team: Don't Smell My Shoes would have to

leave us behind. I know exactly how that feeling is. It leaves a sour feeling in your stomach. Already we had left Gnomes back in Azerbaijan and Mini Adventures in Astana. With them leaving us it meant the one thing nobody wanted to happen. The end of Convoi Exceptionnel.

There were no hard feelings when we hugged each other goodbye. We wanted DSMS to push on to meet Cunning Stunts and other teams for a convoy through Mongolia. Mongolia takes no prisoners, it's one of if not the toughest country on the rally, you need friendship, support and mechanical knowledge to get you through. Me and Lee had already had the conversation about possibly having to skip Mongolia altogether whilst we were in the truck and sadly that plan was looking evermore the best option.
"I hope we get this sorted and catch up with you tomorrow, If not, I wish you all the best and hope our paths meet again" I said to them all, before turning and watching them head down the main road to the Russian border.

"Right, what the bloody hell are we going to do now" I said to Lee in a jokey way. *"We have no money, we need our clothes and passports out the car and somewhere to sleep for the night."* Luckily the young lad had heard us again and made a deal with his friend to take us to a cash point and hotel close to the car. He did just that, within thirty minutes and another drive in a Lada we had cash in our pockets as we turned up to a local hotel. *"Erm, your friends are here"* said the driver. Confused I looked to see seven Mongol Rally cars parked in the car park! *"YES LEE!"* we didn't know any of them and hadn't met up with any of them, we quickly booked into the hotel before heading to the bar. *"You alright lads?"* one bloke

shouted. At this point, I only had one reply. *"Fuck me have we had a bad day boy's! Mine's a pint Lee!"*

A Shattered Dream
Photograph by Lee Marriott

Chapter 19 - Days 34 - 35 - At First Light, We Ride!

Our 8am wakeup call rang through on the bedside telephone, I had a few drinks the night before and completely forgot I had even set a wakeup call. (Well done drunk me) Lee was already up, showered and packing his bag. He was eager to get to the shed to see what was going on with the car, *"First light he said mate, It's already 8am, he might of started"* I was quite sure that 'first light' was a mistranslation and what he really meant was in the morning, but Lee was eager and I was excited to see what would come of the day. I had already showered the night before due to the amount of sand I was covered in from being underneath the car, so packing with haste we were soon out of the hotel and walking back to the car.

"Just be ready for anything mate, the car could look three times worse today, they could have taken the back end completely apart and it still be sitting next to the car or they may not have even started" Lee said to me. He was right, we both had to go there in the mind that this could be the end of the rally for us both.

We reached the shed, the door locked from the inside I tried to take a peep through the gap. *"Our car isn't in there, it's gone!"* I couldn't believe it; the shed was completely empty. Just as I was about to believe we had been robbed of everything the garden gate next to it flung open to show our engineer from the night before and the car standing strong. I instantly got down on the dirty floor to see the rear axle completely fixed. A scaffolding bar had been welded onto the inside followed by two halves of a scaffolding bar welded around the outside. I couldn't believe it! with a huge smile jumped back up to shake the man's hand. He paused for a moment, tapped his watch and pointed at the sun.

"Well what do you know, he actually meant first light. He must have worked all night on the car" After a quick celebration it was back down to business. "Sulka?" which happened to be the Russian word for "How much?" the man raised all of his fingers once, then twice.

"20?"

No.

"200?"

What do you want? 200 dollars?

The man laughed before getting a pen and writing down, '20,000' and holding up Kazakhstani Tenge. Quickly looking at the currency converter we had, it worked out at just under $50. "Well, $50 for the best job we have had done so far on the axle, not only that but he worked on it most of the night" I said to Lee.

We agreed at that point we wouldn't insult the man by haggling. He did a great job in a great time. Not only that but our dream to finish the Mongol rally was once again in action.

We said goodbye to the shed and after a quick stop to get our completely ruined tyre repaired we got rid of quite a few items from the car. If we hadn't used them already, the chances of us using them now were slim. The 12v Travel Kettle was donated to the tyre shop and somehow the toilet bucket still stood strong on the back seats completely unused. Then finally, just before we were about to leave the town of Semey to the Russian border we quickly circled back to the hotel, connected to the wifi and messaged our loved ones we weren't giving up just yet. Although it was close to

3am in England, Caroline called me instantly to wish us luck.
I felt fantastic.

AC/DC Back in Black played on full as we zoomed straight
out of Semey to the Russian border. It didn't take long till we
were greeted with a small row of cars from the border gates.
Lee and I were feeling fantastic listening to loud music and
enjoying a cigarette or two in the sun. Before we knew it we
were straight through Kazakhstan Customs and onto the
Russian side. Driving through no man's land it dawned on us
that not only were we entering the biggest country in the
world, but we were at our second to last country with one of
the most expensive visas.

I instantly fell in love with Russia, as soon as we reached the
border, huge Russian monuments stood high and proud next
to the smooth roads. They stamped each of our passports
and took a brief look at the customs declaration from
Kyrgyzstan before handing them back and announcing
"Welcome to Russia." my smile must have been from ear to
ear, with angry locals trying to push me out of the que, I
stood there happy knowing that I was less than three days
from the finish line. No matter what I could get this car to
Ulan Ude, even if I had to miss out Mongolia all together.
Lee's mood was just as fresh as mine, neither of us seemed
to care when a border guard asked for 90% of our gear and
threatened us with a vicious dog. The Mongol Rally had truly
broken us, re-built us and turned us into Alastair and Lee V2,
the kind of blokes who just 'don't give a shit anymore.' A few
checks later and we were finally out onto Russian soil.
Straight after the border we found a small hut to purchase
car insurance, they gave us chai tea and welcomed us once
again. Then finally by 1pm, we were traveling at 70mph on

the Northern road to our daily destination, Barnaul. 500 km north from Semey.

Every now and again we would hear a tap or creek coming from the rear of the car, neither of us wanted to speak out. Catching each other's eyes now and again each time we could hear it, the music ended up being turned up louder until the sound was completely masked. It wasn't for another 200km when Lee spoke out. *"I don't think we can do Mongolia."*

Lee waited in anticipation of my reply. To this very day I'm positive he was waiting for me to come back with an argument and three hundred reasons why we should, however I felt the very same. *"With two broken axels on normal roads, Mongolia will completely destroy our car. Then it could cost us £1000's to get to the finish line."* Lee nodded in agreement. I need not say any more. It was decided, we would head for the finish line in Ulan Ude Russia. We would no longer enter Mongolia.

Almost complete silence dawned for a few hours whilst we took our decision in. It was a hard decision to make but if we were to go through Mongolia already with a limp, we could come out the other side with a debt of thousands or not make the finish line altogether, end up leaving the car in Mongolia and head home to thousands worth of fines from the Mongolian Embassy. *"I'd rather see my car on the finish line than it in a Mongolian ditch."* I said to myself aloud. Eventually at close to 7pm we made it to the Russian town of Barnaul. We quickly found a cheap hostel and upon parking I saw the cars mile counter *"Lee, we have traveled almost 8,000 miles. Back before we set off, I had people tell me we wouldn't make it to Calais in France, but here we are, 1200 miles from the finish line with only flat, smooth and long Russian roads to go. We are actually going to complete this rally and show everyone who doubted us back home that we achieved everything we said we would and more."* with that said we both decided it was beer o'clock. The Hostel owner informed us that there was a microbrewery next door that we just had to try.

Entering the completely empty bar we ordered two of the man's best beers. All his pumps and kegs were on show to let all visitors see his hand-crafted ales. Not only that but in the fridge next to the counter Chechil cheese was for sale! After a few great tasting beers and as much cheese as we could afford, the decision for an early night was on the cards. It felt strange to be traveling with just me and Lee, there hadn't been a full day so far on the rally since the launch where it had been just myself and Lee driving solo. Even in Turkey when we set off alone from Istanbul, we were with the Convoi that morning and Gnomes in the evening, this was the first 24 hours completely solo. The day felt quiet.

Waking up at 9am our Hostel owners treated us to Eggy Bread, a favorite breakfast of mine. I used to cook it for my Scouts and friends when we were out camping in the Lake District. One of my favorite childhood memories was at the age of 13, I was asked to cook fourteen loaves of eggy bread for a campsite because I made the best, they had ever tasted.

"What's the plan today Lee?" I asked with a smile.

"We did almost five hundred kilometers yesterday. It was a long one, I vote we take it easy today and try to reach a new record of six hundred kilometers, we will be in Ulan Ude in no time." he replied.

Lee my good friend, I couldn't have agreed more. I packed up quickly and tried the spot tracker again to update everyone back home, pressing it again I got the usual red light of doom before placing it on the roof with my morning coffee. Thanks, hugs and a few english coins were given to our host before grabbing my coffee and jumping into the passenger seat for what we were hoping would be the furthest mileage of the trip so far.

Lee quickly navigated us to the main road, and within no time we were on the eat road, the M6 East that would take us all the way to Ulan Ude. As we turned onto the main road I heard a thud coming from the roof *"Ah, the camping chairs must have come loose, I'll sort them when we stop"* I said to Lee. I thought nothing of it until later on that day.

"I'll just try the spot tracker again"

Oh.

Wait, where did I put it?

Oh.

Bollocks.

I'm 99% sure that was the sound I had heard bouncing off the roof and onto the road, now almost one hundred kilometers away from Barnaul, there was no turning back. I quickly covered my tracks before Lee realised how much of a dick I had been *"Ah, the tracker must be in my bag"* I said with a completely flat voice. I'm not the best when it comes to lying. If you ask anyone I know, they will let you know that I'm the biggest exaggerator when it comes to it, I call anyone who happens to be younger than me 12 years old and anything that costs a lot 'a million pounds' the only time I can say I've been completely true to word and tried not to over exaggerate is in this book.

Spot Trackers are a brilliant thing to take with you on the rally. Ours was truly fantastic until it randomly stopped working. I had managed to pick up a spot 3 tracker on eBay just before launch and luckily Marriott Eco Projects had sponsored us a year's subscription. Not only do they update your friends and family of your location but they have an SOS button, a button not to be messed with. If you hold it down it will automatically send a signal to Spot HQ who will instantly send out either local authorities or the military to your location. Its only to be used in the most life-threatening conditions. But a good tool to have by your side. With that said, ours had stopped working back when we entered Kazakhstan and seemed useless ever since.

Southern Russia is beautiful, the amazing hillsides, forests and smooth roads really do put a smile on your face. Every now and again you pass a huge Russian monument covered in communist symbols situated in a field of over a million sunflowers. When I was driving, I stopped as many as I could just for photo opportunities, however both me and Lee were quiet again this morning. We didn't really have much to say to each other so the morning was once again spent singing to the Mongol Rally Spotify playlist and listening to 'The Lancashire Hotpots' We stopped around midafternoon for a wander around the Novosibirsk Shopping Mall, It was meant to be a quick stop for food however I found a stall that sold hats and needed to try all of them on. Since Kazakhstan I had been looking for a military style hat as a souvenir to take home. Many past ralliers had purchased them from military outlets, bazaar's or stolen them from the police when the opportunity showed itself. With once again no luck we had a quick check of our phones to see that Cunning Stunts and DSMS had made it into Mongolia before we returned to the car.

It was a strange feeling to have no one stood around our car taking a look. Usually whenever we left it somewhere in plain sight it attracted enough attention to cause havoc. However, sat by itself, covered in the dirt and mud from what Europe and Asia had thrown at it, it just looked depressed.

I started feeling a little shitty about not going to Mongolia too. This was the last moment we had to say 'Fuck it' and head on the south east road to the border. Instead, we jumped into the car and headed east, two days from Ulan Ude. We drove all day into complete darkness, with another 400km under our wheels we worked out that we had smashed the longest day record by miles completing 789km in a day. That's nothing to some teams, some teams of three never leave their car, driving all day and night in shifts. But for us, we were quite proud.

We looked around for a few hotels but with no luck on the first two we once again began to get a little agitated. Lee hopped out and headed down a dark alleyway out of my sight at one point. I started to worry a little thinking he could be in danger, completely forgetting to check my own surroundings.

A random guy entered my car via the passenger door. Completely shocked and taken by surprise I didn't know what to do at all. With a quick clench of the fist I stared into his eyes as he said "Erm, Taxi?"

No.

"Okay, goodnight friend."

I couldn't help but laugh, how in god's name did this man think a 1995 Ford Fiesta covered in Logos and camping gear could be a taxi, I have no idea. Lee returned sharpish with no luck. I told him what had just happened and the mood was instantly lightened.

We were in the town of Achinsk which luckily housed a small airport. Lee's brilliant logic kicked into action as he announced *"Airports always have hotels next to them, there has to be one next to or nearby."* Well, do you know, he was absolutely right!

Pulling up too 'Hotel Bon Voyage' we headed to the reception that was manned by a small dog. *"Hello goodest boy, we would like a twin room please!"* I asked nicely as the dog remained asleep. *"Erm, excuse me sir, what sort of service do you call this? It's late and I'm in need of a room please"* Once again the dog remains silent.

"Erm, hello sir, can I help?"

Oh god.

Sat down behind another counter was the hotel receptionist who was extremely confused why I was trying book into the hotel by talking to his little dog. Nevertheless, this big Russian dude was happy to take our rubles before showing us to our room. After a quick brew, we were completely conked out on our beds.

Chapter 20 - Days 36 - 37 - From Russia, With Love.

5.15am I woke. Five, bloody fifteen. Unable to sleep and the sun slowly arising, I went outside for a cigarette. The car still looked as depressed as ever and I could tell from the day before that both me and Lee were just as blue. We were soon to be arriving in at the finish line, however without a convoy, two days ahead of the rest of the gang. I whipped out the rainex and a cloth and began cleaning the sponsors names on the car, I wanted them to be seen once we got to the finish line during our thank you letter, once I did that I thought, I may as well finish off the rest of the car. With the car sparkling clean, I decided it should be time I fixed the wing mirror. Traveling at 70mph on a main road with no way to check your side or blind spots, so out came some self-tapping screws, metal brackets and a screwdriver. Within no time the mirror was back on strong. *"Well, if I've done that, I may as well fix the tracking."*

Over the next hour I completely fixed everything wrong with our car, things I should have sorted weeks ago but just couldn't find the time. I wanted my car to stand proud on the finish line.

"What's all this then?" Awake and packed up, Lee had joined me outside, completely gob smacked that I had chosen 05:15 two days before the finish line to fix the car.

It was my turn to drive, with Lee driving close to the entirety of the day before, after a quick morning coffee we were on the road. Lee's DJ skills were on point as banger after banger played. The locals of the city Krasnoyarsk were woken at 08:00 to the sound of 'Mr. Brightside - The Killers' as our car zoomed straight through the city centre. There was a road

313

going right around the city that would have saved us half an hour, but Lee's comment of *"Quick turn left"* whilst looking at Maps.Me turned out he was wrong. Nevertheless, the quick detour was rather nice and even involved us going through a rather beautiful area.

Our day was rather uneventful. I carried on the tradition of stopping at every monument I could to take a photograph. The mood was brilliant, song after song we put hundreds of miles under our tyres *"If we carry on at this rate we could be in Ulan Ude by the morning"*

I had to ruin it didn't I.

SLAM.

I only just managed to stop the car as the traffic ahead of me was at complete standstill. Everyone was out of their cars trying to take a peek of what lay ahead. I took it one extra by standing on the roof of our car. All I could see was traffic. *"I've no idea what the holdup is, however, everyone ahead seems to be stuck and waiting, is there a way round?"* I asked Lee who quickly re-assured me *"There is one main road through the south of Russia, the same one we have been on now for a few days, this is the only way."*

We waited close to an hour.

Until finally we moved, nothing too much just a few car lengths.

Another hour passed until finally we started to move. We reached the end of a long road and sat waiting on a roundabout. From here we could see ahead the traffic continued and the cause of the delay. There was a railway track having maintenance completed at the crossing. Those in charge were allowing 30 mins one side, then 30 mins work than 30 mins the other side. Meaning that every hour we would be allowed though and every half hour they could crack on with resurfacing. After another hour we started to move until we were stopped once again.

Getting impatient, I jumped out of the car, onto the roof and sat there happily on the two spare tyres smoking some lime thin cigarettes. *"Hello, your adventure looks amazing"* said a girl at the back of the car staring at our large map. *"Thank you, it really has been incredible"* I replied. She called for someone out of the car behind when a young lad came over brandishing a bottle of Russian Vodka. *"A toast to complete your adventure, I see you are near the end?"* Whilst waiting for our turn to cross the tracks we drank, smoked and spoke of the wild adventure we had over the past five weeks. Stories all the way from Germany, Azerbaijan and Turkmenistan were told almost as if they had happened yesterday. It reminded me and Lee of exactly what we had accomplished.

Finally, it was time for your turn to cross, I fired up the fiesta as a train passed on the tracks, hundreds of carriages carrying Russian military vehicles charged past. Tanks, Guns, Jeeps, Smaller Tanks, Bigger tanks and even aircraft parts. It was almost the exact sight I expected to see in Russia back when this adventure was just a dream.

Eventually we made it to the town of Tulun. The first hotel on Maps.Me proved to be the cheapest, with no other rally cars in sight we found a parking space next to a motorcycle. Sweden to Mongolia via Russia on an unsuitable motorcycle it read on the side.

"Erm, sorry but, we have done 18 countries in a 1995 ford fiesta, that there is a KTM 550, which isn't unsuitable at all, if anything I'd say it's a wise choice!" Me and Lee couldn't stop laughing. *"Oh boy, I'd hate to have done this in an unsuitable land rover or one of those All-terrain vehicles, that would have*

been tough" Lee announced. From then on, we booked into a cheap hotel and checked our maps. 830 km we had traveled, we could have managed more if it wasn't for our three-hour delay. But we were happy.

"It's 500km, one day's drive to Ulan Ude my friend." 500 km and our Mongol Rally adventure would be over.

Finding a bite to eat we found an open cafe whose staff were eccentric and happy to host us. It was their new chef's first day and he was determined for everybody to try his steak, even me! After explaining I was a vegetarian again and again. I settled to a bowl of chips with a caramel coffee. Lee was more than happy to try the steak, however the next hour consisted of me making jokes such as *"Lee just ate a Russian man's meat"* and *"Do you also hope to try his sausage?"* Lee was unamused.

After filling ourselves up, we returned to our hotel to find the adventure motorcyclist sat on his KTM reading the map on the back of our car. I went over to make conversation and shake the hand of another adventurer; however, I could see his disgust as I went over. A Quick detour to pretend I was grabbing something from the car and the day was done. Tomorrow we would be at the finish line. Tomorrow our Rally would be over.

My phone buzzed loudly in the early hours, grabbing it I could see that Caroline had text me the previous day, however it had only just come through. *"You said yourself before you set off that you shouldn't be upset if your route changes, it's all part of the Adventure. You have traveled thousands of miles and set out to complete exactly what you said you would. You will still come home a hero. We want you home as soon as possible, but make sure you get everything*

316

you want out of this adventure, because I'm not letting you out of my sight after this."

She was right.

I pushed the thought into the back of my head whilst I woke Lee and began the usual packing up and car checks. It didn't feel like the last day of the trip, nor the last time I would have to top up with oil or check the tyres. I felt unsure and uneasy.

Once packed up, I jumped into the driver's seat and jumped back onto the one road east all the way to Ulan-Ude.

Lee turned to me, "It doesn't feel like the last day."

"Tell me about it mate, I don't know what it is, but I don't feel like a celebration, if anything I feel sick" I replied.

I don't know what Lee was expecting me to reply with, however I'm quite sure he was happy to finally get to the finish line and head home to his soon to be bride. My phone pinged on final time on the Hotel Wi-Fi to see that James and Jade from Mini Adventures were three days behind but had finally entered Russia. *"We hope to see you in Ulaanbaatar."*

Shit.

We had completely forgotten to tell them about all of our troubles and they were sticking to a plan that for around three days now, did not exist. With one huge sigh, Lee took one for the team. *"I'll break the news to them."*

The P-255-258 takes you all the way from Semey to Ulan Ude. I will always remember it for its spectacular views, eagle covered canyons, flat tarmac and winding roads. Today we were on the last section, the P-258 from Tulum to Ulan Ude. By midafternoon we had passed the city of Irkutsk and reached the most southerly point of Lake Baikal. Pulling up for photographs and a quick supply run I bumped into a

317

gentleman in a bright orange jumpsuit with a large white bomber jacket. He looked as if he was either about to land on the moon or he was the world's worst disguised escaped convict.

"Your adventure looks incredible" he said in an accent that clearly wasn't Russian. *"It has been, where are you from?"* I asked. It turned out he came from 'just down the road,' a small village outside of Edenborough. I spoke to him about how the rally had been so far, the best and worst moments, how our Convoy had broken one by one and how we were now only a couple of hours from the finish line.

"Nah, you won't be finished today, I'd say give it another week" he said. Confused, I was just about to reply before he continued. *"You are in control of when the adventure ends. Mongolia isn't far, you should go! complete your adventure."*
"But what if the car breaks?" I said quickly.
"Have you learnt nothing on your travels? That's part of the Adventure."

I fell completely silent. Completely lost in my own head. So much so, I don't even recall saying goodbye to the man. I saw him walk away and hitch a ride onto a truck within seconds. My next memory was back in the car driving around the east side of Lake Baikal.

It was then I realised that in my life I'm so busy asking the question *"What if something happens"* and that I never give myself the chance to ask, *"What if something doesn't happen."* Why put the negative first?

Later that evening complete darkness, the city lights of Ulan Ude could be seen. My smile had returned and I was ready to celebrate and catch up with the teams who had also made it to the end. Within no time we were booked into Huskey hostel and on the way to Churchill's. A pub specially selected by The Adventurists as the official pissup for the Mongol Rally, Situated next door to the finish line podium and straight across from the famous Lenin statue.

Whilst passing the podium, I refused to look. I stared at my feet the whole time. I wasn't ready to see the end. I still felt as if there was something more. A hole in my heart that I needed to fill, more so now we were at the finish line.

Lee and I entered Churchills to a cheer from around six other teams all eating, drinking and celebrating. "Well done lads, great to see you here." a quick cheer and pat on the back from Kevin, the Mongol Rally organizer. *"Bloody hell lads, it's good to see you again".* Our friends from Team Breakneck tweed in the 4x4 Fiat Panda who we hadn't seen since the Door to Hell in Turkmenistan, both stood to shake our hands. *"How was Mongolia?"*

And there it was.

The one question I really didn't want to answer.

Lee could see my disappointment and replied, "We didn't go." I was expecting a shocked look, however in reply, I got quite the opposite. *"Not many of the teams here did, we did, and our car is completely fucked. I'm meant to be driving it home, but the gearbox is completely fucked. We lost gear's 2 and 3 on the first day of Mongolia and by the time we reached Ulaanbaatar, it was impossible to move."*

I couldn't believe it. The one car I expected to make it no problem turned out to have one the worst issues. However, with that said, they didn't half rag it around.

Another team shook our hands and introduced themselves. *"We did Mongolia, our rear axle split completely apart and we had to get it welded at a yurt, luckily there are plenty of people offering you a tow to Ulan Ude for the right price"* they said.

It was at that point I fell silent once again.

I drank, smoked and celebrated with the rest of the ralliers, not for completing the rally, more for the Idea I had.

Finishing my pint, I turned to Lee. *"Mate, come outside for a second, I've got an Idea."*

"Why? what's up mate?"

"We should go into Mongolia tomorrow." I said.

Lee smiled.

A little unsure, I continued before he could get a word in. *"I know that If I call it a day now and don't go to Mongolia, I'll never be happy with myself. I'll end up having to do this bloody trip again just to scratch an itch I can do tomorrow.*

It will only take us one day to get to Ulaanbaatar, then we can meet DSMS & Cunning stunts there. We can see the sights, fire some guns, visit the Genghis Khan statue all before convoying back up."

Lee was still smiling.

"Ali, Mate. I was honestly just about to say the same thing"

Chapter 21 - Days 38 - 39 - "We Khan't give up"

Smiles stretched across both of our faces, I asked Lee to show me what he had learnt so far. He did the early morning car checks, inflated the tyres, topped up the oil and even cleaned out the air filter. Our plan was to head to the capital of Mongolia, Ulaanbaatar. Spend some time there waiting for the convoy before heading back up to Ulan Ude. I no longer felt like I had failed or a coward for not going to Mongolia. *"Whatever happens, happens."* like we had been told, plenty of people were offering to take cars to Ulan Ude for a good price.

The sun was high in the sky, Lee set Maps.Me to the Mongolian Border, told me to head straight and fell asleep for an hour clutching his phone. After an hour, I pulled over to wake him.

"Mate, can you check the map for me? I seem to have the sun in my face, this would mean we were heading east, not south."

"It's this way it's just one road south" he said whilst half asleep.

I cracked on for another ten minutes before calling this.

"Sod this!" I called.

Grabbing his phone, he awoke *"What are you...*

Ah Shit.

Right.

Sorry."

We had been heading east towards Chita in completely the wrong direction for over an hour.

Another wrong way tally was added to the dashboard using the paint pen and a little over an hour later we were on the

M-60 south to Mongolia. The scenery changed almost instantly. The landscape had turned tree covered flatland to empty green and brown hills, Eagles flying high in the sky occasionally swooping down to catch its prey. After a few hours we had reached the Russian/Mongolian border. Just before it on the Russian side in the middle of a small desolate down was a huge marked with 'Cash and Carry' written upon it. Feeling peckish and in the need to grab supplies we quickly popped in to grab food, water and treats for our long day of traveling. Lee instantly headed to the deli section to find himself a sausage roll, I however stood in the middle of the 'Cigarettes and Alcohol' section with my jaw to the floor.

It was huge.

Every flavor of cigarette you could ask for along with every type of Russian Vodka. I mean, I couldn't taste the difference with any of the vodka I had tried, to me they all tasted like paint stripper. But whatever you wanted, this place had it. I spent more time looking at the different food and drink it had to offer, I had to force myself to choose some food and snacks, knowing I had to grab what I could and get to the border. After grabbing fruit juice, water, lunch, sweets, crisps and a bulk load of Chechil cheese, we found ourselves as the Mongolian border.

The que consisted of a few cars ahead and around three trucks behind until after an hour of waiting, we were passed the first gates. We saw a Mongol rally car balanced carefully on the back of a pickup truck, clearly broken beyond repair. This could well have been us, broken and battered, being dragged to the finish line.

A quick passport check later we headed over to the main
building, parked the car and followed the locals upstairs to
an office. Everyone spread their car documents out on the
side and went to sit down. Me and Lee not knowing the
situation we did the same. After an hour or so a few border
personnel came to the desk and began stamping the
paperwork. This once calm crowd turned into a stampede of
locals waving their papers in the air as if they were at a
cattle market. It wasn't till a guard turned up that the
situation calmed. Once again, the papers were put in a line
on the desk, however this time they were being sneaky.
Every time myself or Lee looked away, someone would move
their papers ahead of ours. Essentially jumping the que.
Furious and annoyed at the cheek of them, we would move
our papers back whilst their friends tried to push us away
from the desk. It was a game of who would give up first.
Eventually after another hour of waiting, It was my turn.
Much to the disappointment of locals who gave up their
terrible attempts to que jump.
"Passport" she demanded.
"Car Passport!" I handed over the V5.
"Russian Customs"
"Erm, sorry, what?" I said.
"Russian customs document, you get when entering Russia."
We didn't get one.
I had been in charge of keeping all the car documents
together, I knew that if I was to lose a document, it would
mean the end of the trip. So, I purposely placed each
document into its folder in order of receiving.
"We didn't get one!" I said to the woman who was currently
waving a blank one in front of my face. I thought I was

getting somewhere after trying to explain how we entered Russia until she stopped me.

"NO CUSTOMS, NO STAMP"

The one thing I didn't want to hear.

I picked up the entire folder and poured everything down onto the desk. Pulling up pieces of paper from all around the world.

I was nervous, fidgeting around when she reached onto the desk and pulled out a sheet.

"This."

The sheet she had pulled out was a customs declaration I received when I entered Tajikistan. I had no idea what it said as it was written in an unreadable language. Nevertheless, this document seemed to make her smile.

Finally, after another hour we were free to leave and ready to cross no man's land onto the Mongolian side of the border.

Both myself and Lee were already exhausted from our game of tug of war with the locals, jumping into the car I got in front of as many as I could, every now and again I foolishly overtake a few and push right in. Eventually I made it to the front of the line. To everyone on the Mongolian side, I must have looked like a complete knob head, however I'm sure those on the Russian understood my frustration.

A quick sheep dip and we were officially on the Mongolian side. We both jumped out the car and jogged over to the main building ready to be first.

"Stop"

Shouted a border guard.

"Are you in the rally? If so, have you spoken to Kevin?"

I had to ask her to repeat the question. I we both looked at her and expected a. She was a good-looking woman, more so in a Mongolian army uniform. *"She can boss me around anytime mate"* I said to Lee.

"Have you spoken to Kevin?"

It turns out she was just making sure we weren't getting into trouble, we knew our cars couldn't be left in Mongolia or we would have HUGE fines to pay. Technically, she was being helpful, however in this time of brief conversation. The locals had overtaken us.

"Wait here" she said.

A few minutes passed. Before we knew it, everyone had gotten past us and once again we were at the back of line. She returned, telling Lee to walk into the main office, she made me follow her into a small office where she began the paperwork on my car.

Everything suddenly felt out of the ordinary.

"Do you come for work or pleasure?" she asked. This was the start of many, many strange questions. She knew I was part of the rally however asked the question anyway.

"Pleasure" I replied.

"Good boy"

Wait.

What?

Every now and again she would ask a question and tick a box off the paper she was writing. It wasn't till I got the sheet back that I saw half the questions she asked me weren't even on the sheet.

I can't remember everything she asked, but the strangest ones where *"Do you plan on sexual activity within Mongolia?"* and *"Are you looking to find a bride?"*

At this point, I was rather scared of this woman. She was either trying it on or thought I was off to some sort of Mongolian pick your own bride event.

A couple of hours later, we were leaving the Mongolian border with our passports, car insurance and customs document in hand.

We had done it.

We had made it to Mongolia.

Just as we left the exit gate, we passed Highlander I and Highlander II, two teams from the top of Scotland who we met on day one of the rally. They were in identical 1.1 Ford Fiestas and by the looks of things, their rear axles were holding up well. *"Good luck in there"* they shouted as we roared the engine out of the town and into the most incredible landscape I had ever seen.

Snowcapped mountains in the distance, large green and brown hills even closer, stretching for nearly one hundred miles, completely clear. White Yurts were scattered around and wilt horses roamed the landscape. Everything I expected from such an amazing country, I experienced within the first few seconds of entering.

We still had around six hours of driving to go to get to Ulaanbaatar, the road was tarmacked (for now), with the sun setting quickly we pushed on for the capital before nightfall. One of the last things our friends in Team: Breakneck Tweed said to us in Ulan Ude was *"DON'T do the North/South road in the dark, it's just wider than a single lane, pitch black and people like to use their full beam."*

But with the border taking so much longer than we expected, it would be our only hope.

Pushing on in the final light we slowed down occasionally by the odd official looking toll. It cost 4 Tugrik, the equivalent of around 20p. However, each time we were stopped and asked to pay, the ticket we received was Identical to the last. Lee turned to me, *"I think they are having us on here mate."* I couldn't have agreed more, however for the sake of what was 60p so far, I didn't mind. In the last bit of light during the brilliant progress we had made, we hatched a plan for the next toll. .

"You use road, you pay toll" he said.

I turned toward the man with my sunglasses resting upon my head and quoted 'Back to the Future' perfectly.

"Roads" I flicked my glasses down over my eyes, *"Where we're going, we don't need roads"* All of a sudden the Bluetooth speaker roars the first few bars of the 'Back to the Future theme that Lee had setup for this very moment. Dropping the car into 1st, I floored it though the toll.

"Well were 20p better off" I shouted.

The thin road was pitch black and busy. Occasionally a man made, non-regulation size Mongolian speed bump would thud against the underside of your car. Locals had placed these mounds throughout the country to make you slow down through their town. This gave them the opportunity to run out and try sell you something, or if it was raining, send their kids begging. Needless to say, with us, it never worked. At one point the road narrowed just after passing through a town called Baruunkharaa, it was pitch black with only our headlights lighting up the road ahead. I took the car back up to a steady 70 mph before instantly having to slam back on. A large black 4x4 with no lights on pulled out on us instantly.

Swerving in front and slowing down, he tried getting us to stop.

"Well this man is friendly" I said with a smile to Lee trying to break the tension. However, we both knew what this was. With neither of us wanting to admit it. The windows came down on both sides of the truck as heads poked out looking back. I managed to take over the truck and gain some speed before its powerful engine overtook us once more and began to crawl.

Taking the car off road, back on and off again I did all I could to shake him whilst Lee hid our passports & wallets. Eventually I was forced back onto the road right behind him, we lost speed quickly. I was ready to put the car into reverse when a set of headlights came over the hill in front. The truck then switched its headlights on, performed the quickest U-turn and before we knew it, they had vanished. We both knew that this situation could have been a lost worse, our savior's who came over the hill at that point probably had no idea what they had stopped.

Just before we reached Ulaanbaatar we were stopped in slow moving traffic, the river of brake lights ahead showed us that our progress was going to be a lot slower from now on, with cars and people surrounding us we were feeling a lot safer than before. "I wonder if this is just the que into the city?" Lee pondered before closing his eyes to try sneak in a quick nap. I forced my eyes to stay open as we slowly creeped to the front the que. Everyone seemed to be waiting in line for something.

"Lee its another bloody toll" I shouted, waking Lee.

"You are joking, is there a way around?"

Looking around we could see that there was no way round, however every now and again the opposite lane would have a gap big enough for us to squeeze through.

"I'm going to go for it, I'll just wait for this big truck in front to block my view of the guards, then I'll do it."

Lee agreed, we weren't paying another toll.

With the truck now obscuring the view of the guards, I floored it through the gap of opposing traffic, locals behind me followed suit and before the barrier dropped, we were through.

I turned to check if anyone saw to see a very strange sight. Around twenty men in hazmat suits were washing and rinsing down the cars entering the city, one turned and waved his hands in the air frantically towards us.

"What the bloody hell did we just do?" I shouted.

Then we saw the sign.

'Bubonic Plague Decontamination'

Oh,

well.

"Were fucked!"

Wondering if we had started a national health scare, we finally pulled into Ulaanbaatar at just gone 11pm. The bright lights woke us up completely as we looked around.

"Pint?" I said to Lee who quickly agreed. The best idea was to find somewhere to have a celebratory pint and somewhere to stay for the evening. After driving around for quite a while we eventually settled on a small bar in the centre. Pints drawn, we sat there sipping on our cold Mongolian beers, we clinked glasses.

"Well we did it, we came to Mongolia, just like we said we would. The roads are poor and sometimes nonexistent, but where here."

We tried again and again to connect to the Wi-Fi, with no luck at all I remembered back to when we were planning. For the Visa application into Mongolia you have to book your accommodation beforehand. Both me and Lee had 4 nights at the 'Good Karma Hostel' booked in and as luck would have it, it started tonight!

With an idea of a comfy bed a good night's sleep and minimal driving on the cards the next day we downed our pints and headed off in search of our hostel.

We were a few corners away when we came to a dead end. *"It must be the other way"* Lee said. No bother, we drove around to the other side of the dead end only to find another one. *"Well there is a third way but it's down a thin road"* he said, *"how thin?"* We then pulled up to an alleyway that was just about the width of the car. *"Looks like it's this way."*

I asked Lee to walk in front to keep an eye on the car, the last thing I wanted to do was destroy the car down a huge pot hole or take out the side of someone's business.

I drove slowly for close to half a mile, when the road suddenly just ended. Well, I say ended. It was a sheer drop down. I could have continued but I'd never of made it out alive. With all that said, I then had to slowly reverse the car all the way back down.

It was now past midnight, we were both exhausted.

"Right, I'm sleeping in the car" snapped Lee.

"It's okay, we will find somewhere" I said calmly.

"No, I'm sleeping in the car" he snapped again. Lee really didn't do tired well.

"Well, you can sleep in the car all you want, but it will be in the car park of the hostel that I will be sleeping in" I shouted back.

I know I probably shouldn't have shouted but I was feeling brilliant that we had made it to Ulaanbaatar Mongolia, nothing was going to dampen my mood.

I checked Maps.Me one last time to see a hostel, dead centre 'Modern Mongol Hostel' "Let's give this one a try.
Perfect.

I pulled down a one-way street, navigated though a labyrinth of cars coming the other way to see students and travelers sat outside smoking on a low balcony. *"Is this a hostel?"* I shouted. *"Yeah sort of, where are you from?"* they shouted back. *"Brilliant, England"*

Wait.

"You drove here!!" they shouted.

Grabbing things from the car and looking up we made friends with the chaps on the balcony. Showing us inside we booked a room for two, one night with the possibility of staying another. I turned to Lee and sarcastically said "Mate, I thought you were sleeping in the car?" but he wasn't amused at all. Finally, at 1am we had made it to our room.

"It looks nothing like the photo's Lee"

I didn't get a reply.

"It's not very modern is it? Anyway, goodnight mate."

I went over to the window, grabbed the curtains ready to close.

"For fuck sake, really?" I said not able to control my laughter.

"Lee come look at this mate!"

Outside of the window on the other side of a large wall was the most amazing looking hostel, large car park and a large sign that read 'Modern Mongol Hostel'

Sod it.

"I'm going to bed."

We woke, packed our bags into the car and quickly drove around one corner to the hostel we thought we were in the night before. Checking in quickly, our first point of call as to grab Wi-Fi and check up on our friends and families.

DSMS: *"Mongolia is vile, AFK your axle won't make it, don't do Mongolia."*
Caroline: *"Sweetheart, it's been days! I hope everything is okay, we love you so much! Call us when you can xxx"*
Mini Adventures: *"We are days behind you, we hope to see you at the finish line"*
And finally, Grandma:
"Hello Alastair, it's Grandma. I hope you are having a good holiday, is the car broken yet? '/'x/'s oh sorry I don't know how to delete that. Grandma.
Fantastic!
I messaged Caroline first letting her know about mine and Lee's safety. Lee did the same to Mica. I wanted to call her more than anything, but the eight-hour difference now mean that for her it was the middle of the night.
I replied to DSMS letting them know we were in Ulaanbaatar in 'Modern Mongol Hostel' and that when they arrive, they should join us. I quickly got google maps up on my phone and drew them a map on how to find it. I didn't want them in the same situation as us the night before.
I replied to Mini Adventures saying I hoped to see their picture on the finish line and finally, Grandma. I'm sorry I didn't reply, it's £4.50 a text message. But I love you!

Today the plan was to visit the Genghis Khan Equestrian Statue around an hour's drive east of Ulaanbaatar. It's one of the 'not to be missed' places on the rally and a real ending point to the trip.   It took a little longer to get there than originally planned as it was market day in Ulaanbaatar and the road out to the east takes you right past the Ulaanbaatar Black Market. Yes, that's right! the Black Market, the one market they say you can get anything and everything for the right price. Along with that there are toll's with unpassable sand traps around, making it so you have to drive through the toll.

But there it was, the GIANT Genghis Khan Statue standing before us in all of its glory. Both myself and Lee could hardly hold back the tears. It's the most spectacular ending to an amazing adventure. Feel good music blasted as we reached the furthest point east, we would ever travel in our little fiesta.

I parked up with the biggest smile on my face and began to take hundreds and hundreds of photos of the car, myself and Lee all in front of this amazing statue. *"We actually did it mate! Here we are in Ulaanbaatar Mongolia in a Ford Fiesta we drove from Blackpool England. 10,000 miles west of us!"* The realization of getting to Mongolia had finally kicked in. We spent a good few hours at the statue, paying to walk upon the back of the horse, checking out a few gift shops, posting a letter, learning about nomad culture and finally dressing up in traditional Mongolian clothing for some of the funniest pictures of the trip. I could have spent the entire day there, it truly was an amazing place. Outside traditional yurts were scattered around and in the distance nomad horses ran wild. It was perfect. The only thing that let the image down was a company who were running quad bike trips on the circular road around the monument. It's pretty pointless and takes away from the heritage.

Nevertheless, we took this opportunity to drive around the ring road ourselves to the non-touristy side, park up on the grass and film one of the most amazing parts of the trip. A thank you video to all of our friends, family and sponsors who without them, we wouldn't be there. We planned to do the same at the finish line as well, but we couldn't miss an amazing thank you shot from the heart of Mongolia. Before it got too emotional, we said goodbye to Genghis and headed back to our hostel, laughing occasionally at cars who had gotten stuck in the sand because they refused to pay the toll. We parked up back at the hostel, grabbed a few drinks and spent a good few hours updating our social media pages to tell everyone where we were.

In all my life, I had never felt so emotional, so full, so complete.

By late afternoon our stomachs began to rumble for some good food. No bother, there was a pub just across the road. A traditional Irish pub known as the Grand Khan. Wanting to continue our love for Genghis, we chose this pub for food and a few drinks. *"Excuse me my good sir, where are you staying, do you have a hotel?"* said a well-spoken Mongolian. *"erm, hi, were just down the road, why?"*

I should have seen this coming.

"I get you lady for the night, you have sex, you pay me what you think is fair."

I began to laugh, I was just about to reply with my decline when I looked onto the balcony of the pub. Gob smacked, I completely ignored the man and ran upstairs, *"Sir its three dollars to sit on the balcony"*

I ignored the second man and continued to run towards the balcony as quick as I could with the biggest smile from ear to ear. Lee caught up behind confused to why I was running.

Then, finally after a week without them, I embraced Danny, Oli and Adam from Don't Smell my Shoes.
"Boys it's been a while! Lime thin anyone?"

We sat for over two hours smoking (Adam on his vape so he wouldn't be back on the fags when he got home), drinking and chatting about Mongolia. They told us that there is a smooth tarmac road currently running though most of the southern route now, however its up a steep locked off banking that you just can't get your car onto, so instead you are pushed onto the soft sand and gravel. It was annoying but comforting to hear them say repeatedly *"You're so lucky you didn't do it; your car would not have made it."* Comforting to hear that we didn't take the risk, but annoying that we didn't do the route we had originally planned. But still here we were, all sat drinking in the centre of Mongolia! Something we dreamed of 5 and a half weeks ago back in Prague.
I say all, we were missing two of our convoy still. James who would be in Ulan Ude within the next 30 hours and Cunning Stunts.
Wait.
"I thought you met up with Cunning Stunts?" I said.
"Ah, yeah." Danny replied whilst looking around at the others. I could see by the look they gave each other that it wasn't good news.
"They have had some bad times, the last we heard was yesterday morning, I think their engine had fallen out"
WHAT!
I couldn't believe it, we had heard some horror stories from the road so far but this was by far the worst. *"They are with some guy in a 4x4, so at least they aren't by themselves"*

Danny added to comfort our thought as little more. I couldn't stop thinking that that was my worst nightmare, something happening in the Gobi Desert and not being able to find the help. *"So, besides all the hate, what was the funniest part of Mongolia?"* I asked to try and change subject.

"I don't know about Mongolia, but we had a CRAZY time in Russia."

One Night in Russia
A Short Story by Oliver Milverton:

We crossed into Russia first thing in the morning having slept in no man's land. First impressions of Russia were amazing landscapes and even better roads, we sped along! We made it to Barnaul in good time, where we stopped for food and Adam bought a new Vape, we were getting near the end now and he had to get himself off the cigarettes before he faced his Mrs.

Our target that day was Biysk and we got there just as it started to get dark, I was driving with Dan navigating, he punched 'hotel' into maps.me and the search began. I don't remember how many places we tried but we were looking for hours, there was the usual problem of some not existing, some being full, some being brothels masquerading as hotels and one being astronomically expensive, we were ready to give up and camp, but even that wasn't an option. Due to the steep landscape around us there wasn't anywhere we could camp away from the road safely, especially with there being a rumor of bears in the area. It looked like we were going to be sleeping in the car. "Ok" said Dan after another failed attempt "last one".

We drove down a narrow track and came to a high fence with no obvious signage, we continued past this to a small cluster of houses. No sign of life, sleeping in the car looked ever more likely. An old man suddenly appeared from behind a shed and looked slightly shocked at up being there, he spoke no English but understood why we were the. He pointed in the direction we had come so we retraced our steps. What we had thought to be just a continuous fence had a gate in it where a woman had just appeared from.

The gate was flung open and we were ushered into a compound with log cabins around the outside. Just as I was parking up by the gate Adam saw a group of young Russians under a pergola in the compounds centre, *"go further"* he said *"let them get a good look at the car"*, this did the trick. We were suddenly surround by the group with them all speaking at once in broken English; *"Where. From?"* - *"Drive here?"* - *"Name?"*. Mugs of beer and bowls of food were thrust at us. Soon the questions became a chorus of *"Banya, Banya"* accompanied with an action that looked like they wanted to flog us. After a couple of minutes of this and us being utterly confused the owner came over to translate. *"They have booked three hours in our sauna and want you to join them"*, so we now knew what they wanted, although the flogging actions they had made still seemed a bit ominous.

We dumped our bags in our log cabin (yes we had a whole log cabin to ourselves for about $10), donned our swimming trunks and were led down a dark path, through a hole in a fence, down another narrower and darker path - "Where are they taking us" - to a clearing with a shed at one side and swimming pool at the other. We were shown to the sauna and sat in the billowing steam passing around a bottle of some mead-type drink. Bliss. Suddenly everyone got up and dragged us outside, pointing at the swimming pool, we jumped in. Going from a sauna at a freezing cold plunge pool is invigorating, after weeks on the road it was just what we needed. But it wasn't over there, the chorus of "Banya, Banya" was restarted. I was led back to the sauna and made to lie on my front, two of the girls then bought in tree branches poured hot water over them and proceeded to thrash my back from my neck down to the soles off my feet, over and over, it was both painful and relaxing at the same time. Now the flogging actions made sense.

The next three hours was spent between the sauna, being physically beaten, plunge pool, and sat in a room in the sauna hut drinking, smoking shisha and getting to know our new friends using hand signals and broken English. We them moved to the 'disco' hut, more food and drink was produced and the party continued long into the night.

- *Oliver Milverton.*

We booked DSMS into our hostel, showered and told them how they had to visit the Genghis Khan statue the next day on which they agreed. It really was a fantastic ending to a truly remarkable journey. Meanwhile we would go for a quick browse around the city and take in a few tourist spots. I really did have my eye on getting something strange from the Black Market or even a pair of traditional Mongolian Riding boots. My phone buzzed thanks to the hostel Wi-Fi. 'You have been added to the WhatsApp group 'Grand Kahn'. It turned out that many other teams had successfully made it

to Ulaanbaatar today, old faces and new started to chat,
Team: The Bongolians, Team: Around the world in 998cc's,
Team: Silky pandas, Team: Over 9000 and one other name, a
team I missed more than the others Team: Cunning Stunts.
I instantly sent a message to Ritchie however after few hours
with no reply, I started to fear the worst for them all.

That evening we all met up in the Grand Khan, slowly we
were joined by team after team as the rounds of drinks got
bigger and more expensive. Everyone was talking about
Mongolia. How their cars either didn't miss a beat and they
had no problems at all or they just completely broke
altogether. DSMS only had one flat tyre. An easy, quick
change and they were away again. Their Micra was truly
built of brilliance, with next to no problems the entire trip
and the only problems they did have were down to the
driver's fault. I stood with an empty glass in hand, turned
and bumped straight into Ritchie, James and Baz. Almost
spilling their pints, I shook their hands and congratulated
them about arriving in Ulaanbaatar. I could see in their faces
that they were happy to be with us all after such a long time
however reading their body language, I could see they had a
tough time getting here.
"So, how was it?" I mumbled to Ritchie.
"Well, I may as well sit down and tell you all" he said like a
father about to read a bedtime story to his young.
"It all went wrong when James said the engine fell out"
Oh fuck.
Ritchie began to tell us about all the troubles, It turned out
that over the four days they had managed to dislodge the
radiator, drag it along the floor, buckle both front wheels,
completely destroy the front suspension that the front

339

wheels cambered in and a fresh tyre would be completely bald within a few hundred miles of driving. The Mk4 Fiesta was completely fucked. Story upon story was told, including how they had met a man in a Willy's Jeep called Amadeo who convoyed with them the entire way though even though they were such a heavy burden, even so at the point they cracked their sump, he drove two hours back to the closest town just to get them some oil to keep on going.

All that put together with Ritchie's mechanical knowledge, James's strive to help the best he can and Baz's skill of drumming beats off the broken parts from the car, they had managed to coast it into Ulaanbaatar all the way to the hostel. Their story of Mongolia will be one told for years throughout the Mongol Rally, which is exactly what the Mongol Rally was all about.

Celebrating In style, we drank until our wallets were completely empty and our heads full of memories.

Chapter 22 - Days 40 - 41 - The Re-Creation of Convoi Exceptionnel.

DSMS set off early to the Genghis Khan statue leaving Myself, Lee, James and Ritchie to spend the morning having a wander around the Black Market. Baz had jumped in the Willy's Jeep with their new friend, eager to get to Ulan Ude and finish the rally. It was a sad goodbye knowing we were not going to finish together, but at least all our cars would be.

Mongolia doesn't have many touristy places, however one place really tickled our fancy 'Military Arms Training - Fire an RPG for $100.' It was a steep price, but imagine that, firing all the guns we could get out hands on along with an RPG! We knew if there was time, this would be an opportunity not to be missed.

With the Black Market a short walk away, in the blasting heat of Ulaanbaatar we began walking, this was an instant regret. Ulaanbaatar is the most polluted city in the world, you cannot see the sky within the city, only a large blast of smog that occasionally makes your nose drip a little black. We ended up heading into an air-conditioned supermarket for cash however it was more to just cool down.

"It's different, but it's the same." James said.

This must be the most used phrase on the rally at all times when in a supermarket. You have a little excitement to see what sort of brands and food the locals eat, but most of the time it's the same stuff in different packaging.

Eventually we arrived at the Black Market, it's everything you expect it to be. Like out of a film you see all these foreign wares for sale. The market itself if huge! A labyrinth of anything and everything you could possibly want all laid out in specific sections, you could easily spend a full day there just looking around, following the crowds and drinking chai tea from the vendors cycling around. However, we had a timeframe to stick too.

Our plan was to wait for DSMS to get back, if it was still early in the day we would make a break for the Mongolian border however if it got late, our best bet would be wait until the morning. Both me and Lee had seen too well the troubles of traveling at night in Mongolia, not only did the Jeep want to run us off the road but just the roads themselves are dangerous enough, I could tell that Ritchie and James were a little unsure their car would make it also.

We spent a few hours looking around at Mongolian riding boots, hats and even the cheapest suits we had ever seen. I ended up getting almost completely naked in the middle of the market to try on this suit that looked amazing on the model, but on me not so much. I had decided I didn't want it when this English-speaking woman starts shouting about how I have wasted her time.

The Black Market is another unmissable place to visit. It's truly unique and even if you don't buy anything, it's definitely worth taking the time to visit. Along with this Mongolia is home to many stunning Monastery's one large national park and enough yurts to take anyone's fancy. You can even buy your own yurt and have it shipped over to you within a month for less than $1000USD.

On our search for lunch our phones began to buzz, DSMS were on their way back to the hostel, ready to make a break for the Mongolian border this afternoon.

By 4pm we had all the cars loaded up, the smog over the city means that as it gets later and the sun sets, the rays of bright light suffer to break through the smog. (I don't know if that is actually a fact, but it sure felt like it) This wasn't a good feeling for me and Lee knowing what was to come. Nevertheless, with our old friend by our sides, we handed in our keys, fired up our cars and began the rush hour journey out of the city. It didn't matter it was getting dark, heck, it didn't matter we were in standstill traffic for another hour, we were back together once again after such a long time, once again we were Convoi Exceptionnel.

The traffic pushing in from all angles with no sort of any indication of where they wished to go, we were soon completely split up, luckily there is only one way out of Ulaanbaatar to the north and it can't be missed. Just outside of the city were-grouped, said goodbye to the one location we were all so eager to get too and passed over the first hill into the Mongolian wilderness. It wasn't long until we got to the first stop, the stop that on the way in both me and Lee presumed was a toll, only to find out it was biohazard car washing to stop the black death.
"We may be in this que a while lad" Lee shouted behind.
But no,
I had other plans.
"Follow me boys!" with a quick acceleration we all whizzed through the checkpoint along with some local trucks who also spied the gap. Once again, we had missed the all-important stop, once again we could have caused a major pandemic. But why should we care? *"Mongol Rally!"*
Darkness soon hit. The vile roads on the way in were just the same on the way out, tight corners, thin roads and car after

truck blasting their full beams into your eyes in the opposite direction. Cunning Stunts car weaved left and right on its completely bald tyres whilst Ritchie tried to keep it in a straight line. We could see them sat behind DSMS with only one working headlight. I dare to think what was going through Ritchie's head at this point. Their spare tyres were bald with the metal wiring pushing out the sides. If they were to have a blowout now their 17-inch alloys would be tough to find rubbers for, unlink ours and the Micra's 15-inch steelies.

After almost three hours on the road it was now completely pitch black, a quick fuel up and toilet break gave us time to come up with a plan.

Eventually we confirmed on the idea of pushing on until one of us finally calls it a night, then pull over near a yurt, pitch our tents and do the border in the morning, however the closer we got to the border, we were greeted with more motivation to push on. We guessed the border would be quiet in the early hours, and saw little reason to sleep before it, only to wake in the morning joining the back of a long queue. On we went through the darkness over large pothole and car killer speed bumps in the road. We were getting closer and closer to the border, I started to recognize where we were from the small blurs I could see in the darkness, we passed a few tolls, purchased a ticket at the first then floored it through the rest.

Without any notice, we were pulled over by the police at the side of the road. They had waved us down because Cunning Stunts had a headlight out. A quick blow on the connectors to get rid of the dust and we were away. We were lucky it was darkness when he saw us as their little Fiesta looked like a wreck in the day, they would have never allowed them to continue.

"Is that what I think it is?" Lee said to me with a smile.

"Lee my good friend, I think you are right!" I replied.

It was a large lit up archway stretching across the road featuring the Mongolian flag on one side and Russian on the other. There it was, we had made it to the Russian border.

At the gates we were stopped by the guard who instructed us to wait. We all jumped out of our cars supporting huge smiles. We had made it to the border, it was just a smooth 3-hour drive to Ulan Ude and the finish line. Our tiredness had completely vanished as pure adrenaline kicked into us all. Mongolian vodka and other leftovers made and appearance as we started to drink everything we could in celebration. Sweets, chocolate and rations were all consumed including some Chet-cha cheese I had saved for a special occasion. Ritchie had completely lost his mind at this point, he put on a Kazakhstani policeman's hat in which he had purchased earlier on the rally, a cape and some aviator sunglasses as he began shouting and ordering everyone around. Even the border guard couldn't stop himself from laughing.

Before we knew it, we were through the gates, V5's, passports and customs documents out for the last time. The Mongolian side was easy for me and Lee due to only passing through a few days back, a few stamps off a guard I had to wake up, a few car checks and we were directed to the Russian side on the other side of no man's land as we waited for Cunning and DSMS to fill out a bundle of paperwork. The road involved a very sandy, steep road. One final challenge Mongolia had to throw at us all before we left that we then passed with flying colors. It was now 2am and with Russia just though one set of gates, the excitement could not be subdued. No matter how we were spoken too, no matter how we were treated, absolutely nothing could break our spirits. Two hours later at 4am we filled out our tourist cards and we were on Russian soil. I parked the car up just on the other side of the border, switched the engine off and instantly fell asleep.

At 9am the heat of the car woke me, almost as if I had eaten a biscuit of death, with the driest mouth I reached for some fruit juice. Startling Lee he almost shouted himself awake; He had fallen asleep just before I parked so I'm sure he woke with the thought that we had fallen asleep driving.
Car doors opened on either side of us to show that DSMS and Cunning had the same idea. Sleep after the border and cruise into Ulan Ude in the morning.
The cash and carry we nipped into on the way into Mongolia had just opened, a perfect opportunity to grab breakfast, treats for the road and a few bottles of dirt-cheap champagne for the finish line. We regrouped outside in the car park with the same smiles from the night before. Today we were to complete the Mongol Rally. Something we had all dreamed of but never thought possible. Cunning Stunts had thought their rally was over in the dunes of Mongolia, Me and Lee (AFK) thought back in Kazakhstan and Turkey our Rally dreams were over, Don't Smell My Shoes on the other hand thought outside of Germany their rally dreams were at an end when their car kept on cutting out.
But there we were, two Fiestas and one Micra, three hours outside of Ulan Ude where our rally would be complete.

We spent plenty of time on the drive north messing around, overtaking, cutting each other up, breaking, throwing things out the car and even Cunning Stunts had dangled meat on the back of my car knowing I was a vegetarian. Their prank was soon responded to by a dose of karma when they burst a tyre on a small pothole. Their car was just holding on to its life, dragging itself on completely bald tyres their blowout meant that they had to use another bald tyre with its metal mesh hanging out the side that somehow had not punctured yet. With a record breaking tyre change in traffic, within nine minutes the had caught us up. We had pulled over to wait for them in a safe layby and were watching huge winged locusts devour other insects on the grass besides us.

"Look over there" I turned to see James and Ritchie with a huge smile looking down the valley.

There it was, Ulan Ude.

Jumping into the cars we raced for the final half an hour into the town, almost close to tears the celebration music blasted out of our speaker as Lee filmed us all on the approach.

'Ulan Ude - Russia' could be read upon the entrance. A huge mixture of emotions overcame me as I realised this was it, this was the ending I was expecting. I could never had called it a day without doing Mongolia, these were the exact emotions I was missing the first time around, a feeling of accomplishment, achievement and happiness.

The coordinates of the finish line were pressed into Maps.me as we tootled through the city. Locals waving, beeping and smiling at us knowing this was the finish line and we were on our way to completing the biggest rally in the world. We were one street away.

The small blue flag on the Maps.me app flashed and began to get greater in size for each roll of the wheels. I turned the final corner to see the most spectacular sight.

"I can't believe it" I shouted at Lee with huge excitement. It wasn't the finish line my eyes had fixed upon, it was Mini Adventures, they were driving in with us in the most amazing Convoy. I beeped, cheered and blasted the siren. We were once again all together. With the most amazing feeling of accomplishment, Lee grabbed the loudspeaker and shouted.

"Convoi Exceptionnel have completed the Mongol Rally!!"

At exactly 12:43 the wheels of Mini Adventures rolled onto the finish line, followed by Cunning Stunts, Don't Smell My Shoes and Team Away from Keyboard.

The end of an adventure, the creation of lifelong friendships.
-   *Photograph by some bloke who happened to be passing at the time.*

Chapter 23- Days 42 - 43 – Living the Dream

Kevin from The Adventurists congratulated us all and assisted in filming our celebrations. Champagne covered our clothes and cars as we posed for photo after photo. I had never felt a feeling like it before, the most mixed emotion of my entire life. Extreme happiness along with a pinch of sadness. I was ecstatic that we had made it, excited to see my family and proud of both myself and Lee however sadness that the greatest adventure of my life so far had come to an end. Two whole years of planning, sponsorship proposals, filming and heartache had led to this most amazing moment.

After filling all our memory cards up with photos, we filmed a short video for friends, family and sponsors before heading over to the finishing tent and doing something I was dreading.
Singing my car over to be scrapped.
Our tiny 1995 Ford Fiesta Mk3 had completely blown us away, its engine ran smoothly and perfect the entire trip never letting us down. The rear axle gave up on us so many times but it was at these points where we felt the lowest that made the world the greatest. People from both sides of the earth offering their time and help to keep us on the road and keep our rally alive. Throughout the trip I had broken so many personal boundaries that Id forever been hiding behind, my anxiety was almost nonexistent and I had made the most wonderful friends.
I found my love for the open road with every mile that our wheels turned and the best bit about it all, I did it with my best friend.

"Lee, mate come here" I shouted.
"I need you to sign here to say were scrapping the car"
Lee looked at me briefly with a confused look until he
understood, nodded, ticked the box and signed his name.
He knew that I wanted to keep the car more than anything
however the cost outweighed the value of the car. What
would be the point in spending thousands to get a almost
worthless car home.
I then took the time to hug James and Jade, I'd missed them
so much since we left them behind in Kazakhstan and It was
perfect surprise to have them in convoy when we got to the
finish line. It turned out they had been waiting across the
road from the finishing line all morning knowing that we
were on our way. It wouldn't have been the same, finishing
without them.

We booked into a hotel on the other side of town before
jumping on the Wi-Fi to upload picture after picture of us all
on the finish line. I took the time to call Caroline and the girls
back home, it was so amazing to tell them that we made it.
They supported me every step of the journey and I love them
all so much. I remember Caroline's final words before I hung
up. *"Now come home and MARRY ME!"*
We spent the evening eating burgers, partying and eating
more burgers. It was fantastic to celebrate the end of the
rally with the most incredible friends. I took the liberty to
drink as much Russian vodka my body could hold and smoke
as many lime-flavored cigarettes as I could manage. This was
because as soon as I was home, I'd be off the cigarettes again
completely. I don't smoke around my children.
When the night came to an end, Myself, Danny, Jade and
James decided to take the long walk back to the hotel instead

of an Uber. It was so nice to not be in a rush to get somewhere and know that the next morning we wouldn't have to drive anywhere. We could finally take our time. Passing a large crowd in the town centre we watched a great Russian band perform in the square before taking a stroll through the park. We were all a little drunk when...
"Ali, hold this!" all of a sudden Danny threw his wallet and phone into my hand as he jumped headfirst into a park fountain. *"Shit, I didn't expect it to be that deep"*
I hit the floor in pure laughter as Danny popped out of the water shouting *"MONGOL RALLY."*
Shortly after we were all back at the hotel, exhausted and ready for some sleep.

At 13:10 the next day we had driven our cars to 'Donation Point' setup by The Adventurists. A fantastic place where you can drop off all your equipment to be sent to Mongolian charities instead of sending it all to landfill.
We had complete gutted our car for everything we wanted to take home and left it all at the hotel. Everything remaining was donated. Including the COMPLETELY UNUSED TRAVEL TOILET we drove all the way to Mongolia and never even used! I told you Lee!
It was sad to see the car empty, we even donated the roof rack and LED bar. The car was to be crushed so someone may as well have found a use for it. All that remained on and in the car were the sponsors on the outside and our scribbles inside.

Half an hour later we arrived at the Auto link drop off point, I signed the car over to them and agreed for it to be crushed one last time. The entire yard was a Mongol Rally car graveyard. Everyone who had arrived before us had parked up before heading home only a few paint indications on the cars showed their fate. Red - Scrapped. Blue - Pickup, Green - Shipped on. A large dollop of red sprayed on our windscreen I said my final goodbyes by writing on the bonnet.

"Goodbye my little Fiesta, I'm so proud of you"

Lee took plenty of photographs before we caught bus back to town. We all fell completely silent as we left our trust steeds to their final resting place. I was so upset to be leaving my little Fiesta 10,000 miles away from home, knowing that within the next few months It would be crushed. The only thing I regret about the rally is not driving my car home and keeping it. Yes, it would have needed a lot of work for the MOT back home, but I knew from that point I would regret signing the paper to have her crushed.

Back in Ulan Ude town centre plenty more burgers were eaten whilst we browsed Skyscanner. The most annoying thing about Skyscanner is that every time someone books onto a flight the price goes up. It was every man for himself as we all fought for the cheapest price home.

I locked my flight in and booked it quick getting it cheaper than most, Adam did the same meaning we could head to the airport together and have one final meal and a beer before our last goodbye.

Knowing I had such an early taxi ride the next morning, I spent the evening saying goodbye to my convoy family, they had been there for me though everything. True friendship had bloomed throughout us all as we group hugged and shed a few tears.

"I best see you all at my wedding"

By 5am the next morning I had said my goodbye to James from Mini adventures and wished him luck in his week long drive home, A quick drive to the airport brought back the realization that the rally was finally over. All that time planning, preparing and worrying.
It was all over.
My god, I did it,
I completed the Mongol Rally!
I couldn't wait to be home with my family. I flew Ulan Ude - Moscow - Belarus - Manchester where I was greeted at arrivals by my beautiful partner Caroline. Upon seeing her I went completely weak as she wrapped her arms around me. She cried, *"I'm just so happy you are home."*

Chapter 24 - Our Mongol Rally.

It's been Six months since I completed the Mongol Rally, in that time I have married my beautiful wife Caroline, added baby Oakley to the family and changed my job industry completely. Thanks to newly formed friendships, I even asked James from Mini Adventures to be the Godfather to baby Oakley.

The Mongol Rally has completely changed my life. As cheesy as it sounds, I have a whole new perspective on the world, I don't care for things or objects anymore. My whole life is now completely focused on family, friends and adventures old & new.

Do yourself the biggest favor you possibly can.

Do the Mongol Rally.

Mongol Rally - Convoi Exceptionnel:

Team Away from Keyboard:
Ford Fiesta Mk3 - 1995 - 2018
Alastair Cameron
Lee Marriott

Team Don't Smell my Shoes:
Nissan Micra - 1994 - 2018
Adam Skerritt
Oliver Milverton
Daniel Lampard

Team Cunning Stunts:
Ford Fiesta Mk4 - 2000-2018
Richard Turner
Sebastian Inwood
James Ridges

Team Mini Adventure:
Austin Mini 1986 - Today
James Hornig
Jade Rowing

Team: Rally Mc Rally Face
Nissan Micra - 1994-Today
Kate Jarman
Gareth Bain
Carmel Fagen

Team: Two Fake Yanks and a Scott (Gnomes)
Renault Clio 2005 - 2018
Harriott Wood
Jessie Brandt
Russell Brandt

Thank you to everyone who made our Mongol Rally the best adventure I could have ever asked for. Below is a picture from left to right of Oli and Danny of Team: Don't Smell my shoes. Me (Alastair) from Team: Away from Keyboard, Ritchie from Team: Cunning Stunts, Lee my best man from Team: Away from Keyboard and finally James from Mini Adventures. Photograph taken the evening of my Wedding. *A Mongol Wedding with Convoi Exceptionnel.*
-    *Photo by Andrew Davies.*

Chapter 25 – The Confession.

At the start of this book, I spoke about how I told Lee and Peter (Lee's father) that I took apart the entire engine, had the car looked over by a competent mechanic and did everything I possibly could to make it 'Rally ready', I just want you all to know, this was a lie.

I lied because I wanted to remain within the spirit of the rally, I wanted the problems to happen on the road in the thick of the adventure. Although this most definitely lead to the breaking of our rear axle 3 times and our exhaust falling off countless times, these stories are what makes this book and our adventure interesting. I have absolutely no regrets and I do hope you can forgive me.

I urge anyone who wishes to do the Mongol rally to follow suit, sure check the few things that can destroy your adventure such as your engine health and oil levels, but everything else wait until it becomes a problem. This is what makes the difference between an adventure and a holiday.

Thanks,
Alastair Bruce Cameron.

A beginner's guide to the Mongol Rally

So, you think you want to take on the Mongol Rally?
Great! Here is some advice: **DO NOT READ ON.**

The Mongol Rally is all about adventure. Throwing yourself
into the unknown and finding a way to climb out of the
shithole you just jumped into. Getting lost, robbed and
beaten until you can't take it anymore before laughing it off
and just getting on with the adventure. That is the Mongol
Rally. So, if your serious about doing it, either stop right
here, SPOILER ALERT or if you feel the need for a bit more
information, just to kick you up the arse and start planning,
then read on.
But I must stress. Plan your own rally, not a copy/paste of
mine.

The next few chapters answer all the questions that I have
been asked since completing the rally. If I have missed
anything out, I probably did it on purpose. I don't want you
knowing too much now do I?

Thank you for reading about our adventure, I hope you have
the chance to write your own. Do the Mongol Rally.

Chapter I - Do's and Don'ts.

Do the Transfagarasan Highway - Lee (AFK)

Don't set off each morning without a coffee. - Alastair (AFK)

Do take a Nissan Micra- Oli (DSMS)

Don't take a Ford fiesta. - Oli (DSMS)

Do check you visa dates - Adam (DSMS)

Do double check visa dates - Adam (DSMS)

Do triple check visa dates - Adam (DSMS)

Do eat Oli if he hasn't checked his visa dates - Adam (DSMS)

Do Jack your car up before Turkmenistan - Kate (RMcRF)

Do Take a feather pillow, to sleep anywhere - Kate (RMcRF)

Do Take as long as you can for the rally. - Kate (RMcRF)

Do film as much as you can. - Kate (RMcRF)

Don't visit Azerbaijan. Ever - Danny (DSMS)

Don't make plans, go with the flow. - Kate (RMcRF)

Don't take a tent that takes ages to put up -Kate (RMcRF)

Do it in a Lada if you can - Richie (CS)

Do not forget Imodium - Jade (MiniAd)

Don't eat food that isn't cooked or peeled - Oli (DSMS)

Don't be suspicious of the locals, they do help! - Oli (DSMS)

Do piss in the Gate to Hell - Danny (DSMS)

Don't get your VISA's wrong - Oli (DSMS)

Do swap cars - Kate (RMcRF)

Don't feel ashamed to shit yourself - Anonymous (???)

Do take a shit on the closed Mongol roads - Danny (DSMS)

Don't trust the Gate to hell motor bikers - Philo (Over 9000)

Do take steel rim spares - Lee (AFK)

Don't buy the 80-octane fuel if you are up in the mountains.
Go for the expensive stuff because your pistons will barely
turn over on that shit - Danny (DSMS)

Do buy a drone and take loads of camera footage - Danny (DSMS)

Don't be shocked or upset if your car only cost £300 and you spend £700 on the rally on repairs. That's the whole point.

Don't worry. It will only hold you back

Do tell everyone to buy this book (I've got to try somehow!)

Do take no notice of this chapter if you plan on doing the Mongol rally, take everything in as it comes, enjoy the shits, laugh about the fines and make your adventure yours.

Chapter II - Putting rumors to death.

The Mongol Rally is full of rumors and incorrect Information from those who have either lied to put you off or been misled along the way, this section is here to put these to rest and are accurate from our experiences in the 2018 Mongol Rally.

1) Uzbekistan, Tajikistan, Kyrgyzstan and Turkmenistan border guards do not check your car or phones for pornography or nudes.

2) The Turkmenistan Ferry is a complete sham and is not worth your time or money, do the extra work and go through Iran.

3) It's easier to get rid of your car in Uzbekistan than any other of the Stan countries, the DVLA will give you a hard time but you won't have to pay any fines.

4) You cannot go from Armenia to Azerbaijan, although they are no longer at war, they hate each other and will tell you this daily.

5) Mongolia will kill your car in every way it possibly can. The northern route is harder and more liable to flooding than the central route.

6) You can go from Armenia into Georgia; the border is open.

7) When entering Turkmenistan, you are given a sheet with the exact border you enter and wish to exit from, YOU HAVE TO EXIT FROM THAT BORDER, NO OTHER BORDER WILL ALLOW YOU TO EXIT, so make sure its correct when created.

8) Benzin (Petrol) is not Illegal in Uzbekistan, you can find it EVERYWHERE at all fuel stations, in the pump as normal, if you can't, you are blind.

9) The Genghis Khan statue is worth the drive no matter what, it's a very iconic end to the trip.

10) In 2010 a rally participant died in an extremely serious road traffic accident. This rally is an extremely dangerous risk to take and you do it completely at your own risk.

11) You don't have to stop at the hundreds of police checkpoints in Kazakhstan unless you are waved down by the police, just slow down to 10 mph and cruise though. They then may choose to chase you down, but that will be to either get a bribe or a cheeky photograph.

12) Never pay for a bribe, always ask for a receipt and say you will pay at the station, then play the *'I do not understand, waiting game'* eventually they will get bored and send you on your way. NEVER PAY FOR A BRIBE. Unless you're at a border. Don't risk visa refusal.

13) You don't HAVE to go into Mongolia, (You can drive around through Russia) but you will be shunned.

14) Borders DO NOT allow photocopies of your V5, you WILL need the original. The driver must be the one who takes the car through the border.

Chapter III - Days/Mileage - Team AFK

Day:	From/To:	Country:	Total Mileage:
1	Blackpool - Deal:	*(England)*	326 miles.
2	Deal - Frankfurt:	*(Germany)*	777 miles.
3	Frankfurt - Prague	*(Czech Republic)*	1142 miles.
4	Prague - DPRGA	*(Start Line)*	1175 miles.
5	DPRGA - Bratislava	*(Slovakia)*	1402 miles.
6	Bratislava - Deva	*(Romania)*	1833 miles.
7	Deva - Bucharest		2120 miles.
8	Bucharest - Varma Vecha		2272 miles.
9	Varma Vecha - Istanbul	*(Turkey)*	2630 miles.
10	Istanbul - Hendek		2762 miles.
11	Hendek - Samsun		3104 miles.
12	Samsun - Batumi	*(Georgia)*	3466 miles.
13	Batumi - Tbilisi		3682 miles.
14	Tbilisi - Aghstafa	*(Azerbaijan)*	3750 miles.
15	Aghstafa - Baku		4070 miles.
16	Baku - Turkmenbashi	*(Black Sea)*	Ferry Day (1)
17	Baku - Turkmenbashi		Ferry Day (2)
18	Turkmenbashi - Ashgabat	(Turkmenistan)	4439 miles.
19	Ashgabat - Darvaza Gas Crater		4654 miles.
20	Darvaza - Dashoguz		4855 miles.
21	Dashoguz - Khiva	*(Uzbekistan)*	4933 miles.
22	Khiva - Bukhara		5196 miles.
23	Bukhara - Samarkand		5388 miles.
24	Samarkand - Buston		5526 miles.
25	Buston - Osh	*(Kyrgyzstan)*	5815 miles.

Day:	From/To:	Total Mileage:
26	Osh - Yerish, Naryn River	5959 miles.
27	Yerish, Naryn River - Bishkek	6233 miles.
28	Bishkek - Almaty *(Kazakhstan)*	6399 miles.
29	Almaty - Priozersk	6718 miles.
30	Priozersk - Karagandy	7047 miles.
31	Karagandy - Astana	7191 miles.
32	Astana - Pavlodar	7478 miles.
33	Pavlodar - Semey	7606 miles.
34	Semey - Barnaul *(Russia)*	7885 miles.
35	Barnaul - Achinsk	8383 miles.
36	Achinsk - Tulun	8899 miles.
37	Tulun - Ulan-Ude	9418 miles.
38	Ulan-Ude - Ulaanbaatar *(Mongolia)*	9845 miles.
39	Ulaanbaatar - Chinggis Statue	9918 miles.
40	Chinggis Statue - Khyagt *(Russia)*	10135 miles.
41	Khyagt - Ulan-Ude	10285 miles.
42	Ulan-Ude - Autolink Drop Off	10291 miles.

Ford Fiesta MK3 (1995)- N746 JAF - Total Mileage: 67,604.

Chapter IV - Kit List - Car

Item	Notes
Jerry Cans 25l x2	Used daily in the Stans
Wheels (Spare) x2	We went through three.
CB Radio - Antenna	Used Daily
12v Tyre Pump	We forgot ours, had to borrow.
Front Spring	Not Used
Rear Spring	Not Used
Engine Belts (Alternator, drive ect..)	Not Used
Oil (Enough to get you started)	Used over 50l
Roof Rack	Used Daily
Roof Bars	Used Daily
Fuses	Used Daily
LED Bar	Used Daily
12v Loudspeaker	Used Daily
USB Slots	Used Daily
Paint Pens	Used Daily
Tool Kit	Used Daily
Axle Stands x2	Needed with our Scissor Jack.
Car Jack	A MUST.
Spark Plugs x4	Not Needed
Spark Plug Remover	Not Needed
Spare Bulbs	Not Needed
Fuel Funnel	Used Daily
Warning Triangle	Legal Requirement
Hi Vis Jacket	Legal Requirement
12v Ice Box	Not Used
Radio	Used Daily
Maps	Used Daily (Sort Of)
Ratchet Straps x4	Used Daily
Air Filter	Not Used (Cleaned Old One)
Sump Guard	WE DIDN'T HAVE ONE

V5	HAVE THIS AT ALL
TIMES	
Shock Absorbers	WE WISH WE TOOK A SPARE
Chicken Wire	Used Rather Often
Cable Ties	Used Rather Often
Duct Tape	Used Rather Often
Tow Rope	Used Twice
Fire Extinguisher	Not Used
JB Weld	Not Used

Chapter V - Kit List - Personal

Passport	Used Daily
Visas for all Countries	Used Daily
Travel Insurance Documents	Used Daily
Money (In Dollars & Bank)	Used Daily
Tent/Hammock	Used Rather Often
Sleeping bag	Used Rather Often
Stove/Pots/Pans	Used Rather Often
Plate/Bowl/Cutlery	Used Rather Often
Travel Kettle	Not Used
Toilet	Not Used
Toilet Paper	Used Rather Often
Torch	Used Daily
Matches/Lighter	Used Daily
Cigarettes	Used Hourly
First Aid Kit	Not Used (Thankfully)
Camping Chairs	Used Daily
Food (Long Lasting)	Used Daily

Chapter VI - FULL COST BREAKDOWN "It's all down to money."

Total cost of the Rally for Myself and Lee: **£6,902.97**
Total Cost each: **£3,451.48**
What the cost would have been without sponsors:
£9,252.97

Signup:	-£1750
Car:	- £1948,57
Travel:	-£1615.20
Camping Equipment:	-£112.99
Fuel:	-£694.49
Hotels/Camping:	-£636.08
Tax/Insurance:	-£322.03
Mechanics/Parts/Breakdowns:	-£306.41
Additional/Flights Home:	-£1885.02
Sponsors:	+£2350

Here is how it all went down...

PRE RALLY:

SIGN UP:

Mongol Sign Up	£550
Adventurists Car Deposit	£1200
Total: £1750	

CAR:

Ford Fiesta Mk3 1995 1.1l	£595
Car Insurance (Ali, YEAR)	£490

Spring Front	£9.80
Spring Rear	£13
Roof Rack	£20
Fuses	£3
Tools	FREE
Spark Plugs	£7.99
First Aid Kit	FREE
Mario hats	FREE
Paint Pens	£12
CB Radio & Upgraded Ariel	£70
Ratchet Straps	£26
Health Check	£40
Roof Bars	£55
MOT	FREE
Tyres	£30
Full Car Wrap	FREE
Additional Sponsor Vinyl's	£5.99
Breathalyzers	£2.95
JB Weld	£6.60
Sun Strip	£10.99
New Fuse Box & Wiring	£70
Loudspeaker	£10
Air Filter	£5.39
Alternator Belt	£7.74
Clutch Cable	£9.29
Axle Stands	£10.50
Phone/Accessory Mounts	£7.77
Spray Paint	£20
Torx Keys	£4.95
Cup Holders	£7.16
Dual Band Radio	£22.99
Windscreen Wipers	£5.90

CB Mounting and Speaker	£20
Car Manual	£5.99
LED Light bar	£45.59
Rain-X	£8.99
LED Flares	£19.99
Spot Tracker	£25
Spot Tracker Subscription	£180
Insurance (Lee)	£118

Total: £1948.57

TRAVEL:	FOR TWO
Travel Insurance	£209
Russian Visa @£161.20	£322.40
Turkmenistan LOI @ £50.90	£101.80
Visa Machine Admin Fees @ £178	£356
Visa Machine Embassy Visas @ £313	£626

Total: £1615.20

CAMPING EQUIPMENT:	
Travel Kettle	£12.99
Solar Shower	£6
Bungees	£4
Flag Pole	£15
BBQ Tripod	£35
Tent	FREE
Travel Toilet	£15
Camp beds	£25
Sleeping Bags	FREE
Trangia	FREE

Stove	FREE
Icebox/Cooler	FREE

Total: £112.99

SPONSORSHIP:

M&B Logistics	+£1000
Blackpool Van Signs	+FREE WRAP
Marriott Eco Projects	+£500
Baler Services Limited	+£500
Pied Piper Educational Resources	+£200
Barrage Esports	+£50
Dark Veil Paranormal	+£100
PixelSky	+FREE FILM

Total: +£2350

ON THE ROAD:

FUEL:

12th July:	£55.30
13th July:	£52.48
14th July:	£44.24
16th July:	£32.59
17th July:	£37.01
18th July:	£38.47
20th July:	£33.35
21st July:	£23.03
22nd July:	£25.00
23rd July:	£28.78
24th July:	£17.30

25th July:	£16.92
26th July:	£13.27
29th July:	£16.54
30th July:	£15.04
31st July:	£3.01
2nd Aug:	£5.30
3rd Aug:	£16.54
4th Aug:	£13.99
5th Aug:	£8.48
7th Aug:	£12.11
9th Aug:	£4.40
10th Aug:	£14.00
11th Aug:	£6.94
12th Aug:	£11.00
13th Aug:	£3.28
14th Aug:	£11.00
15th Aug:	£30.64
16th Aug:	£26.40
17th Aug:	£25.44
18th Aug:	£26.09
19th Aug:	£12.66
20th Aug:	£13.98

Total: £694.49

HOTELS & ACCOMMODATION (For two):

Prague Hotel	£53.00
Camping Slovakia	£7
Romanian Beach Camp	£13.46
Turkish Ramada	£42
Samsun Camping	£5.76
Georgia Camping	£4.62

Fabrika Hostel Georgia	£20
Azerbaijan Late Night Hotel	£22
Baku Hotel	£40.60
Ashgabat Hotel	£91
North Turkmenistan Hotel	£81
Khiva Hotel	£18.05
Uzbekistan Hotel	£18.80
Apple Hostel	£26.32
Kazakhstan Hotel - Kyrgyzstan	£22
Sky Hostel	£16.41
Military Town Hotel	£12.30
Karagandah Apartment	£12.19
Kazakhstan Capital Hostel	£16.41
I love Semi Hotel	£15.30
Barnaul Hostel	£11.94
Random Russian Hotel	£16.72
Husky Hostel Ulan Ude	£11.20
Modern Mongol Hostel	£34.60
Altan Hotel Ulan Ude	£23.40

Total: £636.08
(Honestly, you don't need this. WILD CAMP)

TAX & INSURANCE:

CZ Vignette	£10.55
SLV Vignette	£8.85
HU Vignette	£10.53
ROM Vignette	£3.53
BUL Vignette	£6.79
Turkish Car Insurance	£50
Georgian Car Insurance	£32
Turkmenistan Car Tax	£108.27

Tajikistan Car Tax	£18.80
Kazakhstan Car Insurance	£20.21
Russian Insurance	£37.00
Mongolia Road Tolls	£3.50
Mongolia Road Tax	£12

Total: £322.03

MECHANICS, BREAKDOWNS & PARTS:

Turkish Mechanic Istanbul	£24.67
Turkish Recovery	£16.45
Turkish Mechanic	£49.34
Oil	£21.38
Uzbekistan Mechanic Khiva (1)	£3.76
Uzbekistan Mechanic Khiva (2)	£7.52
Uzbekistan Mechanic Bukhara	£74.19
Oil	£3.76
DOT4	£3.72
Kazakhstan Break Fix	£7.23
Kazakhstan Semey Recovery	£73
Kazakhstan Semey Mechanic	£21.39

Total: £306.41

ADDITIONALS:

Food	£350
Laundry	£21.50
Turkmenistan VISA @ £71.30	£142.60
Baku - Turkmenbashi Ferry @£150	£300
Flights Home Ali	£512

Flights Home Lee	£540
Random Tolls	£18.42
Bribes/Fines	THEY GOT NOTHING

Total: £1885.02

So, there we have it. Our full cost breakdown. You are probably thinking you can't afford to do the rally, or another year saving is in order after reading that, but please take into account this was a once in a lifetime trip for me. I didn't want to go cheap. We stayed in hotels, ate good food and did the occasional touristy thing. You can instantly save over £2000 by driving home & £500 by camping every night.

Chapter VII - Turkmenbashi Border - 9 Hours and $900 Dollars.

This is the order that you need to stick too, there is no reason to it so please don't try and find one. Also, you will need someone who speaks Russian with you, if you don't, it will take even longer.

1) **Visa Counter** - First to check you LOI & Passport.
2) **Bank** - To pay for your VISA and get proof of payment.
3) **Visa Counter** - To give in your slip and get your Visa.
4) **Bank** - No idea why, we just handed over money.
5) **Transport Check** - V5 check and Insurance
6) **Veterinarian Check**- No smuggling goats and chickens.
7) **Vegetation Check** - Make sure you have no plants
8) **Bank** - Pay for your car's entry into Turkmenistan
9) **Back to your car** - take it to Inspection.
10) **Inspection** - To see what they want to steal from you.
11) **Tax** -Ask a bloke in an office to write a slip you can't read
12) **Printer** - Show he the slip for no reason.
13) **Bank** - Pay for the slip and find out its road tax
14) **Printer** - Give her the slip and she stamp.
15) **Car** - Get everything together and smile at guards.
16) **Exit**

I feel like giving you all this information is cheating, you shouldn't know how this works, it's a complete mindfuck and will test your patience until you wish to cry.
The whole process takes a minimum of 9 Hours with a translator, expect more 12 hours without.

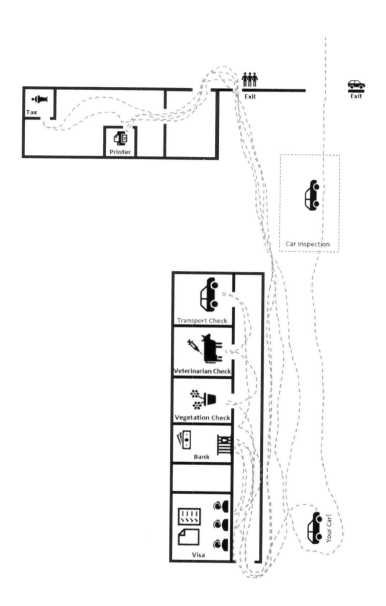

Chapter VIII – The Darvaza Gas Crater

Being one of the main checkpoints/must do's, the Darvaza Gas Crater is not to be missed. Also known as 'The Door to Hell' It is a natural gas field that had since collapsed into an underground cavern back in the 1960's where it lead untouched until the 1970's when geologists set it on fire to prevent the spread of methane gas, Its thought to have been burning continuously since 1971 The diameter of the crater is 69 metres (226 ft), and its depth is 30 metres (98 ft).

But how do you get there?
Follow the northern road from Ashgabat to the halfway point of Erbent, then continue north to Darvaza. You will see this sign.
THIS IS THE SIGN YOU TURN RIGHT AT, that dirt track, right there. That's the one. If you go before or after, your car will be on the wrong road and the chances to get stuck will be even greater.

Chapter IX - FAQ

Should I take a 4x4?

No, don't even think about it. Take the smallest car you can find and make this an adventure not a luxury holiday.

My friends have pulled out, should I still do it?

Yes, 100%. There are so many solo teams who join a convoy and have the most fantastic of times. Also, other teams will happily help you out along the way.

Work won't give me the time off, what should I do?

Quit your job. They are obviously dickheads. You won't realise that at first but you will once you have completed the rally. Whilst they worry about production and deadlines, you will worry about pistons and punctures on the most amazing adventure. I quit my job as soon as I got back and It was the best thing I ever did; I now work at a company that means I can travel the world whilst at work.

I want space and comfort, what car should I take?

Take a plane you gap year sod. If you want comfort, you are in the wrong place. Give Pontins a ring.

Which route should I take?

Go any way you wish, the longer the better. Just try to avoid the Caspian Sea ferry. In fact, Don't! Make your adventure that bit more tedious and give it a go, you will come back with some amazing memories.

I have 2 weeks to do the rally what's the quickest route?

Through Russia. But I'm completely against this idea, take as long as you possibly can and go as far as you possibly can.

I'm worried about 'this' Country.
Don't be. Everywhere we were warned about turned out to be the nicest place with lovely people. Except Azerbaijan, they are dickheads.

Do I need sponsors?
No, you don't NEED them. However, getting anything for free is fantastic. Anything to help you and your charities on this fantastic adventure. I would recommend getting a graphics company with you first, once you have them, companies are eager to join.

I don't know what VISA's to get?
Check out 'The Visa Machine' they did all of ours and It saved us heaps of time with only a little cost on the top.

Should I pay bribes?
No, not unless you really have too. Always ask for a receipt to take to the police station. They will eventually get bored and send you on your way.

How much does petrol cost?
It differs in each country, UK, Turkey and Germany are the most expensive, cheapest was in Turkmenistan and Russia. but remember to take note of how many litres your tank is as you will need to pre pay. Our overall total was £694.49

Chapter X - How to install additional electronics:

You may be wondering some of the best mods for a rally car? below is an example of how I personally wired up our additional including 50" LED Strip Bar, CB Radio, 12v Power Adaptors & Loudspeaker.

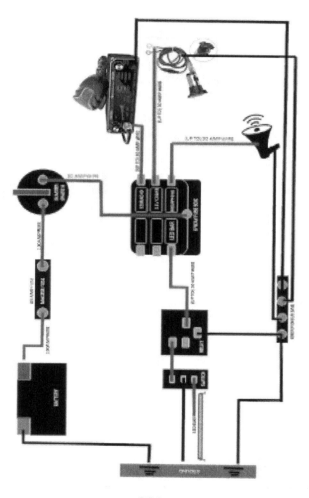

Chapter XI - Sponsors

Sponsors can make or break your rally. Myself and Lee managed to bag some quality sponsors. Saving us thousands, donating to our charities and helping us out with equipment. Not only that but the friends I made with local companies along their generosity was truly remarkable.

You don't technically need them but If you do go down the road of getting sponsors, just be sure that you deliver on what you say you can offer. There is no point offering news coverage and a documentary video if you aren't even taking a camera. Make sure both sides are happy before striking a deal. Here's how we bagged some gems...

Blackpool Van Signs
Steve and Rob are truly fantastic. They were the first company on board with sponsorship once they saw the promotional video on Facebook. I remember getting the call and thinking Id won the lottery when they were interested. They gave us full vehicle graphics completely free, the only thing they asked in return was their logo displayed on the car and a little publicity for them where I could get it. The day I collected the car I was truly amazed at their fantastic work, attention to detail and design. I would honestly recommend their services to anyone. Thanks guys!

Baler Services Limited

Nick, Jackie, Andy, Becky, Ryan and the rest of the team. With Andy and Becky soon to be my brother and sister in law, they were both extremely generous to sponsor me. Not only that but the interest that Ryan, Andy and Nick had about the rally kept me on track with all pre planning and modifications, lending a hand everywhere they could. Also, whilst on the trip, during many times of much needed repairs I stopped to think *"What would Andy do in this situation"* before kicking myself up the arse and getting on with what was needed. I knew that the baler lads would have done anything to join me on the rally. With their fantastic donation towards the trip and our charities they made so much of our trip possible. Thank you.

Barrage esports

Jeff, James and the rest of Barrage Esports. As soon as they heard about SpecialEffect being our main charity a huge donation was sent to them via our fundraising page. Those lads would do anything and everything to support a gaming charity. The world of esports and competitive gaming means so much to them. Thank you for your donation to SpecialEffect you know it's being spent well.

M&B Logistics - Marriott Eco Projects - Pied Piper Educational Resources

Three families that have always been very close, the Moss's Marshall's & Marriott's. And through regular gatherings, be it at their homes, restaurants, their shared country retreat in Northern France or their local pub which the three families brought together, when one is convinced about something or wants to show off the other to men usually follow suit. Especially if it will support their friends. My dad Peter Marriott was first to offer sponsorship although this offer of £1000 to charity if we would admit it was a stupid idea and not do it at all. He eventually accepted I couldn't be convinced otherwise and his new company Marriott Eco Projects, a residential project development company building eco-friendly houses offered £500 to us, covering the hire of our GPS Spot Tracker, so we could keep our loved ones informed of our good progress. Adi Moss, company director of M&B (Felixstowe) Limited, a logistics company that imports fruit & veg to the UK generously offered us £1000 one evening at a party when celebrating my engagement. Although surrounded by his friends would like my dad were not convinced, Adi was most interested in our adventure. That £1000 would help pay for the car and the mods. Gareth, managing director of Pied Piper Educational resources like the others had seen me grow up but thought I was insane for taking up this challenge. He asked me how I could promote his business by traveling to Mongolia in a rust bucket, but my answers didn't win him over. He told me that same evening that Adi had offered, he would save his money to support my family when I inevitably die or wind up in some Gulag while on the rally. His opinion changed however when his friend's companies were on the car and his wasn't. He had to sponsor, and gracefully gave us £200 to cover safety supplies such as first aid kit, fire extinguisher and breakdown accessories. Because he still thought our lives were in peril. - *Lee Marriott*

Pixel Sky - Drones
Brendon spent an entire day in the cold and snow with us filming our promotional video up in Yorkshire. He gave his services completely free so that we could try and land some sponsorship opportunities. Without this I most definitely don't think we would have been as lucky as we were. Along with Andy and Andy, thank you for filming me and my crappy little car. I told you i'd make it all the way!

Dark Veil Paranormal

Thanks Mum! When my mother isn't teaching, she can be found train hopping all over the north with her partner David. They run paranormal investigations and ghost hunts everywhere they can from graveyards to haunted hotels. Their first ever profits were donated to SpecialEffect in return for a small sponsorship sticker on the car. Thank you for believing in us.

Chapter XII - Currency Converter

All currencies were correct on March 1st 2019, however if you are reading this after June 2019, I'm sure that Brexit will have messed everything up and this information will be wrong.

Currency:	Amount Per £1 GBP
Euro	1.13
US Dollar	1.28
Turkish Lira	6.79
Russian Ruble	85.75
Czech Koruna	29.27
Ukrainian Hryvnia	34.75
Romanian Leu	5.38
Georgian Lari	3.38
Belarusian Ruble	2.77
Uzbekistani Som	10759.62
Bulgarian Lev	2.21
Iranian Rial	53958.18
Kazakhstani Tenge	484.83
Azerbaijan Manat	2.17
Mongolian Tughrik	3372.04
Tajikistani Somoni	12.09
Kyrgyzstani Som	89.40
Turkmenistani Manat	4.48

Chapter XIII - Choosing the right vehicle

This topic is highly opinionated throughout the Mongol Rally, but at the end of the day it's all down to you and The Adventurists. Just go by the rules, please.

They have invested a lot of time, money and stupidity into making the Mongol Rally what it is today. So, if you want an adventure, a memory of a lifetime, stick to their rules and enjoy the breakdowns. I know it sounds stupid but some of the most amazing memories I have from the rally were watching my car break itself and meeting the most incredible people in the middle of nowhere. So, to hell with four-wheel drive, big engines, ambulances, ice cream vans and anything that give you that little bit of extra comfort.

The CONVOI EXCEPTIONNEL top ten vehicle to complete the Mongol Rally:

1.   **Nissan Micra** (If you want a minimal fault rally)
The mighty Nissan Micra is a rally favourite, known for its durability and reliability. It laughs in the face of danger as its tiny engine roars through each country. Both Team: Don't Smell My Shoes and Rally McRally Face had this chosen steed, their only problems were flat tyres and minor overheating. What more could you ask for?

2.   **Fiat Panda** (Easy to fix, small issues & extra leg room)
The Fiat Panda is the rally rival of the Nissan Micra, both have fantastic statistics when it comes to completing the Mongol Rally. You can't go wrong with it, A little extra leg

room and spares can be found almost anywhere. If you want to be a bit of a knob, you can also find the Panda 4x4, but if you do, be prepared to have your car sabotaged.

3.   **Citroen 2CV** (Fancy a challenge?)
The Citroen 2CV is a hard to come by car, but if you can get one for the right price and attempt the Mongol Rally, you will achieve 'Legend' status within an instant. Although many have completed before the troubles and hardships are not for the faint hearted.

4.   **Aprilia Mojito** (If you are completely Insane)
Does crying in a ditch completely alone with no water sound like a good idea? Fantastic! One bloke completed the rally on this tiny beast, it took him over three months. I can't begin to imagine the shit this man had to put up with. Sign up, buy a Mojito and adventure!

5.   **Double Decker Bus** (Comfortable & Completely Impractical)
A 2018 team purchased a double decker bus, kitted it up with beds, white goods, a dart board and working warm showers! Don't think they had it easy however, they completed the Pamir Highway & Mongolia, their original plan was to drive it to Australia, but the Mongol Rally beat them.

6.   **Austin Mini** (You will love it and hate it every day)
'Machina Mr Beana' If you wish to be globally recognised by everyone in the world as Mr Bean, watch your suspension collapse underneath you and have the nearest spares 10,000 miles away back in England. Than please, take a Classic Mini.

7.   **Ford Fiesta Mk3/Mk4** (A true rally experience)
Team: AFK & Cunning Stunts pride and joy. I know what you
are thinking *"Why would I take one of those when I've just
read the problems in this book?"* But please take a moment to
realise, we had a true adventure. This is exactly what the
Mongol Rally is about. Breaking down mentally and
physically before swapping your only bottle of water for a
new clutch cable.

8.   **Vauxhall Agila** (Leg Room & Bulletproof)
Many have chosen the Agila as their trusty steed. They seem
to be built strong, the main problem with them however is
shocks and springs! You will go through plenty!

9.   **Nissan Leaf.** (Electric)
Go completely electric and see if you can be one of the first
five teams to complete the rally in a Nissan Leaf! Remember
to pack some spare batteries and a solar charger.

10.   Monkey Bike
If the Aprilia Mojito is too practical, please go ahead and take
something a little more powerful, but half the size, you will
struggle to keep up with snails and the idea of carrying 10l of
water on you at all times through the stans is completely out
of the window. (Good luck getting travel insurance)

Chapter XIIV - Choosing the right route.

There is no right or wrong route. If you wish to head to Mongolia via Africa then by all means, please do! The more adventurous the better. Many teams had over thirteen countries under their belt before they even reached the start line in Prague.

Below is a brief example of the most common routes and the time they take:

The Northern Route

One of the quickest routes of the Rally is the Northern Route, through Ukraine, Russia and Kazakhstan, taking teams between 8 days and three weeks. It's a route with relatively mild weather conditions, so tends to be viewed as the easiest. The downside is that the roads are rather repetitive until you hit Mongolia – mainly straight highways along flat landscapes. But that also means you'll have more time in Mongolia towards and after the end of the race, where the scenery of plateaus, desert plains and mountains on a monumental scale counts as some of the world's most magnificent.

The Central Route (Our Route)

Our route though the EU, heading into Turkey, Georgia and Azerbaijan. Before crossing the Caspian Sea, heading though everywhere that ends in 'Stan' before heading up through Kazakhstan into Russia and finally Mongolia.

It's the most amazing route and would recommend it to everyone over the northern route. Nothing is repetitive and every country shows off its quirky landscape and governments.

The Southern Route

Identical to the Central route however you go through Iran over the Caspian Sea. I would recommend this over the Central route as the Caspian Sea ferry is a complete overpriced sham. Everyone I have spoken to who completed the Southern route say Iran was their favourite country on the entire trip. Don't let the price put you off.

The Wrong Way

Turn up on foot to the launch, fly out to New York, drive across the entirety of the USA before heading into Canada. Jump on a boat to Russia, do the road of bones to Chita, head into Mongolia then back up to the finish line.

Book Cover Design by
Caroline Cameron - *caroline_graphicdesign@outlook.com*

Book Cover Photo by
The Adventurists

Blurb by
Daniel Lampard

Car Design by
Caroline Cameron - *caroline_graphicdesign@outlook.com*
&
Blackpool Van Signs - *https://www.blackpoolvansigns.co.uk/*

Special Thanks to:
Convoi Exceptionnel - For the Journey
Keith Malpus - For the roof rack & morale support!
George Hargreaves - For the large charity donation
Everyone who donated to our sponsors
The Marriott Family
The Cameron Family
The Hargreaves Family
The Wells Family
The Smith-Wells Family
The Adventurists
All of our Sponsors
Special Effect - Thank you for the most amazing support.
Cool Earth – For making our adventure eco-friendly.
Kevin (The Adventurists) - For finding the best burgers in Ulan Ude.

Printed in Great Britain
by Amazon

38232696R00224